1992 SUPPLEMENT TO
CONSTITUTIONAL LAW
THE AMERICAN CONSTITUTION
CONSTITUTIONAL RIGHTS & LIBERTIES

Seventh Editions

By

William B. Lockhart
*Professor of Law, University of California, Hastings
Dean and Professor of Law Emeritus, University of Minnesota*

Yale Kamisar
*Clarence Darrow Distinguished University Professor of Law,
University of Michigan*

Jesse H. Choper
*Earl Warren Professor of Public Law,
University of California, Berkeley*

Steven H. Shiffrin
*Professor of Law,
Cornell University*

AMERICAN CASEBOOK SERIES®

WEST PUBLISHING CO.
ST. PAUL, MINN., 1992

American Casebook Series, the key symbol appearing on the front cover and the WP symbol are registered trademarks of West Publishing Co. Registered in U.S. Patent and Trademark Office.

COPYRIGHT © 1991 WEST PUBLISHING CO.
COPYRIGHT © 1992 By WEST PUBLISHING CO.

All rights reserved
Printed in the United States of America

ISBN 0–314–01080–7

(L.K.C. & S.) 1992 Supp. 7th Ed. ACB

Preface

This Supplement contains significant developments that have occurred since January 1, 1991—the "cut-off" date of the principal books.

The editorial style of this Supplement follows that of the principal books. In designating the places in the principal books at which the supplementary material is to be inserted, the following abbreviations have been used:

Constitutional Law: Cases, Comments & Questions—CON LAW

The American Constitution: Cases & Materials—AMER CON

Constitutional Rights & Liberties: Cases & Materials—RTS & LIB

Chapter and section titles from the principal books have been reproduced in this Supplement to facilitate identification of the material to be inserted.

WILLIAM B. LOCKHART
YALE KAMISAR
JESSE H. CHOPER
STEVEN H. SHIFFRIN

July, 1992

Table of Contents

	Page
PREFACE	iii
TABLE OF CASES	ix

NATURE AND SCOPE OF JUDICIAL REVIEW ... 1
  POLITICAL QUESTIONS ... 1
    United States Department of Commerce v. Montana ... 1

NATIONAL LEGISLATIVE POWER ... 3
  APPLYING NATIONAL POWER TO STATE GOVERNMENTS: INTERGOVERNMENTAL IMMUNITIES ... 3
    State Immunity From Federal Regulation ... 3
    Gregory v. Ashcroft ... 3

STATE POWER TO REGULATE ... 5
  STATE REGULATION WHEN NO FEDERAL REGULATION ... 5
    Regulation of Outgoing Trade: Burdens on Out-of-State Interests Seeking In-State Resources ... 5
    Chemical Waste Management, Inc. v. Hunt ... 5

STATE POWER TO TAX ... 7
  PRAGMATISM OVER FORMALISM: REQUISITES OF A VALID TAX ... 7
    Jurisdiction to Tax ... 7
    Quill Corp. v. North Dakota ... 7

SUBSTANTIVE PROTECTION OF ECONOMIC INTERESTS ... 9
  "TAKING" OF PROPERTY INTERESTS ... 9
    Taking Through Regulation ... 9
    Yee v. City of Escondido ... 9

PROTECTION OF INDIVIDUAL RIGHTS: DUE PROCESS, THE BILL OF RIGHTS, AND NONTEXTUAL CONSTITUTIONAL RIGHTS ... 19
  NATURE AND SCOPE OF FOURTEENTH AMENDMENT DUE PROCESS; APPLICABILITY OF THE BILL OF RIGHTS TO THE STATES ... 19
    The "Ordered Liberty—Fundamental Fairness," "Total Incorporation" and "Selective Incorporation" Theories ... 19
    Pacific Mut. Life Ins. Co. v. Haslip ... 19
    The Retroactive Effect of a Holding of Unconstitutionality ... 23
      Fallon & Meltzer, New Law, Non-Retroactivity, and Constitutional Remedies ... 23

TABLE OF CONTENTS

Page

PROTECTION OF INDIVIDUAL RIGHTS: DUE PROCESS, THE BILL OF RIGHTS, AND NONTEXTUAL CONSTITUTIONAL RIGHTS—Continued

THE RIGHT OF "PRIVACY" (OR "AUTONOMY" OR "PERSONHOOD") 25
    Rust v. Sullivan 25
    Planned Parenthood of Southeastern Pennsylvania v. Casey 28
    Criticism of Bowers v. Hardwick 87
        Fried, Order and Law 87
    The "Right to Die" 87
THE DEATH PENALTY AND RELATED PROBLEMS: CRUEL AND UNUSUAL PUNISHMENT 88
    Other Constitutional Challenges to Capital (and Life) Sentences 88
        "Grossly Disproportionate" Punishment 88
            Harmelin v. Michigan 88
        "Victim Impact" Evidence 92
            Payne v. Tennessee 93
PROCEDURAL DUE PROCESS IN NON-CRIMINAL CASES 97
    Deprivation of "Liberty" and "Property" Interests 97

FREEDOM OF EXPRESSION AND ASSOCIATION 98
    WHAT SPEECH IS NOT PROTECTED? 98
    Reputation and Privacy 98
        Private Individuals and Public Figures 98
            Masson v. New Yorker Magazine, Inc. 98
IS SOME PROTECTED SPEECH LESS EQUAL THAN OTHER PROTECTED SPEECH? 104
    Near Obscene Speech 104
        Barnes v. Glen Theatre, Inc. 104
CONCEIVING AND RECONCEIVING THE STRUCTURE OF FIRST AMENDMENT DOCTRINE: HATE SPEECH REVISITED—AGAIN 114
    R.A.V. v. St. Paul 114
    Dawson v. Delaware 127
FAIR ADMINISTRATION OF JUSTICE AND THE FIRST AMENDMENT AS SWORD 128
    Justice and the First Amendment as Shield 128
        Gentile v. State Bar 128
GOVERNMENT PROPERTY AND THE PUBLIC FORUM ... 134
    Foundation Cases 134
        Forsyth County v. Nationalist Movement 134
    New Forums 136
        International Society for Krishna Consciousness, Inc. v. Lee 136

FREEDOM OF EXPRESSION AND ASSOCIATION—Continued

 Lee v. International Society for Krishna Consciousness, Inc. 145
 GOVERNMENT SUPPORT OF SPEECH 148
  Subsidies and Tax Expenditures 148
   Leathers v. Medlock 148
   Simon & Schuster, Inc. v. New York State Crime Victims Board 151
   Rust v. Sullivan 155
 THE RIGHT NOT TO SPEAK, THE RIGHT TO ASSOCIATE, AND THE RIGHT NOT TO ASSOCIATE 162
  The Right Not to Be Associated With Particular Ideas 162
  Freedom of Association and Employment 163
   Lehnert v. Ferris Faculty Ass'n 163
   Renne v. Geary 163
  Government Mandated Disclosures and Freedom of Association 163
   Reporter's Privilege 163
   Cohen v. Cowles Media Co. 164

FREEDOM OF RELIGION 169
 ESTABLISHMENT CLAUSE 169
  Official Acknowledgement of Religion 169
   Lee v. Weisman 169

EQUAL PROTECTION 173
 TRADITIONAL APPROACH 173
  Nordlinger v. Hahn 173
 RACE AND ETHNIC ANCESTRY 174
  De Jure v. De Facto Discrimination 174
  Georgia v. McCollum 174
  Remedying Segregation 174
  Freeman v. Pitts 174
 SPECIAL SCRUTINY FOR OTHER CLASSIFICATIONS 178
  Mental Retardation 178
   Gregory v. Ashcroft 178
 "FUNDAMENTAL RIGHTS" 178
  Restrictions on Parties and Candidates 178
  Confinement of "Fundamental Rights" 179

THE CONCEPT OF STATE ACTION 181
 RECENT DEVELOPMENTS 181
  Edmonson v. Leesville Concrete Co. 181

LIMITATIONS ON JUDICIAL POWER AND REVIEW 183
 CASE OR CONTROVERSY 183
  Standing and Ripeness 183

Appendices

App.		Page
A.	The Justices of the Supreme Court	186
B.	The Constitution of the United States	187
C.	**New York v. United States**	188

Table of Cases

The principal cases are in bold type. Cases cited or discussed in the text are in roman type. References are to pages. Cases cited in principal cases and within other quoted materials are also included.

Abood v. Detroit Bd. of Educ., 161
Adamson v. People of State of California, 21
Adkins v. Children's Hospital of District of Columbia, 35, 36, 71
Agins v. City of Tiburon, 11, 12, 15
Akron, City of v. Akron Center for Reproductive Health, Inc., 25, 34, 39, 44, 45, 56, 62, 67, 68, 78, 79, 80, 82, 83
Allegheny, County of v. American Civil Liberties Union Greater Pittsburgh Chapter, 171, 172, 173
Allied–Signal, Inc. v. Director, Div. of Taxation, 8
Alvarez-Machain, United States v., 2
Andrus v. Allard, 13, 17
Arizona v. Roberson, 23
Arkansas Writers' Project, Inc. v. Ragland, 134, 148, 149, 151, 152, 157
Associated Press v. N.L.R.B., 164
Associated Press v. United States, 164, 166
Atascadero State Hosp. v. Scanlon, 3

Baker v. Carr, 1, 2
Baker v. Los Angeles Herald Examiner, 100
Barnes v. Glen Theatre, Inc., 104, 115, 129
Batson v. Kentucky, 174
Baysinger, State v., 111
Bazemore v. Friday, 178
Beauharnais v. People of State of Ill., 114
Blum v. Yaretsky, 185
Board of Regents of State Colleges v. Roth, 13
Boos v. Barry, 119, 155
Booth v. Maryland, 92, 93, 94, 95
Bose Corp. v. Consumers Union of United States, Inc., 114
Bowers v. Hardwick, 64, 72, 78, 106, 107, 111
Brandenburg v. Ohio, 120, 154
Branzburg v. Hayes, 164, 166
Broadrick v. Oklahoma, 114
Brown v. Board of Education of Topeka, Shawnee County, Kan., 36, 38, 71, 72, 177
Buckley v. Valeo, 108
Burdick v. Takushi, 178
Burnham v. Superior Court of California, County of Marin, 21
Burson v. Freeman, 125, 146
Burton v. Wilmington Parking Authority, 184
Butler v. McKellar, 23

Caldwell v. Mississippi, 23
California v. LaRue, 104
Carey v. Population Services Intern., 32

Central Eureka Mining Company, United States v., 15
Chaplinsky v. State of New Hampshire, 114, 115, 123, 125, 126
Chemical Waste Management, Inc. v. Hunt, 5
Citizen Pub. Co. v. United States, 166
City of (see name of city)
Clark v. Community for Creative Non–Violence, 105, 115
Cleburne, Tex., City of v. Cleburne Living Center, 180
Cohen v. Cowles Media Co., 164
Coker v. Georgia, 89, 91
Colautti v. Franklin, 67
Community for Creative Non–Violence v. Watt, 108, 113
Complete Auto Transit, Inc. v. Brady, 7, 8
Connecticut v. Doehr, 183
Cornelius v. NAACP Legal Defense and Educational Fund, Inc., 139
County of (see name of county)
Cox v. New Hampshire, 134, 135, 136
Cruzan by Cruzan v. Director, Missouri Dept. of Health, 34, 51, 59
Curtin v. Benson, 14

Dallas, City of v. Stanglin, 106, 108, 109
Dawson v. Delaware, 127
Dean Milk Co. v. City of Madison, Wis., 5
Doe v. Bolton, 41, 66
Doran v. Salem Inn, Inc., 104
Dred Scott v. Sandford, 78, 84, 85, 86
Dun & Bradstreet, Inc. v. Greenmoss Builders, Inc., 154

Edmonson v. Leesville Concrete Co., Inc., 174, 183
Edwards v. Arizona, 23
Eichman, United States v., 108, 123
Eisenstadt v. Baird, 32, 34, 41
Employment Div., Dept. of Human Resources of Oregon v. Smith, 108, 167
Engel v. Vitale, 170, 172
Enmund v. Florida, 90

F.C.C. v. League of Women Voters of California, 158
Fordice, United States v., 176
Forsyth County, Georgia v. Nationalist Movement, 134

TABLE OF CASES

Fort Gratiot Sanitary Landfill, Inc. v. Michigan Dept. of Natural Resources, 5, 6
Foucha v. Louisiana, 97, 179
Freeman v. Pitts, 174

Garcia v. San Antonio Metropolitan Transit Authority, 3, 4
Gentile v. State Bar of Nevada, 128
Georgia v. McCollum, 174
Gertz v. Robert Welch, Inc., 22, 98, 101
Gideon v. Wainwright, 21
Goldblatt v. Town of Hempstead, N. Y., 14
Green v. County School Bd. of New Kent County, Va., 175, 176, 178
Gregory v. Ashcroft, 3, 180
Griffith v. Kentucky, 24
Griswold v. Connecticut, 30, 32, 33, 34, 53, 57, 60, 68, 73, 87
Grosjean v. American Press Co., 148, 149, 151

Harmelin v. Michigan, 88
Harris v. McRae, 25, 26, 157
Heffron v. International Soc. for Krishna Consciousness, Inc., 144
Henneford v. Silas Mason Co., 7
Hernandez v. New York, 174
Hodgson v. Minnesota, 62, 63, 66, 67, 79
Hoyt v. Florida, 51
Hurtado v. People of State of California, 20
Hustler Magazine v. Falwell, 123, 165, 166, 167

Illinois State Bd. of Elections v. Socialist Workers Party, 178
I.N.S. v. Chadha, 2
International Society for Krishna Consciousness, Inc. v. Lee, 136, 145, 146

Jones v. United States, 97

Kaiser Aetna v. United States, 10
Keyishian v. Board of Regents of University of State of N. Y., 159
Keystone Bituminous Coal Ass'n v. DeBenedictis, 10, 15, 16
Kokinda, United States v., 138, 139
Konigsberg v. State Bar of California, 167
Kras, United States v., 161

Landmark Communications, Inc. v. Virginia, 129
Leathers v. Medlock, 129, 148, 152, 154
Lee v. Weisman, 86, 169
Lee v. International Society for Krishna Consciousness, Inc., 137, 145
Lehnert v. Ferris Faculty Ass'n, 163
Lemon v. Kurtzman, 169
Lochner v. People of State of New York, 17, 35, 69, 70, 71, 85
Lockett v. Ohio, 96
Loretto v. Teleprompter Manhattan CATV Corp., 9, 10, 11, 13
Lovell v. City of Griffin, Ga., 166
Loving v. Virginia, 29, 34, 68
Lucas v. South Carolina Coastal Council, 10

Lugar v. Edmondson Oil Co., Inc., 184
Lujan v. Defenders of Wildlife, 181

Mabee v. White Plains Pub. Co., 149, 151
Maher v. Roe, 25, 26, 41, 157
Maine v. Taylor, 6
Marbury v. Madison, 82
Marsh v. State of Alabama, 170, 184
Massachusetts Bd. of Retirement v. Murgia, 180
Masson v. New Yorker Magazine, Inc., 98
Mathews v. Eldridge, 22
Members of City Council of City of Los Angeles v. Taxpayers for Vincent, 146
Michael H. v. Gerald D., 29, 64, 76
Miller v. Schoene, 16
Mills v. Alabama, 147
Minneapolis Star and Tribune Co. v. Minnesota Com'r of Revenue, 148, 149, 150, 151, 158, 164
Morales v. Trans World Airlines, Inc., 117
Mugler v. Kansas, 18
Mu'Min v. Virginia, 129
Munn v. State of Illinois, 17
Murdock v. Commonwealth of Pennsylvania, 135, 136, 144

National Bellas Hess, Inc. v. Department of Revenue of State of Ill., 7, 8
National Collegiate Athletic Ass'n v. Tarkanian, 184, 185
Near v. State of Minn. ex rel. Olson, 154
Nebraska Press Ass'n v. Stuart, 131, 155
New York v. Ferber, 155
New York v. United States, 3, 188
New York Times Co. v. United States, 154, 167
Niemotko v. State of Maryland, 116
Nollan v. California Coastal Com'n, 12
Nordlinger v. Hahn, 173
Norman v. Reed, 178

O'Brien, United States v., 105, 106, 107, 108, 109, 110, 111, 112, 115, 122, 123, 151, 155
Ohio v. Akron Center for Reproductive Health, 76, 79
Ohralik v. Ohio State Bar Ass'n, 117
Oklahoma Press Pub. Co. v. Walling, 149, 151, 164

Pacific Mut. Life Ins. Co. v. Haslip, 19
Paris Adult Theatre I v. Slaton, 106
Pasadena City Bd. of Ed. v. Spangler, 175
Payne v. Tennessee, 93
Penn Cent. Transp. Co. v. City of New York, 11, 15
Pennsylvania Coal Co. v. Mahon, 11, 12, 15
Penry v. Lynaugh, 23
Philadelphia, City of v. New Jersey, 5, 6
Planned Parenthood Ass'n of Kansas City, Mo., Inc. v. Ashcroft, 80
Planned Parenthood of Central Missouri v. Danforth, 27, 41, 51, 53, 61, 62, 63, 66, 67, 74
Planned Parenthood of Southeastern Pennsylvania v. Casey, 28, 162
Plessy v. Ferguson, 35, 36, 69, 70, 71, 72
Poe v. Ullman, 30, 34, 87

TABLE OF CASES

Police Dept. of City of Chicago v. Mosley, 121
Posadas De Puerto Rico Associates v. Tourism Co. of Puerto Rico, 117
Powell v. McCormack, 2
PruneYard Shopping Center v. Robins, 17

Quill Corp. v. North Dakota By and Through Heitkamp, 7

Rankin v. McPherson, 161
R. A. V. v. City of St. Paul, Minnesota, 114
Regan v. Taxation With Representation of Washington, 149, 151, 157, 158, 160
Renne v. Geary, 163
Renton, City of v. Playtime Theatres, Inc., 105, 110, 113, 117, 118, 119, 154
Riggins v. Nevada, 87
Riggs v. Palmer, 153
Roe v. Wade, 25, 26, 28, 29, 30, 31, 32, 33, 34, 35, 36, 37, 38, 39, 40, 41, 42, 43, 44, 46, 47, 53, 54, 55, 58, 60, 61, 63, 64, 65, 66, 67, 68, 69, 70, 71, 72, 73, 77, 78, 79, 80, 82, 83, 84, 85
Roth v. United States, 106, 114, 119
Rummel v. Estelle, 90, 91, 92
Rust v. Sullivan, 25, 155

Sable Communications of California, Inc. v. F.C.C., 115, 116
Saffle v. Parks, 23
Saia v. People of State of New York, 108
San Diego Gas & Elec. Co. v. City of San Diego, 11
Sawyer v. Smith, 23
Schad v. Borough of Mount Ephraim, 104
Schaumburg, Village of v. Citizens for a Better Environment, 145
Schneider v. New Jersey, 108
School Dist. of Abington Tp., Pa. v. Schempp, 170, 172
Shaffer v. Heitner, 21
Shelley v. Kraemer, 184, 185
Simon & Schuster, Inc. v. New York State Crime Victims Bd., 116, 151
Skinner v. State of Oklahoma, 34
Smith v. Allwright, 94
Smith v. Daily Mail Pub. Co., 164, 165, 166, 167

Sniadach v. Family Finance Corp. of Bay View, 21
Snyder v. Commonwealth of Massachusetts, 20, 22
Solem v. Helm, 89, 90, 91, 92
South Carolina v. Gathers, 93, 94, 95
Stanley v. Georgia, 111
State v. ____(see opposing party)
Strauder v. State of West Virginia, 174
Students Challenging Regulatory Agency Procedures (SCRAP), United States v., 181
Sullivan, United States v., 98, 101

Teague v. Lane, 23, 24
Terry v. Adams, 184
Texas v. Johnson, 108, 120, 123, 155
The Florida Star v. B.J.F., 164, 165
Thornburgh v. American College of Obstetricians and Gynecologists, 25, 27, 34, 39, 44, 45, 56, 61, 62, 67, 68, 83
Tinker v. Des Moines Independent Community School Dist., 108
Trafficante v. Metropolitan Life Ins. Co., 182
Twining v. State of New Jersey, 20

United States v. ____(see opposing party)
United States Dept. of Commerce v. Montana, 1

Village of (see name of village)

Ward v. Rock Against Racism, 115, 154, 155
Warth v. Seldin, 181, 182
Washington v. Davis, 176
Watts v. United States, 116
Webster v. Reproductive Health Services, 25, 26, 34, 58, 61, 64, 66, 67, 68, 74, 76, 85
West Coast Hotel Co. v. Parrish, 35, 36, 71, 72, 85
Williams v. Illinois, 20, 22, 23
Wood v. Georgia, 132
Wooley v. Maynard, 160, 161, 162

Yee v. City of Escondido, Cal., 9
Young v. American Mini Theatres, Inc., 110

Zacchini v. Scripps–Howard Broadcasting Co., 164, 166, 167

1992 SUPPLEMENT TO
CONSTITUTIONAL LAW
THE AMERICAN CONSTITUTION
CONSTITUTIONAL RIGHTS & LIBERTIES

Seventh Editions

*

Chapter

NATURE AND SCOPE OF JUDICIAL REVIEW

SECTION: POLITICAL QUESTIONS

CON LAW: P. 30, addition to fn. f

AMER CON: P. 29, addition to fn. f

RTS & LIB: P. 30, addition to fn. f

For the suggestion that the Guaranty Clause might in some circumstances provide a basis for a state or a subdivision with a basis for enjoining a federal statute, see *New York v. United States*, p. 188 of this Supplement infra.

CON LAW: P. 43, after Powell

AMER CON: P. 41, after Powell

RTS & LIB: P. 43, after Powell

Montana brought suit challenging the method Congress employs to determine the number of congressional representatives each state is afforded. UNITED STATES DEPARTMENT OF COMMERCE v. MONTANA, ___ U.S. ___, 112 S.Ct. 1415, 118 L.Ed.2d 87 (1992), per STEVENS, J., held that the dispute was judicially cognizable: "The Government argues that Congress' selection of any of the alternative apportionment methods involved in this litigation is not subject to judicial review. * * *

"The Government insists that each of the factors identified in *Baker* supports the conclusion that the question presented here is committed to the 'political branches' to the exclusion of the Judiciary. Significantly, however, the Government does not suggest that all congressional decisions relating to apportionment are beyond judicial review. The Government does not, for instance, dispute that a court could set aside an apportionment plan that violated the constitutional requirement that '[t]he number of Representatives shall not exceed one for every thirty Thousand.' Further, with respect to the provision that Representatives 'shall be apportioned among the several States * * * according to their respective Numbers,' the Government acknowledges that Congress has a judicially enforceable obligation to select an apportionment plan that is related to population.

"Our previous apportionment cases concerned States' decisions creating legislative districts; today we review the actions of Congress. Respect for a coordinate branch of Government raises special concerns not present in our prior cases, but those concerns relate to the merits of the controversy rather than to our power to resolve it. As the issue is properly raised in a case otherwise unquestionably within our jurisdiction, we must determine whether Congress exercised its apportionment authority within the limits dictated by the Constitution. See *INS v. Chadha,* 462 U.S. 919, 940–941, 103 S.Ct. 2764, 2778–2779, 77 L.Ed.2d 317 (1983); *Powell v. McCormack,* 395 U.S. 486, 521, 89 S.Ct. 1944, 1964, 23 L.Ed.2d 491 (1969). Without the need for another exploration of the *Baker* factors, it suffices to say that, as in *Baker* itself and the apportionment cases that followed, the political question doctrine does not place this kind of constitutional interpretation outside the proper domain of the Judiciary."

CON LAW: P. 43, addition to note 1

AMER CON: P. 42, addition to note 1

RTS & LIB: P. 43, addition to note 1

Suppose Congress entirely ignores the "27th amendment" (see text set out at p. 187 of this Supplement and the accompanying footnote) and a dispute arises. Is the dispute a "political question?"

CON LAW: P. 44, addition to note 2

AMER CON: P. 43, addition to note 2

RTS & LIB: P. 44, addition to note 2

If the United States arrests a citizen and resident of Mexico at his Mexican home and takes him to the United States in violation of international law for the purpose of bringing him to trial in the United States (for murder of a Drug Enforcement Administration agent in Mexico), is the issue of his abduction a "political question" to be negotiated between the United States and Mexico? Should a federal court exercise jurisdiction over the defendant in these circumstances? Order his repatriation? See *United States v. Alvarez–Machain,* ___ U.S. ___, 112 S.Ct. 2188, ___ L.Ed.2d ___ (1992) (permitting a murder trial to go forward).

Chapter

NATIONAL LEGISLATIVE POWER

SECTION: APPLYING NATIONAL POWERS TO STATE GOVERNMENTS: INTERGOVERNMENTAL IMMUNITIES

STATE IMMUNITY FROM FEDERAL REGULATION

CON LAW: P. 165, after note 5

AMER CON: P. 143, after note 3

See NEW YORK v. UNITED STATES at page 188 of this supplement.

GREGORY v. ASHCROFT, ___ U.S. ___, 111 S.Ct. 2395, 115 L.Ed.2d 410 (1991) per O'CONNOR, J., asserted for a majority of 5 many of the same considerations advanced in the *Garcia* dissents. It ruled that the federal Age Discrimination in Employment Act (ADEA) forbidding discharge for age did not apply to state judges required by the Missouri Constitution to retire at 70 years of age. Accompanied by several pages that stressed the "dual sovereignty between States and Federal Government," the federal government's limited powers, the tenth amendment, the "fundamental" nature of a "sovereign entity's" prescribing the qualifications of its own officers, the Court held that ADEA's exclusion of "appointees on the policy-making level" excluded state judges from ADEA protection. It resolved the ambiguity of statutory terms by a "plain statement rule:"

"Congressional interference with the decision of the people of Missouri defining their constitutional officers, would upset the constitutional balance of federal and state powers. For this reason 'it is incumbent upon the federal courts to be certain of Congress' intent before finding that federal law overides' this balance. 'If Congress intends to alter the "usual constitutional balance between the States and the Federal Government" it must make its intention to do so "unmistakably clear in the language of the statute." ' [a] [This] plain statement rule is nothing more than an acknowledgment that the states retain substantial sovereign powers under our constitutional scheme, powers with which Congress does not readily interfere.

---

a. The Court here cited *and quoted from Atascadero State Hospital v. Scanlon,* 473 U.S. 234, 242, 243, 105 S.Ct. 3142, 3147, 3148, 87 L.Ed.2d 171 (1980), and several other opinions to the same effect.

"[We] will not read the ADEA to cover state judges unless Congress has made it clear that judges are *included*. This does not mean that the act must mention judges [explicitly]. Rather it must be plain to anyone reading the Act that it covers judges. [W]e cannot conclude that the statute plainly covers state judges. Therefore, it does not."

Of the six justices in the *Garcia* majority, the four still on the Court all dissented from this reasoning. Blackmun and Marshall expressly agreed with White and Steven's dissent [b] from this "plain statement" rule. Justice WHITE's opinion summarized their position:

"The majority [chooses] not to resolve that issue of statutory construction. Instead, it holds that whether or not the ADEA can fairly be read to exclude state judges from its scope, '[w]e will not read the ADEA to cover state judges unless Congress has made it clear that judges are *included*.' (emphasis in original). I cannot agree with this 'plain statement' rule because it is unsupported by the decisions upon which the majority relies,[c] contrary to our Tenth Amendment jurisprudence, and fundamentally unsound.

"[The] majority's plain statement rule is not only unprecedented, it directly contravenes our decisions in *Garcia*. [In] those cases we made it clear 'that States must find their protection from congressional regulation through the national political process, not through judicially defined spheres of unregulable state activity.' We also rejected as 'unsound in principle and unworkable in practice' any test for state immunity that requires a judicial determination of which state activities are 'traditional,' 'integral,' or 'necessary.' *Garcia*. The majority disregards those decisions in its attempt to carve out areas of state activity that will receive special protection from federal legislation."

b. Independent of the plain statement rule, White, joined by Stevens, interpreted the ADEA exclusion to cover state judges and so concurred in the majority result. Blackmun, joined by Marshall, dissented.

c. Justice White noted that the decisions relied on by the majority were eleventh amendment cases where the issue was "whether Congress intended a particular statute to extend to the states *at all*."

Chapter

STATE POWER TO REGULATE

SECTION: STATE REGULATION WHEN NO FEDERAL REGULATION

REGULATION OF OUTGOING TRADE: BURDENS ON OUT-OF-STATE INTERESTS SEEKING IN-STATE RESOURCES

CON LAW: P. 264, after note 2

AMER CON: P. 200, after note 3

Philadelphia v. New Jersey reaffirmed. CHEMICAL WASTE MANAGEMENT, INC. v. HUNT, __ U.S. __, 112 S.Ct. 2009, 119 L.Ed.2d 121 (1992) per STEVENS, J., invoked *Philadelphia v. New Jersey* to invalidate a fee of $72 per ton imposed by Alabama on disposing of hazardous waste from out of state in privately-owned hazardous waste landfills in Alabama.[a] Landfills for hazardous waste exist in only 16 states. The largest in any state is owned and operated by Chemical Waste Management at Emelle, Alabama, where 90% of the hazardous waste disposed of originates out of state. The $72 fee was in addition to a $26.50 per ton fee imposed on all hazardous waste accepted by Alabama landfills, whatever the source:

"No State may attempt to isolate itself from a problem common to the several States by raising barriers to the free flow of interstate trade. Today, in *Fort Gratiot Sanitary Landfill, Inc. v. Michigan Dept. of Natural Resources*,[b] we have also considered a Commerce Clause challenge to a Michigan law prohibiting private landfill operators from accepting solid waste originating outside the county in which their facilities operate. In striking down that law, we adhered to our decision in *Philadelphia v. New [Jersey]*.

"The Act's additional fee facially discriminates against hazardous waste generated in States other than Alabama, and the Act overall has plainly discouraged the full operation of petitioner's Emelle facility. Such burdensome taxes imposed on interstate commerce alone are generally forbidden:

---

a. Rehnquist was the sole dissenter, as in *Philadelphia*.

b. __ U.S. __, 112 S.Ct. 2019, 119 L.Ed. 2d 139 (1992). This case applied *Philadelphia* to a Michigan law that authorized counties to exclude from landfills waste from outside the regulating county. Such intercounty discrimination did not immunize interstate discrimination from the commerce clause strictures. See *Dean Milk Co. v. Madison*.

5

"[The] State's argument here does not significantly differ from the Alabama Supreme Court's conclusions on the legitimate local purposes of the additional fee imposed, which were:

> 'The Additional Fee serves these legitimate local purposes that cannot be adequately served by reasonable nondiscriminatory alternatives: (1) protection of the health and safety of the citizens of Alabama from toxic substances; (2) conservation of the environment and the state's natural resources; (3) provision for compensatory revenue for the costs and burdens that out-of-state waste generators impose by dumping their hazardous waste in Alabama; (4) reduction of the overall flow of wastes traveling on the state's highways, which flow creates a great risk to the health and safety of the state's citizens.' 584 So.2d, at 1389.

These may all be legitimate local interests, and petitioner has not attacked them. But only rhetoric, and not explanation, emerges as to why Alabama targets *only* interstate hazardous waste to meet these [goals.]

"Ultimately, the State's concern focuses on the volume of the waste entering the Emelle facility. Less discriminatory alternatives, however, are available to alleviate this concern, not the least of which are a generally applicable per-ton additional fee on *all* hazardous waste disposed of within Alabama, or a per-mile tax on *all* vehicles transporting hazardous waste across Alabama roads, or an evenhanded cap on the total tonnage landfilled at Emelle, which would curtail volume from all sources. To the extent Alabama's concern touches environmental conservation and the health and safety of its citizens, such concern does not vary with the point of origin of the waste, and it remains within the State's power to monitor and regulate more closely the transportation and disposal of *all* hazardous waste within its borders. Even with the possible future financial and environmental risks to be borne by Alabama, such risks likewise do not vary with the waste's State of origin in a way allowing foreign, but not local, waste to be burdened. In sum, we find the additional fee to be 'an obvious effort to saddle those outside the State' with most of the burden of slowing the flow of waste into the Emelle facility. *Philadelphia v. New Jersey.* 'That legislative effort is clearly impermissible under the Commerce Clause of the Constitution.' [*Ibid.*].

"*Maine v. Taylor,* provides no additional justification. Maine there demonstrated that the out-of-state baitfish were subject to parasites foreign to in-state baitfish. This difference posed a threat to the State's natural resources, and absent a less discriminatory means of protecting the environment—and none was available—the importation of baitfish could properly be banned. To the contrary, the record establishes that the hazardous waste at issue in this case is the same regardless of its point of origin. As noted in *Fort Gratiot Sanitary Landfill,* 'our conclusion would be different if the imported waste raised health or other concerns not presented by [Alabama] waste.' Because no unique threat is posed, and because adequate means other than overt discrimination meet Alabama's concerns, *Maine v. Taylor* provides the State no respite."

Chapter

STATE POWER TO TAX

SECTION: PRAGMATISM OVER FORMALISM: REQUISITES OF A VALID TAX

JURISDICTION TO TAX

CON LAW: P. 308, after note 3

4. *Do due process "jurisdiction" and commerce clause "substantial nexus" requirements differ?* In QUILL CORP. v. NORTH DAKOTA, ___ U.S. ___, 112 S.Ct. 1904, 119 L.Ed.2d 91 (1992), per STEVENS, J., five justices ruled that they do differ in refusing 8 to 1 to overrule *National Bellas Hess, Inc. v. Department of Revenue*, 386 U.S. 753, 87 S.Ct. 1389, 18 L.Ed.2d 505 (1967).

Ten years before *Complete Auto, Bellas Hess* had ruled that an Illinois law violated both the due process and commerce clauses by requiring out-of-state mail order sellers with no agents, representatives or places of business in Illinois to collect the use tax imposed on their Illinois mail order buyers in Illinois.[1] In *Quill* the majority rejected the due process basis for invalidating such a mail order collection duty but ruled that it still violated the commrce clause:

"The State contends that the nexus requirements imposed by the Due Process and Commerce Clauses are equivalent and that if, as we concluded above, a mail-order house that lacks a physical presence in the taxing State nonetheless satisfies the due process 'minimum contacts' test, then that corporation also meets the Commerce Clause 'substantial nexus' test. We disagree. Despite the similarity in phrasing, the nexus requirements of the Due Process and Commerce Clauses are not identical. The two standards are animated by different constitutional concerns and policies.

"Due process centrally concerns the fundamental fairness of governmental activity. Thus, at the most general level, the due process nexus analysis requires that we ask whether an individual's connections with a State are substantial enough to legitimate the State's exercise of power over him. We have, therefore, often identified 'notice' or 'fair warning' as the analytic touchstone of due process nexus analysis. In contrast, the Commerce Clause, and its nexus requirement, are informed not so much by concerns about fairness for the

---

1. As applied to the buyer the use tax was valid on those who had escaped the state retail sales tax by purchasing out of state. *Henneford v. Silas Mason Co.*, 300 U.S. 577, 57 S.Ct. 524, 81 L.Ed. 814 (1937).

individual defendant as by structural concerns about the effects of state regulation on the national [economy].

"The *Complete Auto* analysis reflects these concerns about the national economy. The second and third parts of that analysis, which require fair apportionment and nondiscrimination, prohibit taxes that pass an unfair share of the tax burden onto interstate commerce. The first and fourth prongs, which require a substantial nexus and a relationship between the tax and State-provided services, limit the reach of State taxing authority so as to ensure that State taxation does not unduly burden interstate commerce. Thus, the 'substantial-nexus' requirement is not, like due process' 'minimum-contacts' requirement, a proxy for notice, but rather a means for limiting state burdens on interstate commerce. Accordingly, contrary to the State's suggestion, a corporation may have the 'minimum contacts' with a taxing State as required by the Due Process Clause, and yet lack the 'substantial nexus' with that State as required by the Commerce Clause.

"[The] bright-line rule of *Bellas Hess* furthers the ends of the dormant Commerce Clause. Undue burdens on interstate commerce may be avoided not only by a case-by-case evaluation of the actual burdens imposed by particular regulations or taxes, but also, in some situations, by the demarcation of a discrete realm of commercial activity that is free from interstate taxation. *Bellas Hess* followed the latter approach and created a safe harbor for vendors 'whose only connection with customers in the [taxing] State is by common carrier or the United States mail.' Under *Bellas Hess,* such vendors are free from state-imposed duties to collect sales and use [taxes].

"Moreover, a bright-line rule in the area of sales and use taxes also encourages settled expectations and, in doing so, fosters investment by businesses and individuals. Indeed, it is not unlikely that the mail-order industry's dramatic growth over the last quarter-century is due in part to the bright-line exemption from state taxation created in *Bellas Hess.*"

Justice Scalia, joined by Kennedy and Thomas, concurred in the due process ruling and concurred in the refusal to overrule *Bellas Hess,* but withheld judgment on the majority's commerce clause reasoning. Instead, Scalia relied on *stare decisis,* noting that "Congress remains free to alter what we have done," and the majority's concern that "the *Bellas Hess* rule has engendered substantial reliance and has become part of the basic framework of a sizeable industry." In a lengthy opinion Justice White also accepted the due process ruling but disagreed with reaching a different result under the commerce clause.

CON LAW: P. 316, after note 3

Unitary tax rulings reaffirmed. ALLIED–SIGNAL v. DIRECTOR, ___ U.S. ___, 112 S.Ct. 2251, ___ L.Ed.2d ___ (1992) entertained but unanimously declined a proposal to overrule the unitary business tax policy approved in the foregoing cases. In an opinion by Kennedy, J., the Court again ruled, on this issue 5 to 4, that this policy did not permit a unitary tax to include in the apportioned income capital gains derived from the purchase and sale as an investment of stock in a corporation engaged in a wholly unrelated business.[2]

2. O'Connor, J., again dissented on the application of the related business requirement, joined by Rehnquist, Blackmun and Thomas.

Chapter

SUBSTANTIVE PROTECTION OF ECONOMIC INTERESTS

SECTION: "TAKING" OF PROPERTY INTERESTS

TAKING THROUGH REGULATION

CON LAW: P. 373, end of note 4

AMER CON: P. 244, end of note 4

RTS & LIB: P. 242, end of note 4

YEE v. CITY OF ESCONDIDO, ___ U.S. ___, 112 S.Ct. 1522, 118 L.Ed.2d 153 (1992), per O'CONNOR, J., unanimously rejected a claim that the convergence of two laws regulating mobile home parks amounted to uncompensated taking of the owner's property through physical occupation, as in *Loretto*. One was an Escondido ordinance regulating the rents mobile home owners paid for the spaces or "pads" where their difficult-to-move "homes" were placed. The 1988 ordinance fixed the rents at their 1986 rates, subject to the right to request increases at any time, which the Council must approve if it determined them to be "just, fair and reasonable" after considering eleven relevant but noninclusive factors.

The other law was the California Mobile Home Residence Law, which limited the grounds on which a park owner could terminate a mobile home owner's tenancy. These included nonpayment of rent, violation of park rules, and the owner's decision to change the use of his land. "While a rental agreement is in effect, the park owner generally may not require removal of a mobile home when it is sold. The park owner may neither charge a transfer fee for the sale, nor disapprove of [any purchaser with] ability to pay the rent." Because of the high cost and potential for damage when moving such homes, the investment in landscaping and other improvements, mobile homes are sold in place in 99 per cent of the cases when an owner wishes to move. Such factors were noted by the California Legislature as reasons for enacting the California law.

Mobile home park owners contended that since under the California law a park owner could not evict a mobile home owner or easily convert the property to other uses, the mobile home owner is a perpetual tenant with a right to occupy the pad at below-market rent indefinitely, which causes a corresponding increase in the value of the mobile home, and yields the tenant a premium for its sale in place. As a result they contended "the rent control ordinance has transferred a discrete interest in land—the right to occupy the land indefinitely at a sub-market rent—from the park owner to the mobile home owner. Petitioners contend that what has been transferred from the park owner to the mobile home owner is no less than a right of physical occupation of the park owner's land.

"This argument, while perhaps within the scope of our regulatory taking cases, cannot be squared easily with our cases on physical takings. The government effects a physical taking only where it *requires* the landowner to submit to the physical occupation of his land. Thus whether the government floods a landowner's property, or does no more than require the landowner to suffer the installation of a cable, *Loretto,* the Takings Clause requires compensation if the government authorizes a compelled physical invasion of property.

"But the Escondido rent control ordinance, even when considered in conjunction with the California Mobilehome Residency Law, authorizes no such thing. Petitioners voluntarily rented their land to mobile home owners. [N]either the City nor the State compels petitioners, once they have rented their property to tenants, to continue doing so. To the contrary, the Mobilehome Residency Law provides that a park owner who wishes to change the use of his land may evict his tenants, albeit with six or twelve months notice. Put bluntly, no government has required any physical invasion of petitioners' property. Petitioners' tenants were invited by petitioners, not forced upon them by the government. While the 'right to exclude' is doubtless, as petitioners assert, 'one of the most essential sticks in the bundle of rights that are commonly characterized as property,' *Kaiser Aetna v. United States,* 444 U.S. 164, 176 (1979), we do not find that right to have been taken from petitioners on the mere face of the Escondido ordinance.

"Petitioners suggest that the statutory procedure for changing the use of a mobile home park is in practice 'a kind of gauntlet,' in that they are not in fact free to change the use of their land. Because petitioners do not claim to have run that gauntlet, however, this case provides no occasion to consider how the procedure has been applied to petitioners' property, and we accordingly confine ourselves to the face of the statute. See *Keystone Bituminous Coal Assn.* A different case would be presented were the statute, on its face or as applied, to compel a landowner over objection to rent his property or to refrain in perpetuity from terminating a tenancy."

CON LAW: P. 381, before section 5

AMER CON: P. 244, at end of notes

RTS & LIB: P. 110, before section 5

LUCAS v. SOUTH CAROLINA COASTAL COUNCIL, ___ U.S. ___, 112 S.Ct. 2886, ___ L.Ed.2d ___ (1992), per SCALIA, J., considered, for the first time in detail, whether denying all economically beneficial, or productive use of land constituted a compensible taking. In 1986 Lucas bought two lots, then zoned for single family dwellings, 300 feet from a South Carolina beach, intending to build such houses on them. Before any construction, a 1988 state law aimed at preventing erosion caused by such developments was applied to bar any more "occupable improvements" that near the seashore. A state trial court held this a compensible taking for depriving Lucas of "any reasonable economic use of the land." The South Carolina Supreme Court reversed, ruling that since the regulation was designed to "preserve South Carolina's beaches" and thus prevent "serious public harm" the taking clause required no compensation. The Supreme Court reversed.

"*Pennsylvania Coal Co. v. Mahon,* [gave] birth [to] the oft-cited maxim that, 'while property may be regulated to a certain extent, if regulation goes too far it will be recognized as a taking.' [In] 70–odd years [of] 'regulatory takings' jurisprudence, we have generally eschewed any 'set formula' for determining how far is too far, preferring to 'engag[e] in essentially ad hoc, factual inquiries,' *Penn Central.* See Epstein, *Takings: Descent and Resurrection,* 1987 Sup.Ct.Rev. 1, 4. We have, however, described at least two discrete categories of regulatory action as compensable without case-specific inquiry into the public interest advanced in support of the restraint. The first encompasses regulations that compel the property owner to suffer a physical 'invasion' of his property. In general (at least with regard to permanent invasions), no matter how minute the intrusion, and no matter how weighty the public purpose behind it, we have required compensation. *Loretto* * * *.

"The second situation in which we have found categorical treatment appropriate is where regulation denies all economically beneficial or productive use of land. See *Agins v. Tiburon,* 447 U.S. 255, 260, 100 S.Ct. 2138, 2141, 65 L.Ed.2d 106 (1980); see also *Nollan; Keystone Bituminous Coal Co.* As we have said on numerous occasions, the Fifth Amendment is violated when land-use regulation 'does not substantially advance legitimate state interests or denies an owner economically viable use of his land.' *Agins.*

"We have never set forth the justification for this rule. Perhaps it is simply, as Justice Brennan suggested, that total deprivation of beneficial use is, from the landowner's point of view, the equivalent of a physical appropriation. See *San Diego Gas & Electric Co. v. San Diego,* 450 U.S., at 652 (Brennan, J., dissenting). [Surely,] at least, in the extraordinary circumstance when no productive or economically beneficial use of land is permitted, it is less realistic to indulge our usual assumption that the legislature is simply 'adjusting the benefits and burdens of economic life,' *Penn Central,* in a manner that secures an 'average reciprocity of advantage' to everyone concerned, *Mahon.* And the functional basis for permitting the government, by regulation, to affect property values without compensation—that 'Government hardly could go on if to some extent values incident to property could not be diminished without paying for every such change in the general law,' ibid.—does not apply to the relatively rare situations where the government has deprived a landowner of all economically beneficial uses.

"On the other side of the balance, affirmatively supporting a compensation requirement, is the fact that regulations that leave the owner of land without economically beneficial or productive options for its use—typically, as here, by requiring land to be left substantially in its natural state—carry with them a heightened risk that private property is being pressed into some form of public service under the guise of mitigating serious public harm. [The] many statutes on the books, both state and federal, that provide for the use of eminent domain to impose servitudes on private scenic lands preventing developmental uses, or to acquire such lands altogether, suggest the practical equivalence in this setting of negative regulation and [appropriation].

"We think, in short, that there are good reasons for our frequently expressed belief that when the owner of real property has been called upon to sacrifice all economically beneficial uses in the name of the common good, that is, to leave his property economically idle, he has suffered a [taking].

"It is correct that many of our prior opinions have suggested that 'harmful or noxious uses' of property may be proscribed by government regulation without the requirement of compensation. For a number of reasons, however, we think the South Carolina Supreme Court was too quick to conclude that that principle decides the present case. The 'harmful or noxious uses' principle was the Court's early attempt to describe in theoretical terms why government may, consistent with the Takings Clause, affect property values by regulation without incurring an obligation to compensate—a reality we nowadays acknowledge explicitly with respect to the full scope of the State's police [power]. 'Harmful or noxious use' analysis was, in other words, simply the progenitor of our more contemporary statements that 'land-use regulation does not effect a taking if it "substantially advance[s] legitimate state interests". . . .' *Nollan,* (quoting *Agins*).

"The transition from our early focus on control of 'noxious' uses to our contemporary understanding of the broad realm within which government may regulate without compensation was an easy one, since the distinction between 'harm-preventing' and 'benefit-conferring' regulation is often in the eye of the beholder. It is quite possible, for example, to describe in either fashion the ecological, economic, and aesthetic concerns that inspired the South Carolina legislature in the present case. One could say that imposing a servitude on Lucas's land is necessary in order to prevent his use of it from 'harming' South Carolina's ecological resources; or, instead, in order to achieve the 'benefits' of an ecological preserve.

"When it is understood that 'prevention of harmful use' was merely our early formulation of the police power justification necessary to sustain (without compensation) any regulatory diminution in value; and that the distinction between regulation that 'prevents harmful use' and that which 'confers benefits' is difficult, if not impossible, to discern on an objective, value-free basis; it becomes self-evident that noxious-use logic cannot serve as a touchstone to distinguish regulatory 'takings'—which require compensation—from regulatory deprivations that do not require compensation. A fortiori the legislature's recitation of a noxious-use justification cannot be the basis for departing from our categorical rule that total regulatory takings must be compensated. If it were, departure would virtually always be allowed. The South Carolina Supreme Court's approach would essentially nullify *Mahon's* affirmation of limits to the noncompensable exercise of the police power. Our cases provide no support for this: None of them that employed the logic of 'harmful use' prevention to sustain a regulation involved an allegation that the regulation wholly eliminated the value of the claimant's land.

"Where the State seeks to sustain regulation that deprives land of all economically beneficial use, we think it may resist compensation only if the logically antecedent inquiry into the nature of the owner's estate shows that the proscribed use interests were not part of his title to begin with. This accords, we think, with our 'takings' jurisprudence, which has traditionally been guided by the understandings of our citizens regarding the content of, and the State's power over, the 'bundle of rights' that they acquire when they obtain title to property. It seems to us that the property owner necessarily expects the uses of his property to be restricted, from time to time, by various measures newly enacted by the State in legitimate exercise of its police powers; '[a]s long recognized, some values are enjoyed under an implied limitation and must yield to the police power.' *Mahon.* And in the case of personal property, by reason of the State's traditionally high degree of control over commercial dealings, he ought to be aware of the possibility that new regulation might even render his property economically worthless (at least if the property's only economically productive use is sale or manufacture for sale), see *Andrus v. Allard.* In the case of land, however, we think the notion pressed by the Council that title is somehow held subject to the 'implied limitation' that the State may subsequently eliminate all economically valuable use is inconsistent with the historical compact recorded in the Takings Clause that has become part of our constitutional culture.

"Where 'permanent physical occupation' of land is concerned, we have refused to allow the government to decree it anew (without compensation), no matter how weighty the asserted 'public interests' involved, *Loretto,* though we assuredly would permit the government to assert a permanent easement that was a pre-existing limitation upon the landowner's title. We believe similar treatment must be accorded confiscatory regulations, i.e., regulations that prohibit all economically beneficial use of land: Any limitation so severe cannot be newly legislated or decreed (without compensation), but must inhere in the title itself, in the restrictions that background principles of the State's law of property and nuisance already place upon land ownership. A law or decree with such an effect must, in other words, do no more than duplicate the result that could have been achieved in the courts—by adjacent landowners (or other uniquely affected persons) under the State's law of private nuisance, or by the State under its complementary power to abate nuisances that affect the public generally, or otherwise.

"On this analysis, the owner of a lake bed, for example, would not be entitled to compensation when he is denied the requisite permit to engage in a landfilling operation that would have the effect of flooding others' land. Nor the corporate owner of a nuclear generating plant, when it is directed to remove all improvements from its land upon discovery that the plant sits astride an earthquake fault. Such regulatory action may well have the effect of eliminating the land's only economically productive use, but it does not proscribe a productive use that was previously permissible under relevant property and nuisance principles. The use of these properties for what are now expressly prohibited purposes was always unlawful, and (subject to other constitutional limitations) it was open to the State at any point to make the implication of those background principles of nuisance and property law explicit. See Michelman, Property, Utility, and Fairness, Comments on the Ethical Foundations of 'Just Compensation' Law, 80 Harv.L.Rev. 1165, 1239–1241 (1967). In light of our traditional resort to 'existing rules or understandings that stem from an independent source such as state law' to define the range of interests that qualify for protection as 'property' under the Fifth (and Fourteenth) amendments, *Board of Regents v. Roth,* 408 U.S. 564, 577 (1972), this recognition that the Takings Clause does not require compensation when an owner is barred from putting land to a use that is proscribed by those 'existing rules or understandings' is surely unexceptional. When, however, a regulation that declares 'off-limits' all economically productive or beneficial uses of land goes beyond what the relevant background principles would dictate, compensation must be paid to sustain it.

"The 'total taking' inquiry we require today will ordinarily entail (as the application of state nuisance law ordinarily entails) analysis of, among other things, the degree of harm to public lands and resources, or adjacent private property, posed by the claimant's proposed activities, see, e.g., Restatement (Second) of Torts §§ 826, 827, the social value of the claimant's activities and their suitability to the locality in question, see, e.g., id., §§ 828(a) and (b), 831, and the relative ease with which the alleged harm can be avoided through measures taken by the claimant and the government (or adjacent private landowners) alike, see, e.g., id., §§ 827(e), 828(c), 830. The fact that a particular use has long been engaged in by similarly situated owners ordinarily imports a lack of any common-law prohibition (though changed circumstances or new knowledge may make what was previously permissible no longer so, see Restatement (Second) of Torts, supra, § 827, comment g.) So also does the fact that other landowners, similarly situated, are permitted to continue the use denied to the claimant.

"It seems unlikely that common-law principles would have prevented the erection of any habitable or productive improvements on petitioner's land; they rarely support prohibition of the 'essential use' of land, *Curtin v. Benson,* 222 U.S. 78, 86 (1911). The question, however, is one of state law to be dealt with on remand. We emphasize that to win its case South Carolina must do more than proffer the legislature's declaration that the uses Lucas desires are inconsistent with the public interest, or the conclusory assertion that they violate a common-law maxim such as *sic utere tuo ut alienum non laedas.* [Instead], as it would be required to do if it sought to restrain Lucas in a common-law action for public nuisance, South Carolina must identify background principles of nuisance and property law that prohibit the uses he now intends in the circumstances in which the property is presently found. Only on this showing can the State fairly claim that, in proscribing all such beneficial uses, the Beachfront Management Act is taking nothing."

KENNEDY, J., concurred in the judgment but favored a broader standard for deciding such cases than the majority's "background principles of the law of property and nuisance," and also stressed the owner's "reasonable investment backed expectations:"

"In my view, reasonable expectations must be understood in light of the whole of our legal tradition. The common law of nuisance is too narrow a confine for the exercise of regulatory power in a complex and interdependent society. *Goldblatt v. Hempstead.* The State should not be prevented from enacting new regulatory initiatives in response to changing conditions, and courts must consider all reasonable expectations whatever their source. The Takings Clause does not require a static body of state property law; it protects private expectations to ensure private investment. I agree with the Court that nuisance prevention accords with the most common expectations of property owners who face regulation, but I do not believe this can be the sole source of state authority to impose severe restrictions. Coastal property may present such unique concerns for a fragile land system that the State can go further in regulating its development and use than the common law of nuisance might otherwise permit.

"The Supreme Court of South Carolina erred, in my view, by reciting the general purposes for which the state regulations were enacted without a determination that they were in accord with the owner's reasonable expectations and therefore sufficient to support a severe restriction on specific parcels of property. The promotion of tourism, for instance, ought not to suffice to deprive specific property of all value without a corresponding duty to compensate. Furthermore, the means as well as the ends of regulation must accord with the owner's reasonable expectations. Here, the State did not act until after the property had been zoned for individual lot development and most other parcels had been improved, throwing the whole burden of the regulation on the remaining lots. This too must be measured in the balance." *Mahon.*

Justices BLACKMUN and STEVENS each dissented separately: [a]

BLACKMUN, J. " * * * If the state legislature is correct that the prohibition on building in front of the setback line prevents serious harm, then, under this Court's prior cases, the Act is constitutional. 'Long ago it was recognized that all property in this country is held under the implied obligation that the owner's use of it shall not be injurious to the community, and the Takings Clause did not transform that principle to one that requires compensation whenever the State asserts its power to enforce it.' *Keystone Bituminous Coal Assn.* The Court consistently has upheld regulations imposed to arrest a significant threat to the common welfare, whatever their economic effect on the [owner].

"Nothing in the record undermines the General Assembly's assessment that prohibitions on building in front of the setback line are necessary to protect people and property from storms, high tides, and beach erosion. Because that legislative determination cannot be disregarded in the absence of such evidence, and because its determination of harm to life and property from building is sufficient to prohibit that use under this Court's cases, the South Carolina Supreme Court correctly found no taking. * * *

"I [question] the Court's rationale in creating a category that obviates a 'case-specific inquiry into the public interest advanced,' if all economic value has been lost. If one fact about the Court's taking jurisprudence can be stated without contradiction, it is that 'the particular circumstances of each case' determine whether a specific restriction will be rendered invalid by the government's failure to pay compensation. *United States v. Central Eureka Mining Co.,* 357 U.S. 155, 168 (1958). This is so because although we have articulated certain factors to be considered, including the economic impact on the property owner, the ultimate conclusion 'necessarily requires a weighing of private and public interests.' *Agins.* When the government regulation prevents the owner from any economically valuable use of his property, the private interest is unquestionably substantial, but we have never before held that no public interest can outweigh it. Instead the Court's prior decisions 'uniformly reject the proposition that diminution in property value, standing alone, can establish a "taking." ' *Penn Central.*

"The Court recognizes that 'our prior opinions have suggested that "harmful or noxious uses" of property may be proscribed by government regulation without the requirement of compensation,' but seeks to reconcile them with its categorical rule by claiming that the Court never has upheld a regulation when the owner alleged the loss of all economic [value].

"These cases rest on the principle that the State has full power to prohibit an owner's use of property if it is harmful to the public. '[S]ince no individual has a right to use his property so as to create a nuisance or otherwise harm others, the State has not "taken" anything when it asserts its power to enjoin the nuisance-like activity.' *Keystone Bituminous Coal.* It would make no sense

---

a. Justice Souter expressed no views on the merits, stating that he would dismiss the writ of certiorari as improvidently granted because, after briefing and arguments, the "assumption that [the] state had deprived the owner of his entire economic interest in the subject property [was] highly questionable," yet unreviewable on the record. In Souter's view, this prevented adequate consideration and explication of both the "uncertain concept of total deprivation" and the nuisance and property law exception advanced by the majority.

under this theory to suggest that an owner has a constitutionally protected right to harm others, if only he makes the proper showing of economic [loss].

"Until today, the Court explicitly had rejected the contention that the government's power to act without paying compensation turns on whether the prohibited activity is a common-law nuisance. The brewery closed in Mugler itself was not a common-law nuisance, and the Court specifically stated that it was the role of the legislature to determine what measures would be appropriate for the protection of public health and safety. In upholding the state action in *Miller v. Schoene,* the Court found it unnecessary to 'weigh with nicety the question whether the infected cedars constitute a nuisance according to common law; or whether they may be so declared by statute.' Instead the Court has relied in the past, as the South Carolina Court has done here, on legislative judgments of what constitutes a [harm].

"The threshold inquiry for imposition of the Court's new rule, 'deprivation of all economically valuable use,' itself cannot be determined objectively. As the Court admits, whether the owner has been deprived of all economic value of his property will depend on how 'property' is [defined]. 'We have long understood that any land-use regulation can be characterized as the "total" deprivation of an aptly defined entitlement * * *. Alternatively, the same regulation can always be characterized as a mere "partial" withdrawal from full, unencumbered ownership of the landholding affected by the regulation * * *.' Michelman, *Takings, 1987,* 88 Colum.L.Rev. 1600, 1614 (1988).

"The Court's decision in *Keystone Bituminous Coal* illustrates this principle perfectly. In *Keystone,* the Court determined that the 'support estate' was 'merely a part of the entire bundle of rights possessed by the owner.' Thus, the Court concluded that the support estate's destruction merely eliminated one segment of the total property. The dissent, however, characterized the support estate as a distinct property interest that was wholly destroyed. The Court could agree on no 'value-free basis' to resolve this dispute.

"Even more perplexing, however, is the Court's reliance on common-law principles of nuisance in its quest for a value-free taking jurisprudence. In determining what is a nuisance at common law, state courts make exactly the decision that the Court finds so troubling when made by the South Carolina General Assembly today: they determine whether the use is harmful. Common-law public and private nuisance law is simply a determination whether a particular use causes harm. See Prosser, Private Action for Public Nuisance, 52 Va.L.Rev. 997, 997 (1966) ('Nuisance is a French word which means nothing more than harm'). There is nothing magical in the reasoning of judges long dead. They determined a harm in the same way as state judges and legislatures do today. If judges in the 18th and 19th centuries can distinguish a harm from a benefit, why not judges in the 20th century, and if judges can, why not legislators? There simply is no reason to believe that new interpretations of the hoary common law nuisance doctrine will be particularly 'objective' or 'value-free.' Once one abandons the level of generality of *sic utere tuo ut alienum non laedas,* one searches in vain, I think, for anything resembling a principle in the common law of [nuisance].

"Finally, the Court justifies its new rule that the legislature may not deprive a property owner of the only economically valuable use of his land, even if the legislature finds it to be a harmful use, because such action is not part of the 'long recognized' 'understandings of our citizens.' These 'understandings' permit such regulation only if the use is a nuisance under the common law. Any other course is 'inconsistent with the historical compact recorded in the Takings Clause.' It is not clear from the Court's opinion where our 'historical compact' or 'citizens' understanding' comes from, but it does not appear to be history."

[After several pages showing limited use of the taking concept in United States history, Justice Blackmun concluded]: "In short, I find no clear and accepted 'historical compact' or 'understanding of our citizens' justifying the Court's new taking doctrine. Instead, the Court seems to treat history as a grab-bag of principles, to be adopted where they support the Court's theory, and ignored where they do not. If the Court decided that the early common law provides the background principles for interpreting the Taking Clause, then regulation, as opposed to physical confiscation, would not be compensable. If the Court decided that the law of a later period provides the background principles, then regulation might be compensable, but the Court would have to confront the fact that legislatures regularly determined which uses were prohibited, independent of the common law, and independent of whether the uses were lawful when the owner purchased."

STEVENS, J.: * * * "In my opinion, the Court is doubly in error. The categorical rule the Court establishes is an unsound and unwise addition to the law and the Court's formulation of the exception to that rule is too rigid and too narrow. * * *

"In addition to lacking support in past decisions, the Court's new rule is wholly arbitrary. A landowner whose property is diminished in value 95% recovers nothing, while an owner whose property is diminished 100% recovers the land's full [value].

"The Court's holding today effectively freezes the State's common law, denying the legislature much of its traditional power to revise the law governing the rights and uses of property. Until today, I had thought that we had long abandoned this approach to constitutional law. More than a century ago we recognized that 'the great office of statutes is to remedy defects in the common law as they are developed, and to adapt it to the changes of time and circumstances.' *Munn v. Illinois,* 94 U.S. 113, 134 (1877). As Justice Marshall observed about a position similar to that adopted by the Court today: 'If accepted, that claim would represent a return to the era of *Lochner,* when common-law rights were also found immune from revision by State or Federal Government. Such an approach would freeze the common law as it has been constructed by the courts, perhaps at its 19th–century state of development. It would allow no room for change in response to changes in circumstance. The Due Process Clause does not require such a result.' *Prune Yard Shopping Center v. Robins,* 447 U.S. 74, 93 (1980) (concurring opinion).

"Arresting the development of the common law is not only a departure from our prior decisions; it is also profoundly unwise. The human condition is one of constant learning and evolution—both moral and practical. Legislatures implement that new learning; in doing so they must often revise the definition of property and the rights of property owners. Thus, when the Nation came to understand that slavery was morally wrong and mandated the emancipation of all slaves, it, in effect, redefined 'property.' On a lesser scale, our ongoing self-education produces similar changes in the rights of property owners: New appreciation of the significance of endangered species, see, e.g., *Andrus v. Allard,* the importance of wetlands, see, e.g., 16 U.S.C. § 3801 et seq.; and the vulnerability of coastal lands, see, e.g., 16 U.S.C. § 1451 et seq., shapes our evolving understandings of property rights.

"Of course, some legislative redefinitions of property will effect a taking and must be compensated—but it certainly cannot be the case that every movement away from common law does so. There is no reason, and less sense, in such an absolute rule. We live in a world in which changes in the economy and the environment occur with increasing frequency and importance. If it was wise a century ago to allow Government ' "the largest legislative discretion" ' to deal with ' "the special exigencies of the moment," ' *Mugler*, it is imperative to do so today. The rule that should govern a decision in a case of this kind should focus on the future, not the past."

Chapter

PROTECTION OF INDIVIDUAL RIGHTS: DUE PROCESS, THE BILL OF RIGHTS, AND NONTEXTUAL CONSTITUTIONAL RIGHTS

SECTION: NATURE AND SCOPE OF FOURTEENTH AMENDMENT DUE PROCESS; APPLICABILITY OF THE BILL OF RIGHTS TO THE STATES

THE "ORDERED LIBERTY—FUNDAMENTAL FAIRNESS," "TOTAL INCORPORATION" AND "SELECTIVE INCORPORATION" THEORIES

CON LAW: P. 399, end of Part I

AMER CON: P. 253, end of Part I

RTS & LIB: P. 128, end of Part I

In PACIFIC MUT. LIFE INS. CO. v. HASLIP, ___ U.S. ___, 111 S.Ct. 1032, 113 L.Ed.2d 1 (1991) the Court, per BLACKMUN, J., held that an award of punitive damages against an insurer, for fraud perpetuated by its agent (an award more than four times the amount of compensatory damages and far in excess of the fine that could be imposed for insurance fraud under Alabama law), did not—considering the constraints imposed by Alabama's procedures—violate the Fourteenth Amendment's Due Process Clause. The Court "concede[d] that unlimited jury discretion—or unlimited judicial discretion for that matter—in the fixing of punitive damages may invite extreme results that jar one's constitutional sensibilities," but concluded, after examining Alabama procedures, that "the award here did not lack objective criteria" and thus "did not cross the line into the area of constitutional impropriety." In the course of his opinion, Justice Blackmun observed:

"So far as we have been able to determine, every state and federal court that has considered the question has ruled that the common-law method for assessing punitive damages does not in itself violate due process. In view of this consistent history, we cannot say that the common-law method for assessing punitive damages is so inherently unfair as to deny due process and be *per se* unconstitutional. * * * [T]he common-law method for assessing punitive damages was well established before the Fourteenth Amendment was enacted. Nothing in that Amendment's text or history indicates an intention on the part of its drafters to overturn the prevailing method.

"This, however, is not the end of the matter. It would be just as inappropriate to say, that because punitive damages have been recognized for so long, their imposition is never unconstitutional. See *Williams v. Illinois,* 399 U.S. 235, 90 S.Ct. 2018, 26 L.Ed.2d 586 (1970) [a] ('Neither the antiquity of a practice nor the fact of steadfast legislative and judicial adherence to it through the centuries insulates it from constitutional attack * * *.') We note once again our concern about punitive damages that 'run wild.' Having said that, we conclude that our task today is to determine whether the Due Process Clause renders the punitive damage award in this case constitutionally unacceptable."

The case prompted JUSTICE SCALIA, who concurred in the judgment, to make some general comments about "due process of law," "'fundamental fairness' under the Fourteenth Amendment," the proper role of history in a due process analysis, "incorporation" within the Fourteenth Amendment of the Bill of Rights guarantees, and the difference between the denial of due process and the denial of equal protection:

"Determining whether common-law procedures for awarding punitive damages can deny 'due process of law' requires some inquiry into the meaning of that majestic phrase. * * *

"*Hurtado v. California,* 110 U.S. 516, 4 S.Ct. 111, 28 L.Ed. 232 (1884) [holding that a murder defendant had not been denied due process because the state prosecution had not been initiated by grand jury indictment, as required by the Fifth Amendment] clarified the proper role of history in a due process analysis: if the government chooses to *follow* a historically approved procedure, it necessarily *provides* due process, but if it chooses to *depart* from historical practice, it does not necessarily *deny* due process. The remaining business, of course, was to develop a test for determining *when* a departure from historical practice denies due process. *Hurtado* provided scant guidance.

"[The] concept of 'fundamental justice' thus entered the due process lexicon not as a description of what due process entails in general, but as a description of what it entails when traditional procedures are dispensed with. As the Court reiterated in *Twining v. New Jersey* (1908), 'consistently with the requirements of due process, no *change* in ancient procedure can be made which disregards those *fundamental principles,* to be ascertained from time to time by judicial action, which have relation to process of law and protect the citizen in his private right, and guard him against the arbitrary action of government' (emphasis added).

"[By] the time the Court decided *Snyder v. Massachusetts* (1934), its understanding of due process had shifted in a subtle but significant way. That case rejected a criminal defendant's claim that he had been denied due process by being prevented from accompanying his jury on a visit to the scene of the crime. Writing for the Court, Justice Cardozo assumed that due process required 'fundamental justice,' or 'fairness' in *all* cases, and not merely when evaluating nontraditional procedures. * * * Even so, however, only the mode of analysis and not the content of the Due Process Clause had changed, since in assessing whether some principle of 'fundamental justice' had been violated, the Court was willing to accord historical practice dispositive weight. [In] the ensuing decades, however, the concept of 'fundamental fairness' under the Fourteenth Amend-

---

a. *Williams* held that a criminal defendant unable to pay the fine could not be incarcerated beyond the maximum term fixed by statute; equal protection requires that the "statutory ceiling" on imprisonment be the same for all "irrespective of their economic status."

ment became increasingly decoupled from the traditional historical approach. The principal mechanism for that development was the incorporation within the Fourteenth Amendment of the Bill of Rights guarantees. Although the Court resisted for some time the idea that 'fundamental fairness' necessarily included the protections of the Bill of Rights, see, e.g., *Adamson,* it ultimately incorporated virtually all of them. * * * *Gideon v. Wainwright,* 372 U.S. 335, 83 S.Ct. 792, 9 L.Ed.2d 799 (1963) established that no matter how strong its historical pedigree, a procedure prohibited by the Sixth Amendment (failure to appoint counsel in certain criminal cases) violates 'fundamental fairness' and must be abandoned by the States.

"To say that unbroken historical usage cannot save a procedure that violates one of the explicit procedural guarantees of the Bill of Rights (applicable through the Fourteenth Amendment) is not necessarily to say that such usage cannot demonstrate the procedure's compliance with the more general guarantee of 'due process.' In principle, what is important enough to have been included within the Bill of Rights has good claim to being an element of 'fundamental fairness,' whatever history might say; and as a practical matter, the invalidation of traditional state practices achievable through the Bill of Rights is at least limited to enumerated subjects. But disregard of 'the procedure of the ages' for incorporation purposes has led to its disregard more generally.

"[In] any case, our due process opinions in recent decades have indiscriminately applied balancing analysis to determine 'fundamental fairness,' without regard to whether the procedure under challenge was (1) a traditional one, and if so (2) prohibited by the Bill of Rights. Even so, however, very few cases have used the due process clause, without the benefit of an accompanying Bill of Rights guarantee, to strike down a procedure concededly approved by traditional and continuing American practice. Most notably, in *Sniadach v. Family Finance Corp.,* 395 U.S. 337, 340, 89 S.Ct. 1820, 23 L.Ed.2d 349 (1969), over the strenuous dissent of Justice Black, the Court declared unconstitutional the garnishment of wages, saying that '[t]he fact that a procedure would pass muster under a feudal regime does not mean it gives necessary protection to all property in its modern forms.' And in *Shaffer v. Heitner,* 433 U.S. 186, 97 S.Ct. 2569, 53 L.Ed.2d 683 (1977), the Court invalidated general *quasi in rem* jurisdiction, saying that ' "traditional notions of fair play and substantial justice" can be as readily offended by the perpetuation of ancient forms that are no longer justified as by the adoption of new procedures that are inconsistent with the basic values of our constitutional heritage.' Such cases, at least in their broad pronouncements if not with respect to the particular provisions at issue, were in my view wrongly decided.

"I might, for reasons of *stare decisis,* adhere to the principle that these cases announce, except for the fact that our later cases give it nothing but lip service, and by their holdings reaffirm the view that traditional practice (unless contrary to the Bill of Rights) is conclusive of 'fundamental fairness.' As I wrote last Term in *Burnham v. Superior Court of Calif.,* 495 U.S. 604, 110 S.Ct. 2105, 109 L.Ed.2d 631 (1990), nothing but the conclusiveness of history can explain why jurisdiction based upon mere service of process within a State—either generally or on the precise facts of that case—is 'fundamentally fair.' Nor to my mind can anything else explain today's decision that a punishment whose assessment and extent are committed entirely to the discretion of the jury is 'fundamentally fair.'

"[When] the rationale of earlier cases (*Sniadach* and *Shaffer*) is contradicted by later holdings—and particularly when that rationale has no basis in constitutional text and itself contradicts opinions never explicitly overruled—I think it has no valid *stare decisis* claim upon me. Our holdings remain in conflict, no matter which course I take. I choose, then, to take the course that accords with the language of the Constitution and with our interpretation of it through the first half of this century. I reject the principle, aptly described and faithfully followed in Justice O'Connor's dissent, that a traditional procedure of our society becomes unconstitutional whenever the Members of this Court 'lose * * * confidence' in it. And like Justice Cardozo in *Snyder,* I affirm that no procedure firmly rooted in the practices of our people can be so 'fundamentally unfair' as to deny due process of law.

"Let me be clear about the scope of the principle I am applying. It does not say that every practice sanctioned by history is constitutional. It does not call into question, for example, the case of *Williams v. Illinois,* relied upon by both the majority and the dissent, where we held unconstitutional the centuries-old practice of permitting convicted criminals to reduce their prison sentences by paying fines. The basis of that invalidation was not denial of due process but denial to indigent prisoners of equal protection of the laws. The Equal Protection Clause and other provisions of the Constitution, unlike the Due Process Clause, are not an explicit invocation of the 'law of the land,' and might be thought to have some counter historical content. Moreover, the principle I apply today does not reject our cases holding that procedures demanded by the Bill of Rights—which extends against the States only *through* the Due Process Clause—must be provided despite historical practice to the contrary. Thus, it does not call into question the proposition that punitive damages, despite their historical sanction, can violate the First Amendment. See, e.g., *Gertz v. Robert Welch* [CON LAW p. 707, AMER CON p. 491, RTS & LIB p. 436] (First Amendment prohibits awards of punitive damages in certain defamation suits).
* * *

"We have expended much ink upon the due-process implications of punitive damages, and the fact-specific nature of the Court's opinion guarantees that we and other courts will expend much more in the years to come. Since jury-assessed punitive damages are a part of our living tradition that dates back prior to 1868, I would end the suspense and categorically affirm their validity."

Dissenting JUSTICE O'CONNOR maintained that "Alabama's common-law punitive damages scheme is void for vagueness." Moreover, applying the test of procedural due process set out in *Mathews v. Eldridge,* CON LAW p. 633, she thought it "clear that the state procedures deprive defendants of property without due process of law." She then addressed Justice Scalia's notion of what due process requires:

"[Justice Scalia] argues that a practice with a long historical pedigree is immune to reexamination. The Court properly rejects this argument. A static notion of due process is flatly inconsistent with *Mathews,* in which this Court announced that the requirements of the Due Process Clause are ' "flexible" ' and may vary with ' "time, place and circumstances." ' * * *

"Due Process is not a fixed notion. Procedural rules, 'even ancient ones, must satisfy contemporary notions of due process.' Although history creates a strong presumption of continued validity, 'the Court has the authority under the [Fourteenth] Amendment to examine even traditionally accepted procedures and declare them invalid.'

"The Court's decision in *Williams v. Illinois* is also instructive. [There,] the Court invalidated on equal protection grounds the time-honored practice of extending prison terms beyond the statutory maximum when a defendant was unable to pay a fine or court costs. * * *

"As in *Williams,* the time has come to reassess the constitutionality of a time-honored practice. The explosion in the frequency and size of punitive damage awards has exposed the constitutional defects that inhere in the common-law system. That we did not discover these defects earlier is regrettable, but it does not mean that we can pretend that they do not exist now. * * * Circumstances today are different than they were 200 years ago, and nothing in the Fourteenth Amendment requires us to blind ourselves to this fact. Just the opposite is true. The Due Process Clause demands that we possess some degree of confidence that the procedures employed to deprive persons of life, liberty, and property are capable of producing fair and reasonable results. When we lose that confidence, a change must be made."

THE RETROACTIVE EFFECT OF A HOLDING OF UNCONSTITUTIONALITY

CON LAW: P. 410, add to note 2

AMER CON: P. 264, add to note 2

RTS & LIB: P. 139, add to note 2

Consider Fallon & Meltzer, *New Law, Non–Retroactivity, and Constitutional Remedies,* 104 Harv.L.Rev. 1731, 1747–49, 1816–20 (1991):

"Only once since *Teague* has the Court found the ruling by a habeas petition to be 'dictated' by relevant precedent.[76] As it has been implemented, *Teague* shields state convictions from collateral attacks based not simply on 'clear breaks' in the law, but, as the Court put it in *Sawyer v. Smith,*[77] even from those based on 'gradual' developments.

"The conception of legal newness implicit in *Teague* and its progeny is difficult to reconcile with the conception of the judicial role embraced by Justice Harlan. Whereas Justice Harlan viewed the law as a fabric stitched together by reason, the current Court often sounds as if in the thrall of the kind of starkly positivist, judicial lawmaking paradigm that Justice Harlan expressly rejected. In *Butler v. McKellar,* for example, the Court denominated as 'new' a decision it had previously characterized as 'controlled' by a settled precedent [see *supra* fn. 76]. Chief Justice Rehnquist's majority opinion dismissed the prior characterization as a polite formula whose claim to descriptive accuracy had dissolved under the acids of legal realism: courts commonly describe 'their decision as being

---

76. *See* Penry v. Lynaugh, 109 S.Ct. 2934, 2946–47 (1989). Butler v. McKellar, 110 S.Ct. 1212 (1990), reflects the Court's characteristic approach. At issue in *Butler* was the retroactive application on habeas of Arizona v. Roberson, 486 U.S. 675 (1988). *Roberson* held that Edwards v. Arizona, 451 U.S. 477 (1981), which bars police from initiating further interrogation once a suspect has requested counsel, applies even when, unlike *Edwards,* the further interrogation concerns a different crime. *See Roberson,* 486 U.S. at 685–88. The Court in *Roberson* had characterized its holding as "controlled" by *Edwards. Id.* In *Butler,* however, the Court held that for purposes of retroactivity doctrine on habeas corpus, *Roberson* established a new rule. *See* 110 S.Ct. at 1217–18. Other cases are to the same effect. *See, e.g.,* Saffle v. Parks, 110 S.Ct. 1257, 1261–63 (1990) (deciding that a rule forbidding an instruction to capital sentencing juries to disregard any influence of sympathy would be new, despite its similarity to a rule found to have been "dictated" by precedent).

77. 110 S.Ct. 2822, 2831–33 (1990) (holding that Caldwell v. Mississippi, 472 U.S. 320, 328–30 (1985), which found an eighth amendment violation when a jury imposing the death penalty was falsely told that responsibility for determining the appropriateness of capital punishment lay elsewhere, was not retroactive under *Teague*).

"controlled" or "governed" by prior opinions' even when the outcome is 'susceptible to debate among reasonable minds.' When debate is possible, Chief Justice Rehnquist reasoned, prior law does not really control; judges must choose. Their choice is controlled by will, and becomes the law only because judges make it so.

Unlike *Griffith [v. Kentucky]*, *Teague* has provoked sharp and continuing divisions within the Supreme Court. For *Teague* directly threatens central concerns of the Court's more liberal Justices by sharply diminishing the role of federal habeas corpus courts in defining and protecting constitutional rights.

* * *

"[H]owever attractive the basic framework, *Teague's* specific application is both unpersuasive and troubling.

"First, *Teague's* definition of the claims that will be deemed to rest on new law—and thus barred from relitigation on habeas unless they qualify for an exception—is far too expansive. By disabling federal habeas courts from granting relief whenever reasonable disagreement is possible about whether a right currently exists, *Teague* reduces the incentives for state courts, and state law enforcement officials, to take account of the evolving direction of the law. A better view would emphasize the continuities in adjudication, and the past reasoning process that links issues not yet clearly resolved to past decisions and principles. In short, new law should be defined more narrowly, to exclude rules and decisions that are clearly foreshadowed, not just those that are 'dictated by precedent.'

"Equally troubling is the narrowness of the exceptions to *Teague's* rule barring consideration of new law claims. The first of these—for new constitutional decisions immunizing primary conduct—is unexceptionable. But the Court's stringent limitation of the second exception to rules that both implicate concerns of fundamental fairness and benefit the innocent restricts federal habeas corpus more sharply than would any of the leading models. * * * Just as disturbing is the Court's refusal to relax *Teague's* strictures in capital cases. In our view allegations of constitutional defects that may have led to an unreliable imposition of a sentence of death requires relaxation of principles that generally favor finality.[481]

* * *

"Analysis of *Teague* * * * yields a mixed verdict. Although the Court's approach rests on a defensible insight that relatively exacting retroactivity standards should prevail on habeas, that insight should mark the beginning, not the end, of an effort to define appropriate principles of review. The Court appears too single-minded in its effort to make new law not simply relevant, but dominant, in shaping the scope of habeas corpus jurisdiction, and too eager to use new law as a tool for sharply restricting habeas courts from either developing or enforcing the constitutional law of criminal procedure."

481. * * * The *Teague* opinion did not consider the need for a third exception for constitutional claims that ordinarily are difficult to raise on direct review—for example, ineffective assistance of counsel, or prosecutorial failure to disclose exculpatory evidence. * * *

SECTION: THE RIGHT OF "PRIVACY" (OR "AUTONOMY" OR "PERSONHOOD")

CON LAW: P. 510, after *Hodgson*

AMER CON: P. 351, after *Hodgson*

RTS & LIB: P. 239, after *Hodgson*

RUST v. SULLIVAN, ___ U.S. ___, 111 S.Ct. 1759, 114 L.Ed.2d 233 (1991) (the free speech aspects of which are discussed infra this Supplement) upheld federal regulations that implement Title X of the Public Health Services Act by (1) prohibiting a Title X project from providing counseling concerning the use of abortion (or providing referral for abortion) as a method of family planning; (2) prohibiting a Title X project from engaging in activities that "encourage, promote or advocate abortion as a matter of family planning"; and (3) requiring that Title X projects be organized so that they are "physically and financially separate" from prohibited abortion activities. The Court, per REHNQUIST, C.J., rejected, inter alia, the arguments (as the majority described them) that the regulations violate a woman's "Fifth Amendment right to medical self-determination and to make informed medical decisions free of government-imposed harm":

"The Government has no constitutional duty to subsidize an activity merely because the activity is constitutionally protected and may validly choose to fund childbirth over abortion and 'implement that judgment by the allocation of public funds' for medical services relating to childbirth but not to those relating to abortion. *Webster*.

"[That] the regulations do not impermissibly burden a woman's Fifth Amendment rights is evident from the line of cases beginning with *Maher* and *McRae* and culminating in our most recent decision in *Webster*. [The] difficulty that a woman encounters when a Title X project does not provide abortion counseling or referral leaves her in no different position than she would have been if the government had not enacted Title X.

"In *Webster* we stated that '[h]aving held that the State's refusal [in *Maher*] to fund abortions does not violate *Roe v. Wade*, it strains logic to reach a contrary result for the use of public facilities and employees.' It similarly would strain logic, in light of the more extreme restrictions in those cases, to find that the mere decision to exclude abortion-related services from a federally funded *pre-conceptual* family planning program, is unconstitutional.

"Petitioners also argue that by impermissibly infringing on the doctor/patient relationship and depriving a Title X client of information concerning abortion as a method of family planning, the regulations violate a woman's Fifth Amendment right to medical self-determination and to make informed medical decisions free of government-imposed harm. They argue that under our decisions in *Akron* and *Thornburgh* the government cannot interfere with a woman's right to make an informed and voluntary choice by placing restrictions on the patient/doctor dialogue.

"* * * Critical to our decisions in *Akron* and *Thornburgh* to invalidate a governmental intrusion into the patient/doctor dialogue was the fact that the laws in both cases required *all* doctors within their respective jurisdictions to provide *all* pregnant patients contemplating an abortion a litany of information, regardless of whether the patient sought the information or whether the doctor thought the information necessary to the patient's decision. Under the Secretary's regulations, however, a doctor's ability to provide, and a woman's right to receive, information concerning abortion and abortion-related services outside the context of the Title X project remains unfettered. It would undoubtedly be easier for a woman seeking an abortion if she could receive information about abortion from a Title X project, but the Constitution does not require that the Government distort the scope of its mandated program in order to provide that information.

"Petitioners contend, however, that most Title X clients are effectively precluded by indigency and poverty from seeing a health care provider who will provide abortion-related services. But once again, even these Title X clients are in no worse position than if Congress had never enacted Title X. 'The financial constraints that restrict an indigent woman's ability to enjoy the full range of constitutionally protected freedom of choice are the product not of governmental restrictions on access to abortion, but rather of her indigency.' *McRae*."

On this issue, BLACKMUN, J., joined by Marshall and Stevens, JJ., dissented:

"By far the most disturbing aspect of today's ruling is the effect it will have on the Fifth Amendment rights of the women who, supposedly, are beneficiaries of Title X programs * * * [E]ven if one accepts as valid the Court's theorizing in [*McRae* and *Webster*], the majority's reasoning in the present cases is flawed.

"Until today, the Court has allowed to stand only those restrictions upon reproductive freedom that, while limiting the availability of abortion, have left intact a woman's ability to decide without coercion whether she will continue her pregnancy to term. *Maher, McRae,* and *Webster* are all to this effect. Today's decision abandons that principle, and with disastrous results.

"Contrary to the majority's characterization, this is not a case in which individuals seek government aid in exercising their fundamental rights. The Fifth Amendment right asserted by petitioners is the right of a pregnant woman to be free from affirmative governmental *interference* in her decision. *Roe* and its progeny are not so much about a medical procedure as they are about a woman's fundamental right to self-determination. Those cases serve to vindicate the idea that 'liberty,' if it means anything, must entail freedom from governmental domination in making the most intimate and personal of decisions. [By] suppressing medically pertinent information and injecting a restrictive ideological message unrelated to considerations of maternal health, the Government places formidable obstacles in the path of Title X clients' freedom of choice and thereby violates their Fifth Amendment rights.

"It is crystal-clear that the aim of the challenged provisions—an aim the majority cannot escape noticing—is not simply to ensure that federal funds are not used to perform abortions, but to 'reduce the incidence of abortion.' 42 CFR § 59.2 (1990) (in definition of 'family planning'). [The] Regulations require Title X physicians and counselors to provide information pertaining only to childbirth, to refer a pregnant woman for prenatal care irrespective of her medical situation, and, upon direct inquiry, to respond that abortion is not an 'appropriate method' of family planning.

"The undeniable message conveyed by this forced speech, and the one that the Title X client will draw from it, is that abortion nearly always is an improper medical option. Although her physician's words, in fact, are strictly controlled by the Government and wholly unrelated to her particular medical situation, the Title X client will reasonably construe them as professional advice to forgo her right to obtain an abortion. As would most rational patients, many of these women will follow that perceived advice and carry their pregnancy to term, despite their needs to the contrary and despite the safety of the abortion procedure for the vast majority of them. Others, delayed by the Regulations' mandatory prenatal referral, will be prevented from acquiring abortions during the period in which the process is medically sound and constitutionally protected.

"In view of the inevitable effect of the Regulations, the majority's conclusion that '[t]he difficulty that a woman encounters when a Title X project does not provide abortion counseling or referral leaves her in no different position than she would have been if the government had not enacted Title X' is insensitive and contrary to common human experience. Both the purpose and result of the challenged Regulations is to deny women the ability voluntarily to decide their procreative destiny. For these women, the Government will have obliterated the freedom to choose as surely as if it had banned abortions outright. The denial of this freedom is not a consequence of poverty but of the Government's ill-intentioned distortion of information it has chosen to provide.

"The substantial obstacles to bodily self-determination that the Regulations impose are doubly offensive because they are effected by manipulating the very words spoken by physicians and counselors to their patients. In our society, the doctor/patient dialogue embodies a unique relationship of trust. The specialized nature of medical science and the emotional distress often attendant to health-related decisions requires that patients place their complete confidence, and often their very lives, in the hands of medical professionals. One seeks a physician's aid not only for medication or diagnosis, but also for guidance, professional judgment, and vital emotional support. Accordingly, each of us attaches profound importance and authority to the words of advice spoken by the physician.

"It is for this reason that we have guarded so jealously the doctor/patient dialogue from governmental intrusion. [The] majority's approval of the Secretary's Regulations flies in the face of our repeated warnings that regulations tending to 'confine the attending physician in an undesired and uncomfortable straitjacket in the practice of his profession,' cannot endure. *Planned Parenthood v. Danforth.*

"The majority attempts to distinguish our holdings in *Akron* and *Thornburgh* on the post-hoc basis that the governmental intrusions into the doctor/patient dialogue invalidated in those cases applied to *all* physicians within a jurisdiction while the Regulations now before the Court pertain to the narrow class of healthcare professionals employed at Title X projects. But the rights protected by the Constitution are *personal* rights. And for the individual woman, the deprivation of liberty by the Government is no less substantial because it affects few rather than many. It cannot be that an otherwise unconstitutional infringement of choice is made lawful because it touches only some of the Nation's pregnant women and not all of them.

"The manipulation of the doctor/patient dialogue achieved through the Secretary's Regulations is clearly an effort 'to deter a woman from making a decision that, with her physician, is hers to make.' *Thornburgh.* As such, it violates the Fifth Amendment."

PLANNED PARENTHOOD OF SOUTHEASTERN PENNSYLVANIA v. CASEY
___ U.S. ___, 112 S.Ct. 2791, ___ L.Ed.2d ___ (1992).

JUSTICE O'CONNOR, JUSTICE KENNEDY, and JUSTICE SOUTER announced the judgment of the Court and delivered the opinion of the Court with respect to Parts I, II, III, V–A, V–C, and VI, an opinion with respect to Part V–E, in which JUSTICE STEVENS joins, and an opinion with respect to Parts IV, V–B, and V–D.

I

Liberty finds no refuge in a jurisprudence of doubt. Yet 19 years after our holding that the Constitution protects a woman's right to terminate her pregnancy in its early stages, *Roe v. Wade,* that definition of liberty is still questioned. Joining the respondents as *amicus curiae,* the United States, as it has done in five other cases in the last decade, again asks us to overrule *Roe.*

At issue in these cases are five provisions of the Pennsylvania Abortion Control Act of 1982 as amended in 1988 and 1989. [The] Act requires that a woman seeking an abortion give her informed consent prior to the abortion procedure, and specifies that she be provided with certain information at least 24 hours before the abortion is performed. § 3205. For a minor to obtain an abortion, the Act requires the informed consent of one of her parents, but provides for a judicial bypass option if the minor does not wish to or cannot obtain a parent's consent. § 3206. Another provision of the Act requires that, unless certain exceptions apply, a married woman seeking an abortion must sign a statement indicating that she has notified her husband of her intended abortion. § 3209. The Act exempts compliance with these three requirements in the event of a "medical emergency," which is defined in § 3203 of the Act. In addition to the above provisions regulating the performance of abortions, the Act imposes certain reporting requirements on facilities that provide abortion services. §§ 3207(b), 3214(a), 3214(f).

Before any of these provisions took effect, the petitioners, who are five abortion clinics and one physician representing himself as well as a class of physicians who provide abortion services, brought this suit seeking declaratory and injunctive relief. Each provision was challenged as unconstitutional on its face. The District Court [held] all the provisions at issue here unconstitutional * * *. The Court of Appeals for the Third Circuit affirmed in part and reversed in part, upholding all of the regulations except for the husband notification requirement.

[The] Court of Appeals found it necessary to follow an elaborate course of reasoning even to identify the first premise to use to determine whether the statute enacted by Pennsylvania meets constitutional standards. And at oral argument in this Court, the attorney for the parties challenging the statute took the position that none of the enactments can be upheld without overruling *Roe.* We disagree with that analysis; but we acknowledge that our decisions after *Roe* cast doubt upon the meaning and reach of its holding. Further, the Chief Justice admits that he would overrule the central holding of *Roe* and adopt the rational relationship test as the sole criterion of constitutionality. State and federal courts as well as legislatures throughout the Union must have guidance as they seek to address this subject in conformance with the Constitution. Given these premises, we find it imperative to review once more the principles that define the rights of the woman and the legitimate authority of the State respecting the termination of pregnancies by abortion procedures.

After considering the fundamental constitutional questions resolved by *Roe*, principles of institutional integrity, and the rule of *stare decisis*, we are led to conclude this: the essential holding of *Roe* should be retained and once again reaffirmed.

It must be stated at the outset and with clarity that *Roe*'s essential holding, the holding we reaffirm, has three parts. First is a recognition of the right of the woman to choose to have an abortion before viability and to obtain it without undue interference from the State. Before viability, the State's interests are not strong enough to support a prohibition of abortion or the imposition of a substantial obstacle to the woman's effective right to elect the procedure. Second is a confirmation of the State's power to restrict abortions after fetal viability, if the law contains exceptions for pregnancies which endanger a woman's life or health. And third is the principle that the State has legitimate interests from the outset of the pregnancy in protecting the health of the woman and the life of the fetus that may become a child. These principles do not contradict one another; and we adhere to each.

II

Constitutional protection of the woman's decision to terminate her pregnancy derives from the Due Process Clause of the Fourteenth Amendment. It declares that no State shall "deprive any person of life, liberty, or property, without due process of law." The controlling word in the case before us is "liberty." Although a literal reading of the Clause might suggest that it governs only the procedures by which a State may deprive persons of liberty, for at least 105 years [the] Clause has been understood to contain a substantive component as well, one "barring certain government actions regardless of the fairness of the procedures used to implement them."

[The] most familiar of the substantive liberties protected by the Fourteenth Amendment are those recognized by the Bill of Rights. We have held that the Due Process Clause of the Fourteenth Amendment incorporates most of the Bill of Rights against the States. It is tempting, as a means of curbing the discretion of federal judges, to suppose that liberty encompasses no more than those rights already guaranteed to the individual against federal interference by the express provisions of the first eight amendments to the Constitution. But of course this Court has never accepted that view.

It is also tempting, for the same reason, to suppose that the Due Process Clause protects only those practices, defined at the most specific level, that were protected against government interference by other rules of law when the Fourteenth Amendment was ratified. See *Michael H. v. Gerald D.*, n. 6 [CON LAW p. 521, AMER CON p. 356, RTS & LIB p. 250] (opinion of Scalia, J.). But such a view would be inconsistent with our law. It is a promise of the Constitution that there is a realm of personal liberty which the government may not enter. We have vindicated this principle before. Marriage is mentioned nowhere in the Bill of Rights and interracial marriage was illegal in most States in the 19th century, but the Court was no doubt correct in finding it to be an aspect of liberty protected against state interference by the substantive component of the Due Process Clause in *Loving v. Virginia* (1967) * * *.

Neither the Bill of Rights nor the specific practices of States at the time of the adoption of the Fourteenth Amendment marks the outer limits of the substantive sphere of liberty which the Fourteenth Amendment protects. See U.S. Const., Amend. 9. As the second Justice Harlan recognized:

"[T]he full scope of the liberty guaranteed by the Due Process Clause cannot be found in or limited by the precise terms of the specific guarantees elsewhere provided in the Constitution. This 'liberty' is not a series of isolated points pricked out in terms of the taking of property; the freedom of speech, press, and religion; the right to keep and bear arms; the freedom from unreasonable searches and seizures; and so on. It is a rational continuum which, broadly speaking, includes a freedom from all substantial arbitrary impositions and purposeless restraints [and] which also recognizes, what a reasonable and sensitive judgment must, that certain interests require particularly careful scrutiny of the state needs asserted to justify their abridgment." *Poe v. Ullman* (1961) (Harlan, J., dissenting from dismissal on jurisdictional grounds).

Justice Harlan wrote these words in addressing an issue the full Court did not reach in *Poe v. Ullman,* but the Court adopted his position four Terms later in *Griswold* [, which held] that the Constitution does not permit a State to forbid a married couple to use contraceptives. That same freedom was later guaranteed, under the Equal Protection Clause, for unmarried couples. [It] is settled now, as it was when the Court heard arguments in *Roe,* that the Constitution places limits on a State's right to interfere with a person's most basic decisions about family and parenthood, as well as bodily integrity.

The inescapable fact is that adjudication of substantive due process claims may call upon the Court in interpreting the Constitution to exercise that same capacity which by tradition courts always have exercised: reasoned judgment. Its boundaries are not susceptible of expression as a simple rule. That does not mean we are free to invalidate state policy choices with which we disagree; yet neither does it permit us to shrink from the duties of our office. As Justice Harlan observed:

"Due process has not been reduced to any formula; its content cannot be determined by reference to any code. The best that can be said is that through the course of this Court's decisions it has represented the balance which our Nation, built upon postulates of respect for the liberty of the individual, has struck between that liberty and the demands of organized society. If the supplying of content to this Constitutional concept has of necessity been a rational process, it certainly has not been one where judges have felt free to roam where unguided speculation might take them. The balance of which I speak is the balance struck by this country, having regard to what history teaches are the traditions from which it developed as well as the traditions from which it broke. That tradition is a living thing. A decision of this Court which radically departs from it could not long survive, while a decision which builds on what has survived is likely to be sound. No formula could serve as a substitute, in this area, for judgment and restraint." *Poe v. Ullman* (Harlan, J., dissenting). * * *

Men and women of good conscience can disagree, and we suppose some always shall disagree, about the profound moral and spiritual implications of terminating a pregnancy, even in its earliest stage. Some of us as individuals find abortion offensive to our most basic principles of morality, but that cannot control our decision. Our obligation is to define the liberty of all, not to mandate our own moral code. The underlying constitutional issue is whether the State can resolve these philosophic questions in such a definitive way that a woman lacks all choice in the matter, except perhaps in those rare circumstances in which the pregnancy is itself a danger to her own life or health, or is the result of rape or incest.

It is conventional constitutional doctrine that where reasonable people disagree the government can adopt one position or the other. That theorem, however, assumes a state of affairs in which the choice does not intrude upon a protected liberty. Thus, while some people might disagree about whether or not the flag should be saluted, or disagree about the proposition that it may not be defiled, we have ruled that a State may not compel or enforce one view or the other.

Our law affords constitutional protection to personal decisions relating to marriage, procreation, contraception, family relationships, child rearing, and education. [These] matters, involving the most intimate and personal choices a person may make in a lifetime, choices central to personal dignity and autonomy, are central to the liberty protected by the Fourteenth Amendment. At the heart of liberty is the right to define one's own concept of existence, of meaning, of the universe, and of the mystery of human life. Beliefs about these matters could not define the attributes of personhood were they formed under compulsion of the State.

These considerations begin our analysis of the woman's interest in terminating her pregnancy but cannot end it, for this reason: though the abortion decision may originate within the zone of conscience and belief, it is more than a philosophic exercise. Abortion is a unique act. It is an act fraught with consequences for others: for the woman who must live with the implications of her decision; for the persons who perform and assist in the procedure; for the spouse, family, and society which must confront the knowledge that these procedures exist, procedures some deem nothing short of an act of violence against innocent human life; and, depending on one's beliefs, for the life or potential life that is aborted. Though abortion is conduct, it does not follow that the State is entitled to proscribe it in all instances. That is because the liberty of the woman is at stake in a sense unique to the human condition and so unique to the law. The mother who carries a child to full term is subject to anxieties, to physical constraints, to pain that only she must bear. That these sacrifices have from the beginning of the human race been endured by woman with a pride that ennobles her in the eyes of others and gives to the infant a bond of love cannot alone be grounds for the State to insist she make the sacrifice. Her suffering is too intimate and personal for the State to insist, without more, upon its own vision of the woman's role, however dominant that vision has been in the course of our history and our culture. The destiny of the woman must be shaped to a large extent on her own conception of her spiritual imperatives and her place in society.

It should be recognized, moreover, that in some critical respects the abortion decision is of the same character as the decision to use contraception, to which [our cases] afford constitutional protection. We have no doubt as to the correctness of those decisions. They support the reasoning in *Roe* relating to the woman's liberty because they involve personal decisions concerning not only the meaning of procreation but also human responsibility and respect for it. As with abortion, reasonable people will have differences of opinion about these matters. One view is based on such reverence for the wonder of creation that any pregnancy ought to be welcomed and carried to full term no matter how difficult it will be to provide for the child and ensure its well-being. Another is that the inability to provide for the nurture and care of the infant is a cruelty to the child and an anguish to the parent. These are intimate views with infinite variations, and their deep, personal character underlay our decisions in *Griswold, Eisenstadt,* and *Carey.* The same concerns are present when the woman confronts the reality that, perhaps despite her attempts to avoid it, she has become pregnant.

It was this dimension of personal liberty that *Roe* sought to protect, and its holding invoked the reasoning and the tradition of the precedents we have discussed, granting protection to substantive liberties of the person. *Roe* was, of course, an extension of those cases and, as the decision itself indicated, the separate States could act in some degree to further their own legitimate interests in protecting pre-natal life. The extent to which the legislatures of the States might act to outweigh the interests of the woman in choosing to terminate her pregnancy was a subject of debate both in *Roe* itself and in decisions following it.

While we appreciate the weight of the arguments made on behalf of the State in the case before us, arguments which in their ultimate formulation conclude that *Roe* should be overruled, the reservations any of us may have in reaffirming the central holding of *Roe* are outweighed by the explication of individual liberty we have given combined with the force of *stare decisis*. We turn now to that doctrine.

III

The obligation to follow precedent begins with necessity, and a contrary necessity marks its outer limit. With Cardozo, we recognize that no judicial system could do society's work if it eyed each issue afresh in every case that raised it. See B. Cardozo, *The Nature of the Judicial Process* 149 (1921). Indeed, the very concept of the rule of law underlying our own Constitution requires such continuity over time that a respect for precedent is, by definition, indispensable. At the other extreme, a different necessity would make itself felt if a prior judicial ruling should come to be seen so clearly as error that its enforcement was for that very reason doomed.

Even when the decision to overrule a prior case is not, as in the rare, latter instance, virtually foreordained, it is common wisdom that the rule of *stare decisis* is not an "inexorable command," and certainly it is not such in every constitutional case. Rather, when this Court reexamines a prior holding, its judgment is customarily informed by a series of prudential and pragmatic considerations designed to test the consistency of overruling a prior decision with the ideal of the rule of law, and to gauge the respective costs of reaffirming and overruling a prior case. Thus, for example, we may ask whether the rule has proved to be intolerable simply in defying practical workability; whether the rule is subject to a kind of reliance that would lend a special hardship to the consequences of overruling and add inequity to the cost of repudiation; whether related principles of law have so far developed as to have left the old rule no more than a remnant of abandoned doctrine; or whether facts have so changed or come to be seen so differently, as to have robbed the old rule of significant application or justification.

So in this case we may inquire whether *Roe*'s central rule has been found unworkable; whether the rule's limitation on state power could be removed without serious inequity to those who have relied upon it or significant damage to the stability of the society governed by the rule in question; whether the law's growth in the intervening years has left *Roe*'s central rule a doctrinal anachronism discounted by society; and whether *Roe*'s premises of fact have so far changed in the ensuing two decades as to render its central holding somehow irrelevant or unjustifiable in dealing with the issue it addressed.

Although *Roe* has engendered opposition, it has in no sense proven "unworkable," representing as it does a simple limitation beyond which a state law is unenforceable. While *Roe* has, of course, required judicial assessment of state laws affecting the exercise of the choice guaranteed against government infringement, and although the need for such review will remain as a consequence of today's decision, the required determinations fall within judicial competence.

The inquiry into reliance counts the cost of a rule's repudiation as it would fall on those who have relied reasonably on the rule's continued application. Since the classic case for weighing reliance heavily in favor of following the earlier rule occurs in the commercial context, where advance planning of great precision is most obviously a necessity, it is no cause for surprise that some would find no reliance worthy of consideration in support of *Roe*.

While neither respondents nor their *amici* in so many words deny that the abortion right invites some reliance prior to its actual exercise, one can readily imagine an argument stressing the dissimilarity of this case to one involving property or contract. Abortion is customarily chosen as an unplanned response to the consequence of unplanned activity or to the failure of conventional birth control, and except on the assumption that no intercourse would have occurred but for *Roe*'s holding, such behavior may appear to justify no reliance claim. Even if reliance could be claimed on that unrealistic assumption, the argument might run, any reliance interest would be *de minimis*. This argument would be premised on the hypothesis that reproductive planning could take virtually immediate account of any sudden restoration of state authority to ban abortions.

To eliminate the issue of reliance that easily, however, one would need to limit cognizable reliance to specific instances of sexual activity. But to do this would be simply to refuse to face the fact that for two decades of economic and social developments, people have organized intimate relationships and made choices that define their views of themselves and their places in society, in reliance on the availability of abortion in the event that contraception should fail. The ability of women to participate equally in the economic and social life of the Nation has been facilitated by their ability to control their reproductive lives. The Constitution serves human values, and while the effect of reliance on *Roe* cannot be exactly measured, neither can the certain cost of overruling *Roe* for people who have ordered their thinking and living around that case be dismissed.

No evolution of legal principle has left *Roe*'s doctrinal footings weaker than they were in 1973. No development of constitutional law since the case was decided has implicitly or explicitly left *Roe* behind as a mere survivor of obsolete constitutional thinking.

It will be recognized, of course, that *Roe* stands at an intersection of two lines of decisions, but in whichever doctrinal category one reads the case, the result for present purposes will be the same. The *Roe* Court itself placed its holding in the succession of cases most prominently exemplified by *Griswold*. When it is so seen, *Roe* is clearly in no jeopardy, since subsequent constitutional developments have neither disturbed, nor do they threaten to diminish, the scope of recognized protection accorded to the liberty relating to intimate relationships, the family, and decisions about whether or not to beget or bear a child.

Roe, however, may be seen not only as an exemplar of *Griswold* liberty but as a rule (whether or not mistaken) of personal autonomy and bodily integrity, with doctrinal affinity to cases recognizing limits on governmental power to mandate medical treatment or to bar its rejection. If so, our cases since *Roe* accord with *Roe*'s view that a State's interest in the protection of life falls short of justifying any plenary override of individual liberty claims. *Cruzan v.*

Director, Missouri Dept. of Health [CON LAW p. 543, AMER CON p. 383, RTS & LIB p. 272].

Finally, one could classify *Roe* as *sui generis*. If the case is so viewed, then there clearly has been no erosion of its central determination. The original holding resting on the concurrence of seven Members of the Court in 1973 was expressly affirmed by a majority of six in 1983, see *Akron I*, and by a majority of five in 1986, see *Thornburgh* * * *. More recently, in *Webster*, although two of the present authors questioned the trimester framework in a way consistent with our judgment today, a majority of the Court either decided to reaffirm or declined to address the constitutional validity of the central holding of *Roe*.

Nor will courts building upon *Roe* be likely to hand down erroneous decisions as a consequence. Even on the assumption that the central holding of *Roe* was in error, that error would go only to the strength of the state interest in fetal protection, not to the recognition afforded by the Constitution to the woman's liberty. The latter aspect of the decision fits comfortably within the framework of the Court's prior decisions including *Skinner, Griswold, Loving,* and *Eisenstadt*, the holdings of which are "not a series of isolated points," but mark a "rational continuum." *Poe v. Ullman* (Harlan, J., dissenting). * * *

The soundness of this prong of the *Roe* analysis is apparent from a consideration of the alternative. If indeed the woman's interest in deciding whether to bear and beget a child had not been recognized as in *Roe*, the State might as readily restrict a woman's right to choose to carry a pregnancy to term as to terminate it, to further asserted state interests in population control, or eugenics, for example. Yet *Roe* has been sensibly relied upon to counter any such suggestions. [In] any event, because *Roe*'s scope is confined by the fact of its concern with postconception potential life, a concern otherwise likely to be implicated only by some forms of contraception protected independently under *Griswold* and later cases, any error in *Roe* is unlikely to have serious ramifications in future cases.

We have seen how time has overtaken some of *Roe*'s factual assumptions: advances in maternal health care allow for abortions safe to the mother later in pregnancy than was true in 1973, and advances in neonatal care have advanced viability to a point somewhat earlier. But these facts go only to the scheme of time limits on the realization of competing interests, and the divergences from the factual premises of 1973 have no bearing on the validity of *Roe*'s central holding, that viability marks the earliest point at which the State's interest in fetal life is constitutionally adequate to justify a legislative ban on nontherapeutic abortions. The soundness or unsoundness of that constitutional judgment in no sense turns on whether viability occurs at approximately 28 weeks, as was usual at the time of *Roe*, at 23 to 24 weeks, as it sometimes does today, or at some moment even slightly earlier in pregnancy, as it may if fetal respiratory capacity can somehow be enhanced in the future. Whenever it may occur, the attainment of viability may continue to serve as the critical fact, just as it has done since *Roe* was decided; which is to say that no change in *Roe*'s factual underpinning has left its central holding obsolete, and none supports an argument for overruling it.

The sum of the precedential inquiry to this point shows *Roe*'s underpinnings unweakened in any way affecting its central holding. While it has engendered disapproval, it has not been unworkable. An entire generation has come of age free to assume *Roe*'s concept of liberty in defining the capacity of women to act in society, and to make reproductive decisions; no erosion of principle going to liberty or personal autonomy has left *Roe*'s central holding a doctrinal remnant; *Roe* portends no developments at odds with other precedent for the analysis of personal liberty; and no changes of fact have rendered viability more or less appropriate as the point at which the balance of interests tips. Within the bounds of normal *stare decisis* analysis, then, and subject to the considerations on which it customarily turns, the stronger argument is for affirming *Roe*'s central holding, with whatever degree of personal reluctance any of us may have, not for overruling it.

In a less significant case, *stare decisis* analysis could, and would, stop at the point we have reached. But the sustained and widespread debate *Roe* has provoked calls for some comparison between that case and others of comparable dimension that have responded to national controversies and taken on the impress of the controversies addressed. Only two such decisional lines from the past century present themselves for examination, and in each instance the result reached by the Court accorded with the principles we apply today.

The first example is that line of cases identified with *Lochner v. New York* (1905), which imposed substantive limitations on legislation limiting economic autonomy in favor of health and welfare regulation, adopting, in Justice Holmes' view, the theory of *laissez-faire*. The *Lochner* decisions were exemplified by *Adkins v. Children's Hospital* (1923), in which this Court held it to be an infringement of constitutionally protected liberty of contract to require the employers of adult women to satisfy minimum wage standards. Fourteen years later, *West Coast Hotel Co. v. Parrish* (1937) signalled the demise of *Lochner* by overruling *Adkins*. In the meantime, the Depression had come and, with it, the lesson that seemed unmistakable to most people by 1937, that the interpretation of contractual freedom protected in *Adkins* rested on fundamentally false factual assumptions about the capacity of a relatively unregulated market to satisfy minimal levels of human welfare. [The] facts upon which the earlier case had premised a constitutional resolution of social controversy had proved to be untrue, and history's demonstration of their untruth not only justified but required the new choice of constitutional principle that *West Coast Hotel* announced. Of course, it was true that the Court lost something by its misperception, or its lack of prescience, and the Court-packing crisis only magnified the loss; but the clear demonstration that the facts of economic life were different from those previously assumed warranted the repudiation of the old law.

The second comparison that 20th century history invites is with the cases employing the separate-but-equal rule for applying the Fourteenth Amendment's equal protection guarantee. They began with *Plessy v. Ferguson* [CON LAW p. 1226, AMER CON p. 939, RTS & LIB p. 955], holding that legislatively mandated racial segregation in public transportation works no denial of equal protection, rejecting the argument that racial separation enforced by the legal machinery of American society treats the black race as inferior. The *Plessy* Court considered "the underlying fallacy of the plaintiff's argument to consist in the assumption that the enforced separation of the two races stamps the colored race with a badge of inferiority. If this be so, it is not by reason of anything found in the act, but solely because the colored race chooses to put that construction upon it." Whether, as a matter of historical fact, the Justices in the *Plessy* majority believed this or not, this understanding of the implication of segregation was the stated justification for the Court's opinion. But this understanding of the facts and the rule it was stated to justify were repudiated in *Brown v. Board of Education* [CON LAW p. 1229, AMER CON p. 941, RTS & LIB p. 958]. As one commentator observed, the question before the Court in *Brown* was "whether discrimination inheres in that segregation which is imposed by law in the twentieth century in certain specific states in the American Union. And that question has meaning and can find an answer only on the ground of history and of common knowledge about the facts of life in the times and places aforesaid." C. Black, *The Lawfulness of the Segregation Decisions,* 69 Yale L.J. 421, 427 (1960).

The Court in *Brown* addressed these facts of life by observing that whatever may have been the understanding in *Plessy*'s time of the power of segregation to stigmatize those who were segregated with a "badge of inferiority," it was clear by 1954 that legally sanctioned segregation had just such an effect, to the point that racially separate public educational facilities were deemed inherently unequal. Society's understanding of the facts upon which a constitutional ruling was sought in 1954 was thus fundamentally different from the basis claimed for the decision in 1896. While we think *Plessy* was wrong the day it was decided, we must also recognize that the *Plessy* Court's explanation for its decision was so clearly at odds with the facts apparent to the Court in 1954 that the decision to reexamine *Plessy* was on this ground alone not only justified but required.

West Coast Hotel and *Brown* each rested on facts, or an understanding of facts, changed from those which furnished the claimed justifications for the earlier constitutional resolutions. Each case was comprehensible as the Court's response to facts that the country could understand, or had come to understand already, but which the Court of an earlier day, as its own declarations disclosed, had not been able to perceive. As the decisions were thus comprehensible they were also defensible, not merely as the victories of one doctrinal school over another by dint of numbers (victories though they were), but as applications of constitutional principle to facts as they had not been seen by the Court before. In constitutional adjudication as elsewhere in life, changed circumstances may impose new obligations, and the thoughtful part of the Nation could accept each decision to overrule a prior case as a response to the Court's constitutional duty.

Because the case before us presents no such occasion it could be seen as no such response. Because neither the factual underpinnings of *Roe*'s central holding nor our understanding of it has changed (and because no other indication of weakened precedent has been shown) the Court could not pretend to be reexamining the prior law with any justification beyond a present doctrinal disposition to come out differently from the Court of 1973. To overrule prior law for no other reason than that would run counter to the view repeated in our cases, that a decision to overrule should rest on some special reason over and above the belief that a prior case was wrongly decided. * * *

The examination of the conditions justifying the repudiation of *Adkins* by *West Coast Hotel* and *Plessy* by *Brown* is enough to suggest the terrible price that would have been paid if the Court had not overruled as it did. In the present case, however, as our analysis to this point makes clear, the terrible price would be paid for overruling. Our analysis would not be complete, however, without explaining why overruling *Roe*'s central holding would not only reach an unjustifiable result under principles of *stare decisis,* but would seriously weaken the Court's capacity to exercise the judicial power and to function as the Supreme Court of a Nation dedicated to the rule of law. To understand why this would be so it is necessary to understand the source of this Court's authority, the conditions necessary for its preservation, and its relationship to the country's understanding of itself as a constitutional Republic.

The root of American governmental power is revealed most clearly in the instance of the power conferred by the Constitution upon the Judiciary of the United States and specifically upon this Court. As Americans of each succeeding generation are rightly told, the Court cannot buy support for its decisions by spending money and, except to a minor degree, it cannot independently coerce obedience to its decrees. The Court's power lies, rather, in its legitimacy, a product of substance and perception that shows itself in the people's acceptance of the Judiciary as fit to determine what the Nation's law means and to declare what it demands.

The underlying substance of this legitimacy is of course the warrant for the Court's decisions in the Constitution and the lesser sources of legal principle on which the Court draws. That substance is expressed in the Court's opinions, and our contemporary understanding is such that a decision without principled justification would be no judicial act at all. But even when justification is furnished by apposite legal principle, something more is required. Because not every conscientious claim of principled justification will be accepted as such, the justification claimed must be beyond dispute. The Court must take care to speak and act in ways that allow people to accept its decisions on the terms the Court claims for them, as grounded truly in principle, not as compromises with social and political pressures having, as such, no bearing on the principled choices that the Court is obliged to make. Thus, the Court's legitimacy depends on making legally principled decisions under circumstances in which their principled character is sufficiently plausible to be accepted by the Nation.

The need for principled action to be perceived as such is implicated to some degree whenever this, or any other appellate court, overrules a prior case. This is not to say, of course, that this Court cannot give a perfectly satisfactory explanation in most cases. People understand that some of the Constitution's language is hard to fathom and that the Court's Justices are sometimes able to perceive significant facts or to understand principles of law that eluded their predecessors and that justify departures from existing decisions. However upsetting it may be to those most directly affected when one judicially derived rule replaces another, the country can accept some correction of error without necessarily questioning the legitimacy of the Court.

In two circumstances, however, the Court would almost certainly fail to receive the benefit of the doubt in overruling prior cases. There is, first, a point beyond which frequent overruling would overtax the country's belief in the Court's good faith. [There] is a limit to the amount of error that can plausibly be imputed to prior courts. If that limit should be exceeded, disturbance of prior rulings would be taken as evidence that justifiable reexamination of principle had given way to drives for particular results in the short term. The legitimacy of the Court would fade with the frequency of its vacillation.

That first circumstance can be described as hypothetical; the second is to the point here and now. Where, in the performance of its judicial duties, the Court decides a case in such a way as to resolve the sort of intensely divisive controversy reflected in *Roe* and those rare, comparable cases, its decision has a dimension that the resolution of the normal case does not carry. It is the dimension present whenever the Court's interpretation of the Constitution calls the contending sides of a national controversy to end their national division by accepting a common mandate rooted in the Constitution.

The Court is not asked to do this very often, having thus addressed the Nation only twice in our lifetime, in the decisions of *Brown* and *Roe.* But when the Court does act in this way, its decision requires an equally rare precedential force to counter the inevitable efforts to overturn it and to thwart its implementation. Some of those efforts may be mere unprincipled emotional reactions; others may proceed from principles worthy of profound respect. But whatever the premises of opposition may be, only the most convincing justification under accepted standards of precedent could suffice to demonstrate that a later decision overruling the first was anything but a surrender to political pressure, and an unjustified repudiation of the principle on which the Court staked its authority in the first instance. So to overrule under fire in the absence of the most compelling reason to reexamine a watershed decision would subvert the Court's legitimacy beyond any serious question.

[The] country's loss of confidence in the judiciary would be underscored by an equally certain and equally reasonable condemnation for another failing in overruling unnecessarily and under pressure. Some cost will be paid by anyone who approves or implements a constitutional decision where it is unpopular, or who refuses to work to undermine the decision or to force its reversal. The price may be criticism or ostracism, or it may be violence. An extra price will be paid by those who themselves disapprove of the decision's results when viewed outside of constitutional terms, but who nevertheless struggle to accept it, because they respect the rule of law. To all those who will be so tested by following, the Court implicitly undertakes to remain steadfast, lest in the end a price be paid for nothing. The promise of constancy, once given, binds its maker for as long as the power to stand by the decision survives and the understanding of the issue has not changed so fundamentally as to render the commitment obsolete. From the obligation of this promise this Court cannot and should not assume any exemption when duty requires it to decide a case in conformance with the Constitution. A willing breach of it would be nothing less than a breach of faith, and no Court that broke its faith with the people could sensibly expect credit for principle in the decision by which it did that.

It is true that diminished legitimacy may be restored, but only slowly. Unlike the political branches, a Court thus weakened could not seek to regain its position with a new mandate from the voters, and even if the Court could somehow go to the polls, the loss of its principled character could not be retrieved by the casting of so many votes. Like the character of an individual, the legitimacy of the Court must be earned over time. So, indeed, must be the character of a Nation of people who aspire to live according to the rule of law. Their belief in themselves as such a people is not readily separable from their understanding of the Court invested with the authority to decide their constitutional cases and speak before all others for their constitutional ideals. If the Court's legitimacy should be undermined, then, so would the country be in its very ability to see itself through its constitutional ideals. The Court's concern with legitimacy is not for the sake of the Court but for the sake of the Nation to which it is responsible.

The Court's duty in the present case is clear. In 1973, it confronted the already-divisive issue of governmental power to limit personal choice to undergo abortion, for which it provided a new resolution based on the due process guaranteed by the Fourteenth Amendment. Whether or not a new social consensus is developing on that issue, its divisiveness is no less today than in 1973, and pressure to overrule the decision, like pressure to retain it, has grown only more intense. A decision to overrule *Roe*'s essential holding under the existing circumstances would address error, if error there was, at the cost of both profound and unnecessary damage to the Court's legitimacy, and to the Nation's commitment to the rule of law. It is therefore imperative to adhere to the essence of *Roe*'s original decision, and we do so today.

From what we have said so far it follows that it is a constitutional liberty of the woman to have some freedom to terminate her pregnancy. We conclude that the basic decision in *Roe* was based on a constitutional analysis which we cannot now repudiate. The woman's liberty is not so unlimited, however, that from the outset the State cannot show its concern for the life of the unborn, and at a later point in fetal development the State's interest in life has sufficient force so that the right of the woman to terminate the pregnancy can be restricted.

That brings us, of course, to the point where much criticism has been directed at *Roe*, a criticism that always inheres when the Court draws a specific rule from what in the Constitution is but a general standard. We conclude, however, that the urgent claims of the woman to retain the ultimate control over her destiny and her body, claims implicit in the meaning of liberty, require us to perform that function. Liberty must not be extinguished for want of a line that is clear. And it falls to us to give some real substance to the woman's liberty to determine whether to carry her pregnancy to full term.

We conclude the line should be drawn at viability, so that before that time the woman has a right to choose to terminate her pregnancy. We adhere to this principle for two reasons. First, as we have said, is the doctrine of *stare decisis*. Any judicial act of line-drawing may seem somewhat arbitrary, but *Roe* was a reasoned statement, elaborated with great care. We have twice reaffirmed it in the face of great opposition. See *Thornburgh; Akron I*. Although we must overrule those parts of *Thornburgh* and *Akron I* which, in our view, are inconsistent with *Roe*'s statement that the State has a legitimate interest in promoting the life or potential life of the unborn, the central premise of those cases represents an unbroken commitment by this Court to the essential holding of *Roe*. It is that premise which we reaffirm today.

The second reason is that the concept of viability, as we noted in *Roe,* is the time at which there is a realistic possibility of maintaining and nourishing a life outside the womb, so that the independent existence of the second life can in reason and all fairness be the object of state protection that now overrides the rights of the woman. Consistent with other constitutional norms, legislatures may draw lines which appear arbitrary without the necessity of offering a justification. But courts may not. We must justify the lines we draw. And there is no line other than viability which is more workable. To be sure, as we have said, there may be some medical developments that affect the precise point of viability, but this is an imprecision within tolerable limits given that the medical community and all those who must apply its discoveries will continue to explore the matter. The viability line also has, as a practical matter, an element of fairness. In some broad sense it might be said that a woman who fails to act before viability has consented to the State's intervention on behalf of the developing child.

The woman's right to terminate her pregnancy before viability is the most central principle of *Roe v. Wade*. It is a rule of law and a component of liberty we cannot renounce.

On the other side of the equation is the interest of the State in the protection of potential life. The *Roe* Court recognized the State's "important and legitimate interest in protecting the potentiality of human life." The weight to be given this state interest, not the strength of the woman's interest, was the difficult question faced in *Roe*. We do not need to say whether each of us, had we been Members of the Court when the valuation of the State interest came before it as an original matter, would have concluded, as the *Roe* Court did, that its weight is insufficient to justify a ban on abortions prior to viability even when it is subject to certain exceptions. The matter is not before us in the first instance, and coming as it does after nearly 20 years of litigation in *Roe*'s wake we are satisfied that the immediate question is not the soundness of *Roe*'s resolution of the issue, but the precedential force that must be accorded to its holding. And we have concluded that the essential holding of *Roe* should be reaffirmed.

Yet it must be remembered that *Roe* speaks with clarity in establishing not only the woman's liberty but also the State's "important and legitimate interest in potential life." That portion of the decision in *Roe* has been given too little acknowledgement and implementation by the Court in its subsequent cases. Those cases decided that any regulation touching upon the abortion decision must survive strict scrutiny, to be sustained only if drawn in narrow terms to further a compelling state interest. Not all of the cases decided under that formulation can be reconciled with the holding in *Roe* itself that the State has legitimate interests in the health of the woman and in protecting the potential life within her. In resolving this tension, we choose to rely upon *Roe*, as against the later cases.

Roe established a trimester framework to govern abortion regulations. Under this elaborate but rigid construct, almost no regulation at all is permitted during the first trimester of pregnancy; regulations designed to protect the woman's health, but not to further the State's interest in potential life, are permitted during the second trimester; and during the third trimester, when the fetus is viable, prohibitions are permitted provided the life or health of the mother is not at stake. Most of our cases since *Roe* have involved the application of rules derived from the trimester framework.

The trimester framework no doubt was erected to ensure that the woman's right to choose not become so subordinate to the State's interest in promoting fetal life that her choice exists in theory but not in fact. We do not agree, however, that the trimester approach is necessary to accomplish this objective. A framework of this rigidity was unnecessary and in its later interpretation sometimes contradicted the State's permissible exercise of its powers.

Though the woman has a right to choose to terminate or continue her pregnancy before viability, it does not at all follow that the State is prohibited from taking steps to ensure that this choice is thoughtful and informed. Even in the earliest stages of pregnancy, the State may enact rules and regulations designed to encourage her to know that there are philosophic and social arguments of great weight that can be brought to bear in favor of continuing the pregnancy to full term and that there are procedures and institutions to allow adoption of unwanted children as well as a certain degree of state assistance if the mother chooses to raise the child herself. [It] follows that States are free to enact laws to provide a reasonable framework for a woman to make a decision that has such profound and lasting meaning. This, too, we find consistent with *Roe*'s central premises, and indeed the inevitable consequence of our holding that the State has an interest in protecting the life of the unborn.

We reject the trimester framework, which we do not consider to be part of the essential holding of *Roe*. Measures aimed at ensuring that a woman's choice contemplates the consequences for the fetus do not necessarily interfere with the right recognized in *Roe,* although those measures have been found to be inconsistent with the rigid trimester framework announced in that case. A logical reading of the central holding in *Roe* itself, and a necessary reconciliation of the liberty of the woman and the interest of the State in promoting prenatal life, require, in our view, that we abandon the trimester framework as a rigid prohibition on all previability regulation aimed at the protection of fetal life. The trimester framework suffers from these basic flaws: in its formulation it misconceives the nature of the pregnant woman's interest; and in practice it undervalues the State's interest in potential life, as recognized in *Roe.*

As our jurisprudence relating to all liberties save perhaps abortion has recognized, not every law which makes a right more difficult to exercise is, *ipso facto,* an infringement of that right. An example clarifies the point. We have held that not every ballot access limitation amounts to an infringement of the right to vote. Rather, the States are granted substantial flexibility in establishing the framework within which voters choose the candidates for whom they wish to vote.

The abortion right is similar. Numerous forms of state regulation might have the incidental effect of increasing the cost or decreasing the availability of medical care, whether for abortion or any other medical procedure. The fact that a law which serves a valid purpose, one not designed to strike at the right itself, has the incidental effect of making it more difficult or more expensive to procure an abortion cannot be enough to invalidate it. Only where state regulation imposes an undue burden on a woman's ability to make this decision does the power of the State reach into the heart of the liberty protected by the Due Process Clause.

For the most part, the Court's early abortion cases adhered to this view [quoting from *Maher v. Roe, Doe v. Bolton* and other cases].

These considerations of the nature of the abortion right illustrate that it is an overstatement to describe it as a right to decide whether to have an abortion "without interference from the State," *Danforth.* All abortion regulations interfere to some degree with a woman's ability to decide whether to terminate her pregnancy. It is, as a consequence, not surprising that despite the protestations contained in the original *Roe* opinion to the effect that the Court was not recognizing an absolute right, the Court's experience applying the trimester framework has led to the striking down of some abortion regulations which in no real sense deprived women of the ultimate decision. Those decisions went too far because the right recognized by *Roe* is a right "to be free from unwarranted governmental intrusion into matters so fundamentally affecting a person as the decision whether to bear or beget a child." *Eisenstadt.* Not all governmental intrusion is of necessity unwarranted; and that brings us to the other basic flaw in the trimester framework: even in *Roe*'s terms, in practice it undervalues the State's interest in the potential life within the woman.

Roe was express in its recognition of the State's "important and legitimate interest[s] in preserving and protecting the health of the pregnant woman [and] in protecting the potentiality of human life." The trimester framework, however, does not fulfill *Roe*'s own promise that the State has an interest in protecting fetal life or potential life. *Roe* began the contradiction by using the trimester framework to forbid any regulation of abortion designed to advance that interest before viability. Before viability, *Roe* and subsequent cases treat all governmental attempts to influence a woman's decision on behalf of the potential life within her as unwarranted. This treatment is, in our judgment, incompatible with the recognition that there is a substantial state interest in potential life throughout pregnancy.

The very notion that the State has a substantial interest in potential life leads to the conclusion that not all regulations must be deemed unwarranted. Not all burdens on the right to decide whether to terminate a pregnancy will be undue. In our view, the undue burden standard is the appropriate means of reconciling the State's interest with the woman's constitutionally protected liberty. * * *

A finding of an undue burden is a shorthand for the conclusion that a state regulation has the purpose or effect of placing a substantial obstacle in the path of a woman seeking an abortion of a nonviable fetus. A statute with this purpose is invalid because the means chosen by the State to further the interest in potential life must be calculated to inform the woman's free choice, not hinder it. And a statute which, while furthering the interest in potential life or some other valid state interest, has the effect of placing a substantial obstacle in the path of a woman's choice cannot be considered a permissible means of serving its legitimate ends. To the extent that the opinions of the Court or of individual Justices use the undue burden standard in a manner that is inconsistent with this analysis, we set out what in our view should be the controlling standard. [In] our considered judgment, an undue burden is an unconstitutional burden. Understood another way, we answer the question, left open in previous opinions discussing the undue burden formulation, whether a law designed to further the State's interest in fetal life which imposes an undue burden on the woman's decision before fetal viability could be constitutional. The answer is no.

Some guiding principles should emerge. What is at stake is the woman's right to make the ultimate decision, not a right to be insulated from all others in doing so. Regulations which do no more than create a structural mechanism by which the State, or the parent or guardian of a minor, may express profound respect for the life of the unborn are permitted, if they are not a substantial obstacle to the woman's exercise of the right to choose. [Unless] it has that effect on her right of choice, a state measure designed to persuade her to choose childbirth over abortion will be upheld if reasonably related to that goal. Regulations designed to foster the health of a woman seeking an abortion are valid if they do not constitute an undue burden.

Even when jurists reason from shared premises, some disagreement is inevitable. [That] is to be expected in the application of any legal standard which must accommodate life's complexity. We do not expect it to be otherwise with respect to the undue burden standard. We give this summary:

(a) To protect the central right recognized by *Roe* while at the same time accommodating the State's profound interest in potential life, we will employ the undue burden analysis as explained in this opinion. An undue burden exists, and therefore a provision of law is invalid, if its purpose or effect is to place a substantial obstacle in the path of a woman seeking an abortion before the fetus attains viability.

(b) We reject the rigid trimester framework of *Roe*. To promote the State's profound interest in potential life, throughout pregnancy the State may take measures to ensure that the woman's choice is informed, and measures designed to advance this interest will not be invalidated as long as their purpose is to persuade the woman to choose childbirth over abortion. These measures must not be an undue burden on the right.

(c) As with any medical procedure, the State may enact regulations to further the health or safety of a woman seeking an abortion. Unnecessary health regulations that have the purpose or effect of presenting a substantial obstacle to a woman seeking an abortion impose an undue burden on the right.

(d) Our adoption of the undue burden analysis does not disturb the central holding of *Roe,* and we reaffirm that holding. Regardless of whether exceptions are made for particular circumstances, a State may not prohibit any woman from making the ultimate decision to terminate her pregnancy before viability.

(e) We also reaffirm *Roe*'s holding that "subsequent to viability, the State in promoting its interest in the potentiality of human life may, if it chooses, regulate, and even proscribe, abortion except where it is necessary, in appropriate medical judgment, for the preservation of the life or health of the mother."

These principles control our assessment of the Pennsylvania statute, and we now turn to the issue of the validity of its challenged provisions.

V

The Court of Appeals applied what it believed to be the undue burden standard and upheld each of the provisions except for the husband notification requirement. We agree generally with this conclusion, but refine the undue burden analysis in accordance with the principles articulated above. We now consider the separate statutory sections at issue.

A

Because it is central to the operation of various other requirements, we begin with the statute's definition of medical emergency. Under the statute, a medical emergency is

"[t]hat condition which, on the basis of the physician's good faith clinical judgment, so complicates the medical condition of a pregnant woman as to necessitate the immediate abortion of her pregnancy to avert her death or for which a delay will create serious risk of substantial and irreversible impairment of a major bodily function."

Petitioners argue that the definition is too narrow, contending that it forecloses the possibility of an immediate abortion despite some significant health risks. If the contention were correct, we would be required to invalidate the restrictive operation of the provision, for the essential holding of *Roe* forbids a State from interfering with a woman's choice to undergo an abortion procedure if continuing her pregnancy would constitute a threat to her health.

The District Court found that there were three serious conditions which would not be covered by the statute: preeclampsia, inevitable abortion, and premature ruptured membrane. Yet, as the Court of Appeals observed, it is undisputed that under some circumstances each of these conditions could lead to an illness with substantial and irreversible consequences. While the definition could be interpreted in an unconstitutional manner, the Court of Appeals construed the phrase "serious risk" to include those circumstances. It stated: "we read the medical emergency exception as intended by the Pennsylvania legislature to assure that compliance with its abortion regulations would not in any way pose a significant threat to the life or health of a woman." [W]e have said that we will defer to lower court interpretations of state law unless they amount to "plain" error. This " 'reflect[s] our belief that district courts and courts of appeals are better schooled in and more able to interpret the laws of their respective States.' " We adhere to that course today, and conclude that, as construed by the Court of Appeals, the medical emergency definition imposes no undue burden on a woman's abortion right.

B

We next consider the informed consent requirement. Except in a medical emergency, the statute requires that at least 24 hours before performing an abortion a physician inform the woman of the nature of the procedure, the health risks of the abortion and of childbirth, and the "probable gestational age of the unborn child." The physician or a qualified nonphysician must inform the woman of the availability of printed materials published by the State describing the fetus and providing information about medical assistance for childbirth, information about child support from the father, and a list of agencies which provide adoption and other services as alternatives to abortion. An abortion may not be performed unless the woman certifies in writing that she has been informed of the availability of these printed materials and has been provided them if she chooses to view them.

Our prior decisions establish that as with any medical procedure, the State may require a woman to give her written informed consent to an abortion. In this respect, the statute is unexceptional. Petitioners challenge the statute's definition of informed consent because it includes the provision of specific information by the doctor and the mandatory 24-hour waiting period. The conclusions reached by a majority of the Justices in the separate opinions filed today and the undue burden standard adopted in this opinion require us to overrule in part some of the Court's past decisions, decisions driven by the trimester framework's prohibition of all previability regulations designed to further the State's interest in fetal life.

[To] the extent *Akron I* and *Thornburgh* find a constitutional violation when the government requires, as it does here, the giving of truthful, nonmisleading information about the nature of the procedure, the attendant health risks and those of childbirth, and the "probable gestational age" of the fetus, those cases go too far, are inconsistent with *Roe*'s acknowledgment of an important interest in potential life, and are overruled. [It] cannot be questioned that psychological well-being is a facet of health. Nor can it be doubted that most women considering an abortion would deem the impact on the fetus relevant, if not dispositive, to the decision. In attempting to ensure that a woman apprehend the full consequences of her decision, the State furthers the legitimate purpose of reducing the risk that a woman may elect an abortion, only to discover later, with devastating psychological consequences, that her decision was not fully informed. If the information the State requires to be made available to the woman is truthful and not misleading, the requirement may be permissible.

We also see no reason why the State may not require doctors to inform a woman seeking an abortion of the availability of materials relating to the consequences to the fetus, even when those consequences have no direct relation to her health. An example illustrates the point. We would think it constitutional for the State to require that in order for there to be informed consent to a kidney transplant operation the recipient must be supplied with information about risks to the donor as well as risks to himself or herself. A requirement that the physician make available information similar to that mandated by the statute here was described in *Thornburgh* as "an outright attempt to wedge the Commonwealth's message discouraging abortion into the privacy of the informed-consent dialogue between the woman and her physician." We conclude, however, that informed choice need not be defined in such narrow terms that all considerations of the effect on the fetus are made irrelevant. As we have made clear, we depart from the holdings of *Akron I* and *Thornburgh* to the extent that we permit a State to further its legitimate goal of protecting the life of the unborn by enacting legislation aimed at ensuring a decision that is mature and informed, even when in so doing the State expresses a preference for childbirth over abortion. In short, requiring that the woman be informed of the availability of information relating to fetal development and the assistance available should she decide to carry the pregnancy to full term is a reasonable measure to insure an informed choice, one which might cause the woman to choose childbirth over abortion. This requirement cannot be considered a substantial obstacle to obtaining an abortion, and, it follows, there is no undue burden.

Our prior cases also suggest that the "straitjacket" of particular information which must be given in each case interferes with a constitutional right of privacy between a pregnant woman and her physician. As a preliminary matter, it is worth noting that the statute now before us does not require a physician to comply with the informed consent provisions "if he or she can demonstrate by a preponderance of the evidence, that he or she reasonably believed that furnishing the information would have resulted in a severely adverse effect on the physical or mental health of the patient."

In this respect, the statute does not prevent the physician from exercising his or her medical judgment.

Whatever constitutional status the doctor-patient relation may have as a general matter, in the present context it is derivative of the woman's position. The doctor-patient relation does not underlie or override the two more general rights under which the abortion right is justified: the right to make family decisions and the right to physical autonomy. On its own, the doctor-patient relation here is entitled to the same solicitude it receives in other contexts. Thus, a requirement that a doctor give a woman certain information as part of obtaining her consent to an abortion is, for constitutional purposes, no different from a requirement that a doctor give certain specific information about any medical procedure.

[The] Pennsylvania statute also requires us to reconsider the holding in *Akron I* that the State may not require that a physician, as opposed to a qualified assistant, provide information relevant to a woman's informed consent. Since there is no evidence on this record that requiring a doctor to give the information as provided by the statute would amount in practical terms to a substantial obstacle to a woman seeking an abortion, we conclude that it is not an undue burden. * * *

Our analysis of Pennsylvania's 24-hour waiting period between the provision of the information deemed necessary to informed consent and the performance of an abortion under the undue burden standard requires us to reconsider the premise behind the decision in *Akron I* invalidating a parallel requirement. In *Akron I* we said: "Nor are we convinced that the State's legitimate concern that the woman's decision be informed is reasonably served by requiring a 24-hour delay as a matter of course."

We consider that conclusion to be wrong. The idea that important decisions will be more informed and deliberate if they follow some period of reflection does not strike us as unreasonable, particularly where the statute directs that important information become part of the background of the decision. The statute, as construed by the Court of Appeals, permits avoidance of the waiting period in the event of a medical emergency and the record evidence shows that in the vast majority of cases, a 24-hour delay does not create any appreciable health risk. In theory, at least, the waiting period is a reasonable measure to implement the State's interest in protecting the life of the unborn, a measure that does not amount to an undue burden.

Whether the mandatory 24-hour waiting period is nonetheless invalid because in practice it is a substantial obstacle to a woman's choice to terminate her pregnancy is a closer question. The findings of fact by the District Court indicate that because of the distances many women must travel to reach an abortion provider, the practical effect will often be a delay of much more than a day because the waiting period requires that a woman seeking an abortion make at least two visits to the doctor. The District Court also found that in many instances this will increase the exposure of women seeking abortions to "the harassment and hostility of anti-abortion protestors demonstrating outside a clinic." As a result, the District Court found that for those women who have the fewest financial resources, those who must travel long distances, and those who have difficulty explaining their whereabouts to husbands, employers, or others, the 24-hour waiting period will be "particularly burdensome."

These findings are troubling in some respects, but they do not demonstrate that the waiting period constitutes an undue burden. We do not doubt that, as the District Court held, the waiting period has the effect of "increasing the cost and risk of delay of abortions," but the District Court did not conclude that the increased costs and potential delays amount to substantial obstacles. Rather, applying the trimester framework's strict prohibition of all regulation designed to promote the State's interest in potential life before viability, the District Court concluded that the waiting period does not further the state "interest in maternal health" and "infringes the physician's discretion to exercise sound medical judgment." Yet, as we have stated, under the undue burden standard a State is permitted to enact persuasive measures which favor childbirth over abortion, even if those measures do not further a health interest. And while the waiting period does limit a physician's discretion, that is not, standing alone, a reason to invalidate it. In light of the construction given the statute's definition of medical emergency by the Court of Appeals, and the District Court's findings, we cannot say that the waiting period imposes a real health risk.

We also disagree with the District Court's conclusion that the "particularly burdensome" effects of the waiting period on some women require its invalidation. A particular burden is not of necessity a substantial obstacle. Whether a burden falls on a particular group is a distinct inquiry from whether it is a substantial obstacle even as to the women in that group. And the District Court did not conclude that the waiting period is such an obstacle even for the women who are most burdened by it. Hence, on the record before us, and in the context of this facial challenge, we are not convinced that the 24-hour waiting period constitutes an undue burden.

We are left with the argument that the various aspects of the informed consent requirement are unconstitutional because they place barriers in the way of abortion on demand. Even the broadest reading of *Roe,* however, has not suggested that there is a constitutional right to abortion on demand. Rather, the right protected by *Roe* is a right to decide to terminate a pregnancy free of undue interference by the State. Because the informed consent requirement facilitates the wise exercise of that right it cannot be classified as an interference with the right *Roe* protects. The informed consent requirement is not an undue burden on that right.

C

Section 3209 of Pennsylvania's abortion law provides, except in cases of medical emergency, that no physician shall perform an abortion on a married woman without receiving a signed statement from the woman that she has notified her spouse that she is about to undergo an abortion. The woman has the option of providing an alternative signed statement certifying that her husband is not the man who impregnated her; that her husband could not be located; that the pregnancy is the result of spousal sexual assault which she has reported; or that the woman believes that notifying her husband will cause him or someone else to inflict bodily injury upon her. A physician who performs an abortion on a married woman without receiving the appropriate signed statement will have his or her license revoked, and is liable to the husband for damages.

The District Court heard the testimony of numerous expert witnesses, and made detailed findings of fact regarding the effect of this statute. These included:

"273. The vast majority of women consult their husbands prior to deciding to terminate their pregnancy * * *.

* * *

"279. The 'bodily injury' exception could not be invoked by a married woman whose husband, if notified, would, in her reasonable belief, threaten to (a) publicize her intent to have an abortion to family, friends or acquaintances; (b) retaliate against her in future child custody or divorce proceedings; (c) inflict psychological intimidation or emotional harm upon her, her children or other persons; (d) inflict bodily harm on other persons such as children, family members or other loved ones; or (e) use his control over finances to deprive of necessary monies for herself or her children * * *.

* * *

"281. Studies reveal that family violence occurs in two million families in the United States. This figure, however, is a conservative one that substantially understates (because battering is usually not reported until it reaches life-threatening proportions) the actual number of families affected by domestic violence. In fact, researchers estimate that one of every two women will be battered at some time in their life * * *.

"282. A wife may not elect to notify her husband of her intention to have an abortion for a variety of reasons, including the husband's illness, concern about her own health, the imminent failure of the marriage, or the husband's absolute opposition to the abortion * * *.

"283. The required filing of the spousal consent form would require plaintiff-clinics to change their counseling procedures and force women to reveal their most intimate decision-making on pain of criminal sanctions. The confidentiality of these revelations could not be guaranteed, since the woman's records are not immune from subpoena * * *.

"284. Women of all class levels, educational backgrounds, and racial, ethnic and religious groups are battered * * *.

"285. Wife-battering or abuse can take on many physical and psychological forms. The nature and scope of the battering can cover a broad range of actions and be gruesome and torturous * * *.

"286. Married women, victims of battering, have been killed in Pennsylvania and throughout the United States * * *.

"287. Battering can often involve a substantial amount of sexual abuse, including marital rape and sexual mutilation * * *.

"288. In a domestic abuse situation, it is common for the battering husband to also abuse the children in an attempt to coerce the wife * * *.

"289. Mere notification of pregnancy is frequently a flashpoint for battering and violence within the family. The number of battering incidents is high during the pregnancy and often the worst abuse can be associated with pregnancy * * *. The battering husband may deny parentage and use the pregnancy as an excuse for abuse * * *.

"290. Secrecy typically shrouds abusive families. Family members are instructed not to tell anyone, especially police or doctors, about the abuse and violence. Battering husbands often threaten their wives or her children with further abuse if she tells an outsider of the violence and tells her that nobody will believe her. A battered woman, therefore, is highly unlikely to disclose the violence against her for fear of retaliation by the abuser * * *.

"291. Even when confronted directly by medical personnel or other helping professionals, battered women often will not admit to the battering because they have not admitted to themselves that they are battered * * *.

* * *

"294. A woman in a shelter or a safe house unknown to her husband is not 'reasonably likely' to have bodily harm inflicted upon her by her batterer, however her attempt to notify her husband pursuant to section 3209 could accidentally disclose her whereabouts to her husband. Her fear of future ramifications would be realistic under the circumstances.

"295. Marital rape is rarely discussed with others or reported to law enforcement authorities, and of those reported only few are prosecuted * * *.

"296. It is common for battered women to have sexual intercourse with their husbands to avoid being battered. While this type of coercive sexual activity would be spousal sexual assault as defined by the Act, many women may not consider it to be so and others would fear disbelief * * *.

"297. The marital rape exception to section 3209 cannot be claimed by women who are victims of coercive sexual behavior other than penetration. The 90–day reporting requirement of the spousal sexual assault statute further narrows the class of sexually abused wives who can claim the exception, since many of these women may be psychologically unable to discuss or report the rape for several years after the incident * * *.

"298. Because of the nature of the battering relationship, battered women are unlikely to avail themselves of the exceptions to section 3209 of the Act, regardless of whether the section applies to them."

These findings are supported by studies of domestic violence. The American Medical Association (AMA) has published a summary of the recent research in this field, which indicates that in an average 12–month period in this country, approximately two million women are the victims of severe assaults by their male partners. In a 1985 survey, women reported that nearly one of every eight husbands had assaulted their wives during the past year. The AMA views these figures as "marked underestimates," because the nature of these incidents discourages women from reporting them, and because surveys typically exclude the very poor, those who do not speak English well, and women who are homeless or in institutions or hospitals when the survey is conducted. According to the AMA, "[r]esearchers on family violence agree that the true incidence of partner violence is probably *double* the above estimates; or four million severely assaulted women per year. Studies suggest that from one-fifth to one-third of all women will be physically assaulted by a partner or ex-partner during their lifetime." Thus on an average day in the United States, nearly 11,000 women are severely assaulted by their male partners. Many of these incidents involve sexual assault. * * *

Other studies fill in the rest of this troubling picture. Physical violence is only the most visible form of abuse. Psychological abuse, particularly forced social and economic isolation of women, is also common. Many victims of domestic violence remain with their abusers, perhaps because they perceive no superior alternative. Many abused women who find temporary refuge in shelters return to their husbands, in large part because they have no other source of income. Returning to one's abuser can be dangerous. Recent Federal Bureau of Investigation statistics disclose that 8.8% of all homicide victims in the United States are killed by their spouse. Thirty percent of female homicide victims are killed by their male partners.

The limited research that has been conducted with respect to notifying one's husband about an abortion, although involving samples too small to be representative, also supports the District Court's findings of fact. The vast majority of women notify their male partners of their decision to obtain an abortion. In many cases in which married women do not notify their husbands, the pregnancy is the result of an extramarital affair. Where the husband is the father, the primary reason women do not notify their husbands is that the husband and wife are experiencing marital difficulties, often accompanied by incidents of violence.

This information and the District Court's findings reinforce what common sense would suggest. In well-functioning marriages, spouses discuss important intimate decisions such as whether to bear a child. But there are millions of women in this country who are the victims of regular physical and psychological abuse at the hands of their husbands. Should these women become pregnant, they may have very good reasons for not wishing to inform their husbands of their decision to obtain an abortion. Many may have justifiable fears of physical abuse, but may be no less fearful of the consequences of reporting prior abuse to the Commonwealth of Pennsylvania. Many may have a reasonable fear that notifying their husbands will provoke further instances of child abuse; these women are not exempt from § 3209's notification requirement. Many may fear devastating forms of psychological abuse from their husbands, including verbal harassment, threats of future violence, the destruction of possessions, physical confinement to the home, the withdrawal of financial support, or the disclosure of the abortion to family and friends. These methods of psychological abuse may act as even more of a deterrent to notification than the possibility of physical violence, but women who are the victims of the abuse are not exempt from § 3209's notification requirement. And many women who are pregnant as a result of sexual assaults by their husbands will be unable to avail themselves of the exception for spousal sexual assault, because the exception requires that the woman have notified law enforcement authorities within 90 days of the assault, and her husband will be notified of her report once an investigation begins. If anything in this field is certain, it is that victims of spousal sexual assault are extremely reluctant to report the abuse to the government; hence, a great many spousal rape victims will not be exempt from the notification requirement imposed by § 3209.

The spousal notification requirement is thus likely to prevent a significant number of women from obtaining an abortion. It does not merely make abortions a little more difficult or expensive to obtain; for many women, it will impose a substantial obstacle. We must not blind ourselves to the fact that the significant number of women who fear for their safety and the safety of their children are likely to be deterred from procuring an abortion as surely as if the Commonwealth had outlawed abortion in all cases.

Respondents attempt to avoid the conclusion that § 3209 is invalid by pointing out that it imposes almost no burden at all for the vast majority of women seeking abortions. They begin by noting that only about 20 percent of the women who obtain abortions are married. They then note that of these women about 95 percent notify their husbands of their own volition. Thus, respondents argue, the effects of § 3209 are felt by only one percent of the women who obtain abortions. Respondents argue that since some of these women will be able to notify their husbands without adverse consequences or will qualify for one of the exceptions, the statute affects fewer than one percent of women seeking abortions. For this reason, it is asserted, the statute cannot be invalid on its face. We disagree with respondents' basic method of analysis.

The analysis does not end with the one percent of women upon whom the statute operates; it begins there. Legislation is measured for consistency with the Constitution by its impact on those whose conduct it affects. For example, we would not say that a law which requires a newspaper to print a candidate's reply to an unfavorable editorial is valid on its face because most newspapers would adopt the policy even absent the law. The proper focus of constitutional inquiry is the group for whom the law is a restriction, not the group for whom the law is irrelevant.

Respondents' argument itself gives implicit recognition to this principle, at one of its critical points. Respondents speak of the one percent of women seeking abortions who are married and would choose not to notify their husbands of their plans. By selecting as the controlling class women who wish to obtain abortions, rather than all women or all pregnant women, respondents in effect concede that § 3209 must be judged by reference to those for whom it is an actual rather than irrelevant restriction. Of course, as we have said, § 3209's real target is narrower even than the class of women seeking abortions identified by the State: it is married women seeking abortions who do not wish to notify their husbands of their intentions and who do not qualify for one of the statutory exceptions to the notice requirement. The unfortunate yet persisting conditions we document above will mean that in a large fraction of the cases in which § 3209 is relevant, it will operate as a substantial obstacle to a woman's choice to undergo an abortion. It is an undue burden, and therefore invalid.

This conclusion is in no way inconsistent with our decisions upholding parental notification or consent requirements. Those enactments, and our judgment that they are constitutional, are based on the quite reasonable assumption that minors will benefit from consultation with their parents and that children will often not realize that their parents have their best interests at heart. We cannot adopt a parallel assumption about adult women.

[If] this case concerned a State's ability to require the mother to notify the father before taking some action with respect to a living child raised by both, [it] would be reasonable to conclude as a general matter that the father's interest in the welfare of the child and the mother's interest are equal.

Before birth, however, the issue takes on a very different cast. It is an inescapable biological fact that state regulation with respect to the child a woman is carrying will have a far greater impact on the mother's liberty than on the father's. The effect of state regulation on a woman's protected liberty is doubly deserving of scrutiny in such a case, as the State has touched not only upon the private sphere of the family but upon the very bodily integrity of the pregnant woman. Cf. *Cruzan.* The Court has held that "when the wife and the husband disagree on this decision, the view of only one of the two marriage partners can prevail. Inasmuch as it is the woman who physically bears the child and who is the more directly and immediately affected by the pregnancy, as between the two, the balance weighs in her favor." *Danforth.* This conclusion rests upon the basic nature of marriage and the nature of our Constitution * * *. The Constitution protects individuals, men and women alike, from unjustified state interference, even when that interference is enacted into law for the benefit of their spouses.

There was a time, not so long ago, when a different understanding of the family and of the Constitution prevailed. * * * Only one generation has passed since this Court observed that "woman is still regarded as the center of home and family life," with attendant "special responsibilities" that precluded full and independent legal status under the Constitution. *Hoyt v. Florida*, 368 U.S. 57, 82 S.Ct. 159, 7 L.Ed.2d 118 (1961). These views, of course, are no longer consistent with our understanding of the family, the individual, or the Constitution.

In keeping with our rejection of the common-law understanding of a woman's role within the family, the Court held in *Danforth* that the Constitution does not permit a State to require a married woman to obtain her husband's consent before undergoing an abortion. The principles that guided the Court in *Danforth* should be our guides today. For the great many women who are victims of abuse inflicted by their husbands, or whose children are the victims of such abuse, a spousal notice requirement enables the husband to wield an effective veto over his wife's decision. Whether the prospect of notification itself deters such women from seeking abortions, or whether the husband, through physical force or psychological pressure or economic coercion, prevents his wife from obtaining an abortion until it is too late, the notice requirement will often be tantamount to the veto found unconstitutional in *Danforth.* The women most affected by this law—those who most reasonably fear the consequences of notifying their husbands that they are pregnant—are in the gravest danger.

The husband's interest in the life of the child his wife is carrying does not permit the State to empower him with this troubling degree of authority over his wife. The contrary view leads to consequences reminiscent of the common law. A husband has no enforceable right to require a wife to advise him before she exercises her personal choices. If a husband's interest in the potential life of the child outweighs a wife's liberty, the State could require a married woman to notify her husband before she uses a postfertilization contraceptive. Perhaps next in line would be a statute requiring pregnant married women to notify their husbands before engaging in conduct causing risks to the fetus. After all, if the husband's interest in the fetus' safety is a sufficient predicate for state regulation, the State could reasonably conclude that pregnant wives should notify their husbands before drinking alcohol or smoking. Perhaps married women should notify their husbands before using contraceptives or before undergoing any type of surgery that may have complications affecting the husband's interest in his wife's reproductive organs. And if a husband's interest justifies notice in any of these cases, one might reasonably argue that it justifies exactly what the *Danforth* Court held it did not justify—a requirement of the husband's consent as well. A State may not give to a man the kind of dominion over his wife that parents exercise over their children.

Section 3209 embodies a view of marriage consonant with the common-law status of married women but repugnant to our present understanding of marriage and of the nature of the rights secured by the Constitution. Women do not lose their constitutionally protected liberty when they marry. The Constitution protects all individuals, male or female, married or unmarried, from the abuse of governmental power, even where that power is employed for the supposed benefit of a member of the individual's family. These considerations confirm our conclusion that § 3209 is invalid.

D

We next consider the parental consent provision. Except in a medical emergency, an unemancipated young woman under 18 may not obtain an abortion unless she and one of her parents (or guardian) provides informed consent as defined above. If neither a parent nor a guardian provides consent, a court may authorize the performance of an abortion upon a determination that the young woman is mature and capable of giving informed consent and has in fact given her informed consent, or that an abortion would be in her best interests.

We have been over most of this ground before. Our cases establish, and we reaffirm today, that a State may require a minor seeking an abortion to obtain the consent of a parent or guardian, provided that there is an adequate judicial bypass procedure. Under these precedents, in our view, the one-parent consent requirement and judicial bypass procedure are constitutional.

The only argument made by petitioners respecting this provision and to which our prior decisions do not speak is the contention that the parental consent requirement is invalid because it requires informed parental consent. For the most part, petitioners' argument is a reprise of their argument with respect to the informed consent requirement in general, and we reject it for the reasons given above. Indeed, some of the provisions regarding informed consent have particular force with respect to minors: the waiting period, for example, may provide the parent or parents of a pregnant young woman the opportunity to consult with her in private, and to discuss the consequences of her decision in the context of the values and moral or religious principles of their family.

E

Under the recordkeeping and reporting requirements of the statute, every facility which performs abortions is required to file a report stating its name and address as well as the name and address of any related entity, such as a controlling or subsidiary organization. In the case of state-funded institutions, the information becomes public.

For each abortion performed, a report must be filed identifying: the physician (and the second physician where required); the facility; the referring physician or agency; the woman's age; the number of prior pregnancies and prior abortions she has had; gestational age; the type of abortion procedure; the date of the abortion; whether there were any pre-existing medical conditions which would complicate pregnancy; medical complications with the abortion; where applicable, the basis for the determination that the abortion was medically necessary; the weight of the aborted fetus; and whether the woman was married, and if so, whether notice was provided or the basis for the failure to give notice. Every abortion facility must also file quarterly reports showing the number of abortions performed broken down by trimester. In all events, the identity of each woman who has had an abortion remains confidential.

In *Danforth,* we held that recordkeeping and reporting provisions "that are reasonably directed to the preservation of maternal health and that properly respect a patient's confidentiality and privacy are permissible." We think that under this standard, all the provisions at issue here except that relating to spousal notice are constitutional. Although they do not relate to the State's interest in informing the woman's choice, they do relate to health. The collection of information with respect to actual patients is a vital element of medical research, and so it cannot be said that the requirements serve no purpose other than to make abortions more difficult. Nor do we find that the requirements impose a substantial obstacle to a woman's choice. At most they might increase the cost of some abortions by a slight amount. While at some point increased cost could become a substantial obstacle, there is no such showing on the record before us.

Subsection (12) of the reporting provision requires the reporting of, among other things, a married woman's "reason for failure to provide notice" to her husband. This provision in effect requires women, as a condition of obtaining an abortion, to provide the Commonwealth with the precise information we have already recognized that many women have pressing reasons not to reveal. Like the spousal notice requirement itself, this provision places an undue burden on a woman's choice, and must be invalidated for that reason.

VI

Our Constitution is a covenant running from the first generation of Americans to us and then to future generations. It is a coherent succession. Each generation must learn anew that the Constitution's written terms embody ideas and aspirations that must survive more ages than one. We accept our responsibility not to retreat from interpreting the full meaning of the covenant in light of all of our precedents. We invoke it once again to define the freedom guaranteed by the Constitution's own promise, the promise of liberty. * * *

JUSTICE STEVENS, concurring in part and dissenting in part.

The portions of the Court's opinion that I have joined are more important than those with which I disagree. I shall therefore first comment on significant areas of agreement, and then explain the limited character of my disagreement.

The Court is unquestionably correct in concluding that the doctrine of *stare decisis* has controlling significance in a case of this kind, notwithstanding an individual justice's concerns about the merits.[1] The central holding of *Roe* has been a "part of our law" for almost two decades. It was a natural sequel to the protection of individual liberty established in *Griswold.* The societal costs of overruling *Roe* at this late date would be enormous. *Roe* is an integral part of a correct understanding of both the concept of liberty and the basic equality of men and women.

1. It is sometimes useful to view the issue of *stare decisis* from a historical perspective. In the last nineteen years, fifteen Justices have confronted the basic issue presented in *Roe.* Of those, eleven have voted as the majority does today: Chief Justice Burger, Justices Douglas, Brennan, Stewart, Marshall, and Powell, and Justices Blackmun, O'Connor, Kennedy, Souter, and myself. Only four—all of whom happen to be on the Court today—have reached the opposite conclusion.

Stare decisis also provides a sufficient basis for my agreement with the joint opinion's reaffirmation of *Roe*'s post-viability analysis. Specifically, I accept the proposition that "[i]f the State is interested in protecting fetal life after viability, it may go so far as to proscribe abortion during that period, except when it is necessary to preserve the life or health of the mother."

I also accept what is implicit in the Court's analysis, namely, a reaffirmation of *Roe*'s explanation of *why* the State's obligation to protect the life or health of the mother must take precedence over any duty to the unborn. The Court in *Roe* carefully considered, and rejected, the State's argument "that the fetus is a 'person' within the language and meaning of the Fourteenth Amendment." * * * Accordingly, an abortion is not "the termination of life entitled to Fourteenth Amendment protection." From this holding, there was no dissent; indeed, no member of the Court has ever questioned this fundamental proposition. Thus, as a matter of federal constitutional law, a developing organism that is not yet a "person" does not have what is sometimes described as a "right to life."[2] This has been and, by the Court's holding today, remains a fundamental premise of our constitutional law governing reproductive autonomy.

My disagreement with the joint opinion begins with its understanding of the trimester framework established in *Roe*. Contrary to the suggestion of the joint opinion, it is not a "contradiction" to recognize that the State may have a legitimate interest in potential human life and, at the same time, to conclude that that interest does not justify the regulation of abortion before viability (although other interests, such as maternal health, may). The fact that the State's interest is legitimate does not tell us when, if ever, that interest outweighs the pregnant woman's interest in personal liberty. It is appropriate, therefore, to consider more carefully the nature of the interests at stake.

First, it is clear that, in order to be legitimate, the State's interest must be secular; consistent with the First Amendment the State may not promote a theological or sectarian interest. Moreover, as discussed above, the state interest in potential human life is not an interest *in loco parentis,* for the fetus is not a person.

Identifying the State's interests—which the States rarely articulate with any precision—makes clear that the interest in protecting potential life is not grounded in the Constitution. It is, instead, an indirect interest supported by both humanitarian and pragmatic concerns. Many of our citizens believe that any abortion reflects an unacceptable disrespect for potential human life and that the performance of more than a million abortions each year is intolerable;

---

2. Professor Dworkin has made this comment on the issue:

"The suggestion that states are free to declare a fetus a person * * * assumes that a state can curtail some persons' constitutional rights by adding new persons to the constitutional population. The constitutional rights of one citizen are of course very much affected by who or what else also has constitutional rights, because the rights of others may compete or conflict with his. So any power to increase the constitutional population by unilateral decision would be, in effect, a power to decrease rights the national Constitution grants to others.

"If a state could declare trees to be persons with a constitutional right to life, it could prohibit publishing newspapers or books in spite of the First Amendment's guarantee of free speech, which could not be understood as a license to kill * * *. Once we understand that the suggestion we are considering has that implication, we must reject it. If a fetus is not part of the constitutional population, under the national constitutional arrangement, then states have no power to overrule that national arrangement by themselves declaring that fetuses have rights competitive with the constitutional rights of pregnant women." Dworkin, *Unenumerated Rights: Whether and How Roe Should be Overruled,* 59 U.Chi.L.Rev. 381, 400–401 (1992).

many find third-trimester abortions performed when the fetus is approaching personhood particularly offensive. The State has a legitimate interest in minimizing such offense. The State may also have a broader interest in expanding the population,[3] believing society would benefit from the services of additional productive citizens—or that the potential human lives might include the occasional Mozart or Curie. These are the kinds of concerns that comprise the State's interest in potential human life.

In counterpoise is the woman's constitutional interest in liberty. One aspect of this liberty is a right to bodily integrity, a right to control one's person. This right is neutral on the question of abortion: The Constitution would be equally offended by an absolute requirement that all women undergo abortions as by an absolute prohibition on abortions. * * *

The woman's constitutional liberty interest also involves her freedom to decide matters of the highest privacy and the most personal nature. A woman considering abortion faces "a difficult choice having serious and personal consequences of major importance to her own future—perhaps to the salvation of her own immortal soul." The authority to make such traumatic and yet empowering decisions is an element of basic human dignity. As the joint opinion so eloquently demonstrates, a woman's decision to terminate her pregnancy is nothing less than a matter of conscience.

Weighing the State's interest in potential life and the woman's liberty interest, I agree with the joint opinion that the State may "'expres[s] a preference for normal childbirth,'" that the State may take steps to ensure that a woman's choice "is thoughtful and informed," and that "States are free to enact laws to provide a reasonable framework for a woman to make a decision that has such profound and lasting meaning." Serious questions arise, however, when a State attempts to "persuade the woman to choose childbirth over abortion." Decisional autonomy must limit the State's power to inject into a woman's most personal deliberations its own views of what is best. The State may promote its preferences by funding childbirth, by creating and maintaining alternatives to abortion, and by espousing the virtues of family; but it must respect the individual's freedom to make such judgments.

This theme runs throughout our decisions concerning reproductive freedom. In general, *Roe*'s requirement that restrictions on abortions before viability be justified by the State's interest in *maternal* health has prevented States from interjecting regulations designed to influence a woman's decision. Thus, we have upheld regulations of abortion that are not efforts to sway or direct a woman's choice but rather are efforts to enhance the deliberative quality of that decision or are neutral regulations on the health aspects of her decision. * * * Conversely, we have consistently rejected state efforts to prejudice a woman's choice, either by limiting the information available to her or by "requir[ing] the delivery of information designed 'to influence the woman's informed choice between abortion or childbirth.'"

---

3. The state interest in protecting potential life may be compared to the state interest in protecting those who seek to immigrate to this country. A contemporary example is provided by the Haitians who have risked the perils of the sea in a desperate attempt to become "persons" protected by our laws. Humanitarian and practical concerns would support a state policy allowing those persons unrestricted entry; countervailing interests in population control support a policy of limiting the entry of these potential citizens. While the state interest in population control might be sufficient to justify strict enforcement of the immigration laws, that interest would not be sufficient to overcome a woman's liberty interest. Thus, a state interest in population control could not justify a state-imposed limit on family size or, for that matter, state-mandated abortions.

In my opinion, the principles established in this long line of cases and the wisdom reflected in Justice Powell's opinion for the Court in *Akron* (and followed by the Court just six years ago in *Thornburgh*) should govern our decision today. Under these principles, §§ 3205(a)(2)(i)–(iii) of the Pennsylvania statute are unconstitutional. Those sections require a physician or counselor to provide the woman with a range of materials clearly designed to persuade her to choose not to undergo the abortion. While the State is free, pursuant to § 3208 of the Pennsylvania law, to produce and disseminate such material, the State may not inject such information into the woman's deliberations just as she is weighing such an important choice.

Under this same analysis, §§ 3205(a)(1)(i) and (iii) of the Pennsylvania statute are constitutional. Those sections, which require the physician to inform a woman of the nature and risks of the abortion procedure and the medical risks of carrying to term, are neutral requirements comparable to those imposed in other medical procedures. Those sections indicate no effort by the State to influence the woman's choice in any way. If anything, such requirements *enhance*, rather than skew, the woman's decisionmaking.

The 24–hour waiting period required by §§ 3205(a)(1)–(2) of the Pennsylvania statute raises even more serious concerns. Such a requirement arguably furthers the State's interests in two ways, neither of which is constitutionally permissible.

First, it may be argued that the 24–hour delay is justified by the mere fact that it is likely to reduce the number of abortions, thus furthering the State's interest in potential life. But such an argument would justify any form of coercion that placed an obstacle in the woman's path. The State cannot further its interests by simply wearing down the ability of the pregnant woman to exercise her constitutional right.

Second, it can more reasonably be argued that the 24–hour delay furthers the State's interest in ensuring that the woman's decision is informed and thoughtful. But there is no evidence that the mandated delay benefits women or that it is necessary to enable the physician to convey any relevant information to the patient. The mandatory delay thus appears to rest on outmoded and unacceptable assumptions about the decisionmaking capacity of women. While there are well-established and consistently maintained reasons for the State to view with skepticism the ability of minors to make decisions, none of those reasons applies to an adult woman's decisionmaking ability. Just as we have left behind the belief that a woman must consult her husband before undertaking serious matters, so we must reject the notion that a woman is less capable of deciding matters of gravity.

In the alternative, the delay requirement may be premised on the belief that the decision to terminate a pregnancy is presumptively wrong. This premise is illegitimate. Those who disagree vehemently about the legality and morality of abortion agree about one thing: The decision to terminate a pregnancy is profound and difficult. No person undertakes such a decision lightly—and States may not presume that a woman has failed to reflect adequately merely because her conclusion differs from the State's preference. A woman who has, in the privacy of her thoughts and conscience, weighed the options and made her decision cannot be forced to reconsider all, simply because the State believes she has come to the wrong conclusion.[5]

5. The joint opinion's reliance on the indirect effects of the regulation of constitutionally protected activity, see *ante,* 31–32, is misplaced; [as I explained in *Hodgson*] what

Part of the constitutional liberty to choose is the equal dignity to which each of us is entitled. A woman who decides to terminate her pregnancy is entitled to the same respect as a woman who decides to carry the fetus to term. The mandatory waiting period denies women that equal respect.

In my opinion, a correct application of the "undue burden" standard leads to the same conclusion concerning the constitutionality of these requirements. A state-imposed burden on the exercise of a constitutional right is measured both by its effects and by its character: A burden may be "undue" either because the burden is too severe or because it lacks a legitimate, rational justification.[6]

The 24-hour delay requirement fails both parts of this test. The findings of the District Court establish the severity of the burden that the 24-hour delay imposes on many pregnant women. Yet even in those cases in which the delay is not especially onerous, it is, in my opinion, "undue" because there is no evidence that such a delay serves a useful and legitimate purpose. As indicated above, there is no legitimate reason to require a woman who has agonized over her decision to leave the clinic or hospital and return again another day. While a general requirement that a physician notify her patients about the risks of a proposed medical procedure is appropriate, a rigid requirement that all patients wait 24 hours or (what is true in practice) much longer to evaluate the significance of information that is either common knowledge or irrelevant is an irrational and, therefore, "undue" burden.

The counseling provisions are similarly infirm. Whenever government commands private citizens to speak or to listen, careful review of the justification for that command is particularly appropriate. In this case, the Pennsylvania statute directs that counselors provide women seeking abortions with information concerning alternatives to abortion, the availability of medical assistance benefits, and the possibility of child-support payments. The statute requires that this information be given to *all* women seeking abortions, including those for whom such information is clearly useless, such as those who are married, those who have undergone the procedure in the past and are fully aware of the options, and those who are fully convinced that abortion is their only reasonable option. Moreover, the statute requires physicians to inform all of their patients of "the probable gestational age of the unborn child." This information is of little decisional value in most cases, because 90% of all abortions are performed during the first trimester when fetal age has less relevance than when the fetus nears viability. Nor can the information required by the statute be justified as relevant to any "philosophic" or "social" argument, either favoring or disfavoring the abortion decision in a particular case. In light of all of these facts, I conclude that the information requirements * * * do not serve a useful purpose and thus constitute an unnecessary—and therefore undue—burden on the woman's constitutional liberty to decide to terminate her pregnancy.

matters is not only the effect of a regulation but also the reason for the regulation.

6. The meaning of any legal standard can only be understood by reviewing the actual cases in which it is applied. For that reason, I discount both Justice Scalia's comments on past descriptions of the standard and the attempt to give it crystal clarity in the joint opinion. The several opinions supporting the judgment in *Griswold v. Connecticut,* 381 U.S. 479 (1965), are less illuminating than the central holding of the case, which appears to have passed the test of time. The future may also demonstrate that a standard that analyzes both the severity of a regulatory burden and the legitimacy of its justification will provide a fully adequate framework for the review of abortion legislation even if the contours of the standard are not authoritatively articulated in any single opinion.

Accordingly, while I disagree with Parts IV, V–B, and V–D of the joint opinion,[8] I join the remainder of the Court's opinion.

JUSTICE BLACKMUN, concurring in part, concurring in the judgment in part, and dissenting in part.

I join parts I, II, III, V–A, V–C, and VI of the joint opinion of Justices O'Connor, Kennedy and Souter.

Three years ago, in *Webster*, four Members of this Court appeared poised to "cas[t] into darkness the hopes and visions of every woman in this country" who had come to believe that the Constitution guaranteed her the right to reproductive choice. (Blackmun, J., dissenting). All that remained between the promise of *Roe* and the darkness of the plurality was a single, flickering flame. Decisions since *Webster* gave little reason to hope that this flame would cast much light. But now, just when so many expected the darkness to fall, the flame has grown bright.

I do not underestimate the significance of today's joint opinion. Yet I remain steadfast in my belief that the right to reproductive choice is entitled to the full protection afforded by this Court before *Webster*. And I fear for the darkness as four Justices anxiously await the single vote necessary to extinguish the light.

Make no mistake, the joint opinion of Justices O'Connor, Kennedy, and Souter is an act of personal courage and constitutional principle. In contrast to previous decisions in which Justices O'Connor and Kennedy postponed reconsideration of *Roe*, the authors of the joint opinion today join Justice Stevens and me in concluding that "the essential holding of *Roe* should be retained and once again reaffirmed." In brief, five Members of this Court today recognize that "the Constitution protects a woman's right to terminate her pregnancy in its early stages."

A fervent view of individual liberty and the force of *stare decisis* have led the Court to this conclusion. Today a majority reaffirms that the Due Process Clause of the Fourteenth Amendment establishes "a realm of personal liberty which the government may not enter"—a realm whose outer limits cannot be determined by interpretations of the Constitution that focus only on the specific practices of States at the time the Fourteenth Amendment was adopted. Included within this realm of liberty is "'the right of the *individual,* married or single, to be free from unwarranted governmental intrusion into matters so fundamentally affecting a person as the decision whether to bear or beget a child.'" "These matters, involving the most intimate and personal choices a person may make in a lifetime, choices central to personal dignity and autonomy, are *central* to the liberty protected by the Fourteenth Amendment." (Emphasis added). Finally, the Court today recognizes that in the case of abortion, "the liberty of the woman is at stake in a sense unique to the human condition and so unique to the law. The mother who carries a child to full term is subject to anxieties, to physical constraints, to pain that only she must bear."

The Court's reaffirmation of *Roe's* central holding is also based on the force of *stare decisis.* [In] the 19 years since *Roe* was decided, that case has shaped more than reproductive planning—"an entire generation has come of age free to assume *Roe's* concept of liberty in defining the capacity of women to act in

---

8. Although I agree that a parental-consent requirement (with the appropriate bypass) is constitutional, I do not join Part V–D of the joint opinion because its approval of Pennsylvania's informed parental-consent requirement is based on the reasons given in Part V–B, with which I disagree.

society and to make reproductive decisions." The Court understands that, having "call[ed] the contending sides [to] end their national division by accepting a common mandate rooted in the Constitution," a decision to overrule *Roe* "would seriously weaken the Court's capacity to exercise the judicial power and to function as the Supreme Court of a Nation dedicated to the rule of law." What has happened today should serve as a model for future Justices and a warning to all who have tried to turn this Court into yet another political branch.

In striking down the Pennsylvania statute's spousal notification requirement, the Court has established a framework for evaluating abortion regulations that responds to the social context of women facing issues of reproductive choice.[1] In determining the burden imposed by the challenged regulation, the Court inquires whether the regulation's "*purpose or effect* is to place a substantial obstacle in the path of a woman seeking an abortion before the fetus attains viability." (Emphasis added). * * * Whatever may have been the practice when the Fourteenth Amendment was adopted, the Court observes, "[w]omen do not lose their constitutionally protected liberty when they marry. The Constitution protects all individuals, male or female, married or unmarried, from the abuse of governmental power, even where that power is employed for the supposed benefit of a member of the individual's family."[2]

Lastly, while I believe that the joint opinion errs in failing to invalidate the other regulations, I am pleased that the joint opinion has not ruled out the possibility that these regulations may be shown to impose an unconstitutional burden. The joint opinion makes clear that its specific holdings are based on the insufficiency of the record before it. I am confident that in the future evidence will be produced to show that "in a large fraction of the cases in which [these regulations are] relevant, [they] will operate as a substantial obstacle to a woman's choice to undergo an abortion."

Today, no less than yesterday, the Constitution and decisions of this Court require that a State's abortion restrictions be subjected to the strictest of judicial scrutiny. Our precedents and the joint opinion's principles require us to subject all non-*de minimis* abortion regulations to strict scrutiny. Under this standard, the Pennsylvania statute's provisions requiring content-based counseling, a 24–hour delay, informed parental consent, and reporting of abortion-related information must be invalidated. * * *

State restrictions on abortion violate a woman's right of privacy in two ways. First, compelled continuation of a pregnancy infringes upon a woman's right to bodily integrity by imposing substantial physical intrusions and significant risks of physical harm. During pregnancy, women experience dramatic physical changes and a wide range of health consequences. Labor and delivery pose additional health risks and physical demands. In short, restrictive abortion laws force women to endure physical invasions far more substantial than those this Court has held to violate the constitutional principle of bodily integrity in other contexts.[3]

1. As I shall explain, the joint opinion and I disagree on the appropriate standard of review for abortion regulations. I do agree, however, that the reasons advanced by the joint opinion suffice to invalidate the spousal notification requirement under a strict scrutiny standard.

2. I also join the Court's decision to uphold the medical emergency provision. * * *

3. As the joint opinion acknowledges, this Court has recognized the vital liberty interest of persons in refusing unwanted medical treatment. *Cruzan.* Just as the Due Process Clause protects the deeply personal decision of the individual to *refuse* medical treatment, it also must protect the deeply personal decision to *obtain* medical treatment, including a woman's decision to terminate a pregnancy.

Further, when the State restricts a woman's right to terminate her pregnancy, it deprives a woman of the right to make her own decision about reproduction and family planning—critical life choices that this Court long has deemed central to the right to privacy. The decision to terminate or continue a pregnancy has no less an impact on a woman's life than decisions about contraception or marriage. Because motherhood has a dramatic impact on a woman's educational prospects, employment opportunities, and self-determination, restrictive abortion laws deprive her of basic control over her life.

[A] State's restrictions on a woman's right to terminate her pregnancy also implicate constitutional guarantees of gender equality. State restrictions on abortion compel women to continue pregnancies they otherwise might terminate. By restricting the right to terminate pregnancies, the State conscripts women's bodies into its service, forcing women to continue their pregnancies, suffer the pains of childbirth, and in most instances, provide years of maternal care. The State does not compensate women for their services; instead, it assumes that they owe this duty as a matter of course. This assumption—that women can simply be forced to accept the "natural" status and incidents of motherhood— appears to rest upon a conception of women's role that has triggered the protection of the Equal Protection Clause.[4] The joint opinion recognizes that these assumptions about women's place in society "are no longer consistent with our understanding of the family, the individual, or the Constitution."

The Court has held that limitations on the right of privacy are permissible only if they survive "strict" constitutional scrutiny—that is, only if the governmental entity imposing the restriction can demonstrate that the limitation is both necessary and narrowly tailored to serve a compelling governmental interest. *Griswold*. We have applied this principle specifically in the context of abortion regulations. *Roe*.[5]

[In] my view, application of [the] analytical framework [set forth in *Roe*] is no less warranted than when it was approved by seven Members of this Court in *Roe*. Strict scrutiny of state limitations on reproductive choice still offers the most secure protection of the woman's right to make her own reproductive decisions, free from state coercion. No majority of this Court has ever agreed upon an alternative approach. The factual premises of the trimester framework have not been undermined and the *Roe* framework is far more administrable, and far less manipulable, than the "undue burden" standard adopted by the joint opinion.

Nonetheless, three criticisms of the trimester framework continue to be uttered. First, the trimester framework is attacked because its key elements do not appear in the text of the Constitution. My response to this attack remains the same as it was in *Webster* * * *.

---

4. A growing number of commentators are recognizing this point. See, *e.g.*, L. Tribe, *American Constitutional Law*, § 15–10, pp. 1353–1359 (2d ed. 1988); Siegel, *Reasoning from the Body: A Historical Perspective on Abortion Regulation and Questions of Equal Protection*, 44 Stan.L.Rev. 261, 350–380 (1992); Sunstein, *Neutrality in Constitutional Law (With Special Reference to Pornography, Abortion, and Surrogacy)*, 92 Colum.L.Rev. 1, 31–44 (1992) * * *.

5. To say that restrictions on a right are subject to strict scrutiny is not to say that the right is absolute. Regulations can be upheld if they have no significant impact on the woman's exercise of her right and are justified by important state health objectives. See, *e.g.*, *Danforth* (upholding requirements of a woman's written consent and record keeping). But the Court today reaffirms the essential principle of *Roe* that a woman has the right "to choose to have an abortion before viability and to obtain it without undue interference from the State." Under *Roe*, any more than *de minimis* interference is undue.

The second criticism is that the framework more closely resembles a regulatory code than a body of constitutional doctrine. Again, my answer remains the same as in *Webster*. * * *

The final, and more genuine, criticism of the trimester framework is that it fails to find the State's interest in potential human life compelling throughout pregnancy. No member of this Court—nor for that matter, the Solicitor General—has ever questioned our holding in *Roe* that an abortion is not "the termination of life entitled to Fourteenth Amendment protection." Accordingly, a State's interest in protecting fetal life is not grounded in the Constitution. Nor, consistent with our Establishment Clause, can it be a theological or sectarian interest. See *Thornburgh* (Stevens, J., concurring). It is, instead, a legitimate interest grounded in humanitarian or pragmatic concerns.

But while a State has "legitimate interests from the outset of the pregnancy in protecting the health of the woman and the life of the fetus that may become a child," legitimate interests are not enough. To overcome the burden of strict scrutiny, the interests must be compelling. The question then is how best to accommodate the State's interest in potential human life with the constitutional liberties of pregnant women. Again, I stand by the views I expressed in *Webster* * * *.

Roe's trimester framework does not ignore the State's interest in prenatal life. Like Justice Stevens, I agree that the State may take steps to ensure that a woman's choice "is thoughtful and informed" and that "States are free to enact laws to provide a reasonable framework for a woman to make a decision that has such profound and lasting meaning." But

> "[s]erious questions arise when a State attempts to 'persuade the woman to choose childbirth over abortion.' Decisional autonomy must limit the State's power to inject into a woman's most personal deliberations its own views of what is best. The State may promote its preferences by funding childbirth, by creating and maintaining alternatives to abortion, and by espousing the virtues of family, but it must respect the individual's freedom to make such judgments." (Opinion of Stevens, J.).

As the joint opinion recognizes, "the means chosen by the State to further the interest in potential life must be calculated to inform the woman's free choice, not hinder it."

In sum, *Roe*'s requirement of strict scrutiny as implemented through a trimester framework should not be disturbed. No other approach has gained a majority, and no other is more protective of the woman's fundamental right. Lastly, no other approach properly accommodates the woman's constitutional right with the State's legitimate interests.

Application of the strict scrutiny standard results in the invalidation of all the challenged provisions. Indeed, as this Court has invalidated virtually identical provisions in prior cases, *stare decisis* requires that we again strike them down.

This Court has upheld informed and written consent requirements only where the State has demonstrated that they genuinely further important health-related state concerns. See *Danforth*. A State may not, under the guise of securing informed consent, "require the delivery of information 'designed to influence the woman's informed choice between abortion or childbirth.'" *Thornburgh*. Rigid requirements that a specific body of information be imparted to a woman in all cases, regardless of the needs of the patient, improperly intrude upon the discretion of the pregnant woman's physician and thereby impose an "'undesired and uncomfortable straitjacket.'" *Thornburgh* (quoting *Danforth*).

Measured against these principles, some aspects of the Pennsylvania informed-consent scheme are unconstitutional. While it is unobjectionable for the Commonwealth to require that the patient be informed of the nature of the procedure, the health risks of the abortion and of childbirth, and the probable gestational age of the unborn child, I remain unconvinced that there is a vital state need for insisting that the information be provided by a physician rather than a counselor. The District Court found that the physician-only requirement necessarily would increase costs to the plaintiff-clinics, costs that undoubtedly would be passed on to patients. And because trained women counselors are often more understanding than physicians, and generally have more time to spend with patients, the physician-only disclosure requirement is not narrowly tailored to serve the Commonwealth's interest in protecting maternal health.

Sections 3205(a)(2)(i)–(iii) of the Act further requires that the physician or a qualified non-physician inform the woman that printed materials are available from the Commonwealth that describe the fetus and provide information about medical assistance for childbirth, information about child support from the father, and a list of agencies [that] provide adoption and other services as alternatives to abortion. *Thornburgh* invalidated biased patient-counseling requirements virtually identical to the one at issue here. What we said of those requirements fully applies in this case * * *.

The 24–hour waiting period following the provision of the foregoing information is also clearly unconstitutional. The District Court found that the mandatory 24–hour delay could lead to delays in excess of 24 hours, thus increasing health risks, and that it would require two visits to the abortion provider, thereby increasing travel time, exposure to further harassment, and financial cost. Finally, the District Court found that the requirement would pose especially significant burdens on women living in rural areas and those women that have difficulty explaining their whereabouts. In *Akron* this Court invalidated a similarly arbitrary or inflexible waiting period because, as here, it furthered no legitimate state interest.[8]

As Justice Stevens insightfully concludes, the mandatory delay rests either on outmoded or unacceptable assumptions about the decisionmaking capacity of women or the belief that the decision to terminate the pregnancy is presumptively wrong. The requirement that women consider this obvious and slanted information for an additional 24 hours contained in these provisions will only influence the woman's decision in improper ways. The vast majority of women will know this information—of the few that do not, it is less likely that their minds will be changed by this information than it will be either by the realization that the State opposes their choice or the need once again to endure abuse and harassment on return to the clinic.[9]

Except in the case of a medical emergency, § 3206 requires a physician to obtain the informed consent of a parent or guardian before performing an

8. The Court's decision in *Hodgson v. Minnesota*, validating a 48–hour waiting period for minors seeking an abortion to permit parental involvement does not alter this conclusion. Here the 24–hour delay is imposed on an *adult* woman. Moreover, the statute in *Hodgson* did not require any delay once the minor obtained the affirmative consent of either a parent or the court.

9. Because this information is so widely known, I am confident that a developed record can be made to show that the 24–hour delay, "in a large fraction of the cases in which [the restriction] is relevant, * * * will operate as a substantial obstacle to a woman's choice to undergo an abortion" [quoting from the joint opinion's discussion of the spousal notification requirement].

abortion on an unemancipated minor or an incompetent woman. Based on evidence in the record, the District Court concluded that, in order to fulfill the informed-consent requirement, generally accepted medical principles would require an in-person visit by the parent to the facility. Although the Court "has recognized that the State has somewhat broader authority to regulate the activities of children than of adults," the State nevertheless must demonstrate that there is a "*significant state interest* in conditioning an abortion [that] is not present in the case of an adult." *Danforth* (emphasis added). The requirement of an in-person visit would carry with it the risk of a delay of several days or possibly weeks, even where the parent is willing to consent. While the State has an interest in encouraging parental involvement in the minor's abortion decision, § 3206 is not narrowly drawn to serve that interest.[10]

Finally, the Pennsylvania statute requires every facility performing abortions to report its activities to the Commonwealth. Pennsylvania contends that this requirement is valid under *Danforth*, in which this Court held that record-keeping and reporting requirements that are reasonably directed to the preservation of maternal health and that properly respect a patient's confidentiality are permissible. The Commonwealth attempts to justify its required reports on the ground that the public has a right to know how its tax dollars are spent. A regulation designed to inform the public about public expenditures does not further the Commonwealth's interest in protecting maternal health. Accordingly, such a regulation cannot justify a legally significant burden on a woman's right to obtain an abortion.

The confidential reports concerning the identities and medical judgment of physicians involved in abortions at first glance may seem valid, given the State's interest in maternal health and enforcement of the Act. The District Court found, however, that, notwithstanding the confidentiality protections, many physicians, particularly those who have previously discontinued performing abortions because of harassment, would refuse to refer patients to abortion clinics if their names were to appear on these reports. The Commonwealth has failed to show that the name of the referring physician either adds to the pool of scientific knowledge concerning abortion or is reasonably related to the Commonwealth's interest in maternal health. I therefore agree with the District Court's conclusion that the confidential reporting requirements are unconstitutional insofar as they require the name of the referring physician and the basis for his or her medical judgment. * * *

At long last, The Chief Justice admits it. Gone are the contentions that the issue need not be (or has not been) considered. There, on the first page, for all to see, is what was expected: "We believe that *Roe* was wrongly decided, and that it can and should be overruled consistently with our traditional approach to *stare decisis* in constitutional cases." If there is much reason to applaud the advances made by the joint opinion today, there is far more to fear from The Chief Justice's opinion.

The Chief Justice's criticism of *Roe* follows from his stunted conception of individual liberty. While recognizing that the Due Process Clause protects more

---

10. The judicial-bypass provision does not cure this violation. *Hodgson* is distinguishable, since this case involves more than parental involvement or approval—rather, the Pennsylvania law requires that the parent receive information designed to discourage abortion in a face-to-face meeting with the physician. The bypass procedure cannot ensure that the parent would obtain the information, since in many instances, the parent would not even attend the hearing. A State may not place any restriction on a young woman's right to an abortion, however irrational, simply because it has provided a judicial bypass.

than simple physical liberty, he then goes on to construe this Court's personal-liberty cases as establishing only a laundry list of particular rights, rather than a principled account of how these particular rights are grounded in a more general right of privacy. This constricted view is reinforced by The Chief Justice's exclusive reliance on tradition as a source of fundamental rights. He argues that the record in favor of a right to abortion is no stronger than the record in *Michael H. v. Gerald D.* (1989), where the plurality found no fundamental right to visitation privileges by an adulterous father, or in *Bowers v. Hardwick* (1986) [CON LAW p. 528, AMER CON p. 368, RTS & LIB p. 257], where the Court found no fundamental right to engage in homosexual sodomy, or in a case involving the "firing of a gun [into] another person's body." In The Chief Justice's world, a woman considering whether to terminate a pregnancy is entitled to no more protection than adulterers, murderers, and so-called "sexual deviates."[11] Given The Chief Justice's exclusive reliance on tradition, people using contraceptives seem the next likely candidate for his list of outcasts.

Even more shocking than The Chief Justice's cramped notion of individual liberty is his complete omission of any discussion of the effects that compelled childbirth and motherhood have on women's lives. The only expression of concern with women's health is purely instrumental—for The Chief Justice, only women's *psychological* health is a concern, and only to the extent that he assumes that every woman who decides to have an abortion does so without serious consideration of the moral implications of their decision. In short, The Chief Justice's view of the State's compelling interest in maternal health has less to do with health than it does with compelling women to be maternal.

Nor does The Chief Justice give any serious consideration to the doctrine of *stare decisis*. For The Chief Justice, the facts that gave rise to *Roe* are surprisingly simple: "women become pregnant, there is a point somewhere, depending on medical technology, where a fetus becomes viable, and women give birth to children." This characterization of the issue thus allows The Chief Justice quickly to discard the joint opinion's reliance argument by asserting that "reproductive planning could take . . . virtually immediate account of a decision overruling *Roe*."

The Chief Justice's narrow conception of individual liberty and *stare decisis* leads him to propose the same standard of review proposed by the plurality in *Webster*. "States may regulate abortion procedures in ways rationally related to a legitimate state interest. * * *" The Chief Justice then further weakens the test by providing an insurmountable requirement for facial challenges: petitioners must "'show that no set of circumstances exists under which the [provision] would be valid.'" In short, in his view, petitioners must prove that the statute cannot constitutionally be applied to *anyone*. Finally, in applying his standard to the spousal-notification provision, The Chief Justice contends that the record lacks any "hard evidence" to support the joint opinion's contention that a "large fraction" of women who prefer not to notify their husbands involve situations of battered women and unreported spousal assault. Yet throughout the explication of his standard, The Chief Justice never explains what hard evidence is, how large a fraction is required, or how a battered woman is supposed to pursue an as-applied challenge.

11. Obviously, I do not share the plurality's views of homosexuality as sexual deviance.

Under his standard, States can ban abortion if that ban is rationally related to a legitimate state interest—a standard which the United States calls "deferential, but not toothless." Yet when pressed at oral argument to describe the teeth, the best protection that the Solicitor General could offer to women was that a prohibition, enforced by criminal penalties, *with no exception for the life of the mother,* "could raise very serious questions." Perhaps, the Solicitor General offered, the failure to include an exemption for the life of the mother would be "arbitrary and capricious." If, as The Chief Justice contends, the undue burden test is made out of whole cloth, the so-called "arbitrary and capricious" limit is the Solicitor General's "new clothes."

Even if it is somehow "irrational" for a State to require a woman to risk her life for her child, what protection is offered for women who become pregnant through rape or incest? Is there anything arbitrary or capricious about a State's prohibiting the sins of the father from being visited upon his offspring?[12]

But, we are reassured, there is always the protection of the democratic process. While there is much to be praised about our democracy, our country since its founding has recognized that there are certain fundamental liberties that are not to be left to the whims of an election. A woman's right to reproductive choice is one of those fundamental liberties. Accordingly, that liberty need not seek refuge at the ballot box.

In one sense, the Court's approach is worlds apart from that of The Chief Justice and Justice Scalia. And yet, in another sense, the distance between the two approaches is short—the distance is but a single vote.

I am 83 years old. I cannot remain on this Court forever, and when I do step down, the confirmation process for my successor well may focus on the issue before us today. That, I regret, may be exactly where the choice between the two worlds will be made.

CHIEF JUSTICE REHNQUIST, with whom JUSTICE WHITE, JUSTICE SCALIA, and JUSTICE THOMAS join, concurring in the judgment in part and dissenting in part.

The joint opinion, following its newly-minted variation on *stare decisis,* retains the outer shell of *Roe* but beats a wholesale retreat from the substance of that case. We believe that *Roe* was wrongly decided, and that it can and should be overruled consistently with our traditional approach to *stare decisis* in constitutional cases. We would adopt the approach of the plurality in *Webster* and uphold the challenged provisions of the Pennsylvania statute in their entirety.

In ruling on this case below, the Court of Appeals for the Third Circuit first observed that "this appeal does not directly implicate *Roe;* this case involves the regulation of abortions rather than their outright prohibition." Accordingly, the

---

12. Justice Scalia urges the Court to "get out of this area" and leave questions regarding abortion entirely to the States. Putting aside the fact that what he advocates is nothing short of an abdication by the Court of its constitutional responsibilities, Justice Scalia is uncharacteristically naive if he thinks that overruling *Roe* and holding that restrictions on a woman's right to an abortion are subject only to rational-basis review will enable the Court henceforth to avoid reviewing abortion-related issues. State efforts to regulate and prohibit abortion in a post-*Roe* world undoubtedly would raise a host of distinct and important constitutional questions meriting review by this Court. For example, does the Eighth Amendment impose any limits on the degree or kind of punishment a State can inflict upon physicians who perform, or women who undergo, abortions? What effect would differences among States in their approaches to abortion have on a woman's right to engage in interstate travel? Does the First Amendment permit States that choose not to criminalize abortion to ban all advertising providing information about where and how to obtain abortions?

court directed its attention to the question of the standard of review for abortion regulations. In attempting to settle on the correct standard, however, the court confronted the confused state of this Court's abortion jurisprudence. After considering the several opinions in *Webster* and *Hodgson* the Court of Appeals concluded that Justice O'Connor's "undue burden" test was controlling, as that was the narrowest ground on which we had upheld recent abortion regulations. * * * Applying this standard, the Court of Appeals upheld all of the challenged regulations except the one requiring a woman to notify her spouse of an intended abortion.

In arguing that this Court should invalidate each of the provisions at issue, petitioners insist that we reaffirm our decision in *Roe* * * *.[1] We agree with the Court of Appeals that our decision in *Roe* is not directly implicated by the Pennsylvania statute, which does not prohibit, but simply regulates, abortion. But, as the Court of Appeals found, the state of our post-*Roe* decisional law dealing with the regulation of abortion is confusing and uncertain, indicating that a reexamination of that line of cases is in order. Unfortunately for those who must apply this Court's decisions, the reexamination undertaken today leaves the Court no less divided than beforehand. Although they reject the trimester framework that formed the underpinning of *Roe,* Justices O'Connor, Kennedy, and Souter adopt a revised undue burden standard to analyze the challenged regulations. We conclude, however, that such an outcome is an unjustified constitutional compromise, one which leaves the Court in a position to closely scrutinize all types of abortion regulations despite the fact that it lacks the power to do so under the Constitution.

In *Roe,* the Court opined that the State "does have an important and legitimate interest in preserving and protecting the health of the pregnant woman [and] that it has still another important and legitimate interest in protecting the potentiality of human life." In the companion case of *Doe* the Court referred to its conclusion in *Roe* "that a pregnant woman does not have an absolute constitutional right to an abortion on her demand." But while the language and holdings of these cases appeared to leave States free to regulate abortion procedures in a variety of ways, later decisions based on them have found considerably less latitude for such regulations than might have been expected.

For example, after *Roe,* many States have sought to protect their young citizens by requiring that a minor seeking an abortion involve her parents in the decision. Some States have simply required notification of the parents, while others have required a minor to obtain the consent of her parents. In a number of decisions, however, the Court has substantially limited the States in their ability to impose such requirements. * * *

In *Roe,* the Court observed that certain States recognized the right of the father to participate in the abortion decision in certain circumstances. Because neither *Roe* nor *Doe* involved the assertion of any paternal right, the Court expressly stated that the case did not disturb the validity of regulations that protected such a right. But three years later, in *Danforth,* the Court extended its abortion jurisprudence and held that a State could not require that a woman obtain the consent of her spouse before proceeding with an abortion. *Danforth.*

---

1. Two years after *Roe,* the West German constitutional court, by contrast, struck down a law liberalizing access to abortion on the grounds that life developing within the womb is constitutionally protected. In 1988, the Canadian Supreme Court followed reasoning similar to that of *Roe* in striking down a law which restricted abortion.

States have also regularly tried to ensure that a woman's decision to have an abortion is an informed and well-considered one. In *Danforth,* we upheld a requirement that a woman sign a consent form prior to her abortion * * *. Since that case, however, we have twice invalidated state statutes designed to impart [full knowledge of the nature of the abortion decision] to a woman seeking an abortion [discussing *Akron* and *Thornburgh*].

We have not allowed States much leeway to regulate even the actual abortion procedure. Although a State can require that second-trimester abortions be performed in outpatient clinics, we concluded in *Akron* and *Ashcroft* that a State could not require that such abortions be performed only in hospitals. * * *

Although *Roe* allowed state regulation after the point of viability to protect the potential life of the fetus, the Court subsequently rejected attempts to regulate in this manner [discussing *Colautti v. Franklin* and *Thornburgh*].

[The] task of the Court of Appeals in the present case was obviously complicated by this confusion and uncertainty. [I]t concluded that in light of *Webster* and *Hodgson,* the strict scrutiny standard enunciated in *Roe* was no longer applicable, and that the "undue burden" standard adopted by Justice O'Connor was the governing principle. This state of confusion and disagreement warrants reexamination of the "fundamental right" accorded to a woman's decision to abort a fetus in *Roe,* with its concomitant requirement that any state regulation of abortion survive "strict scrutiny." * * *

In *Roe* the Court recognized a "guarantee of personal privacy" which "is broad enough to encompass a woman's decision whether or not to terminate her pregnancy." We are now of the view that, in terming this right fundamental, the Court in *Roe* read the earlier opinions upon which it based its decision much too broadly. Unlike marriage, procreation and contraception, abortion "involves the purposeful termination of potential life." The abortion decision must therefore "be recognized as *sui generis,* different in kind from the others that the Court has protected under the rubric of personal or family privacy and autonomy." *Thornburgh* (White, J., dissenting). One cannot ignore the fact that a woman is not isolated in her pregnancy, and that the decision to abort necessarily involves the destruction of a fetus.

[Nor] do the historical traditions of the American people support the view that the right to terminate one's pregnancy is "fundamental." The common law which we inherited from England made abortion after "quickening" an offense. At the time of the adoption of the Fourteenth Amendment, statutory prohibitions or restrictions on abortion were commonplace; in 1868, at least 28 of the then–37 States and 8 Territories had statutes banning or limiting abortion. By the turn of the century virtually every State had a law prohibiting or restricting abortion on its books. By the middle of the present century, a liberalization trend had set in. But 21 of the restrictive abortion laws in effect in 1868 were still in effect in 1973 when *Roe* was decided, and an overwhelming majority of the States prohibited abortion unless necessary to preserve the life or health of the mother. On this record, it can scarcely be said that any deeply rooted tradition of relatively unrestricted abortion in our history supported the classification of the right to abortion as "fundamental" under the Due Process Clause of the Fourteenth Amendment.

We think, therefore, both in view of this history and of our decided cases dealing with substantive liberty under the Due Process Clause, that the Court was mistaken in *Roe* when it classified a woman's decision to terminate her pregnancy as a "fundamental right" that could be abridged only in a manner which withstood "strict scrutiny." * * *

We believe that the sort of constitutionally imposed abortion code of the type illustrated by our decisions following *Roe* is inconsistent "with the notion of a Constitution cast in general terms, as ours is, and usually speaking in general principles, as ours does." *Webster* (plurality opinion). The Court in *Roe* reached too far when it analogized the right to abort a fetus to the rights involved in [*Griswold, Loving* and other cases] and thereby deemed the right to abortion fundamental.

The joint opinion of Justices O'Connor, Kennedy, and Souter cannot bring itself to say that *Roe* was correct as an original matter, but the authors are of the view that "the immediate question is not the soundness of *Roe*'s resolution of the issue, but the precedential force that must be accorded to its holding." Instead of claiming that *Roe* was correct as a matter of original constitutional interpretation, the opinion therefore contains an elaborate discussion of *stare decisis*. This discussion of the principle of *stare decisis* appears to be almost entirely dicta, because the joint opinion does not apply that principle in dealing with *Roe*. *Roe* decided that a woman had a fundamental right to an abortion. The joint opinion rejects that view. *Roe* decided that abortion regulations were to be subjected to "strict scrutiny" and could be justified only in the light of "compelling state interests." The joint opinion rejects that view. *Roe* analyzed abortion regulation under a rigid trimester framework, a framework which has guided this Court's decisionmaking for 19 years. The joint opinion rejects that framework.

Stare decisis is defined in Black's Law Dictionary as meaning "to abide by, or adhere to, decided cases." Whatever the "central holding" of *Roe* that is left after the joint opinion finishes dissecting it is surely not the result of that principle. While purporting to adhere to precedent, the joint opinion instead revises it. *Roe* continues to exist, but only in the way a storefront on a western movie set exists: a mere facade to give the illusion of reality. Decisions following *Roe*, such as *Akron* and *Thornburgh*, are frankly overruled in part under the "undue burden" standard expounded in the joint opinion.

In our view, authentic principles of *stare decisis* do not require that any portion of the reasoning in *Roe* be kept intact. "*Stare decisis* is not [a] universal, inexorable command," especially in cases involving the interpretation of the Federal Constitution. Erroneous decisions in such constitutional cases are uniquely durable, because correction through legislative action, save for constitutional amendment, is impossible. It is therefore our duty to reconsider constitutional interpretations that "depar[t] from a proper understanding" of the Constitution. * * * Our constitutional watch does not cease merely because we have spoken before on an issue; when it becomes clear that a prior constitutional interpretation is unsound we are obliged to reexamine the question.

The joint opinion discusses several *stare decisis* factors which, it asserts, point toward retaining a portion of *Roe*. Two of these factors are that the main "factual underpinning" of *Roe* has remained the same, and that its doctrinal foundation is no weaker now than it was in 1973. Of course, what might be called the basic facts which gave rise to *Roe* have remained the same—women become pregnant, there is a point somewhere, depending on medical technology, where a fetus becomes viable, and women give birth to children. But this is only to say that the same facts which gave rise to *Roe* will continue to give rise to similar cases. It is not a reason, in and of itself, why those cases must be decided in the same incorrect manner as was the first case to deal with the question. And surely there is no requirement, in considering whether to depart from *stare decisis* in a constitutional case, that a decision be more wrong now than it was at the time it was rendered. If that were true, the most outlandish constitutional decision could survive forever, based simply on the fact that it was no more outlandish later than it was when originally rendered.

Nor does the joint opinion faithfully follow this alleged requirement. The opinion frankly concludes that *Roe* and its progeny were wrong in failing to recognize that the State's interests in maternal health and in the protection of unborn human life exist throughout pregnancy. But there is no indication that these components of *Roe* are any more incorrect at this juncture than they were at its inception.

The joint opinion also points to the reliance interests involved in this context in its effort to explain why precedent must be followed for precedent's sake. Certainly it is true that where reliance is truly at issue, as in the case of judicial decisions that have formed the basis for private decisions, "[c]onsiderations in favor of *stare decisis* are at their acme." But, as the joint opinion apparently agrees, any traditional notion of reliance is not applicable here. The Court today cuts back on the protection afforded by *Roe,* and no one claims that this action defeats any reliance interest in the disavowed trimester framework. Similarly, reliance interests would not be diminished were the Court to go further and acknowledge the full error of *Roe,* as "reproductive planning could take virtually immediate account of" this action.

The joint opinion thus turns to what can only be described as an unconventional—and unconvincing—notion of reliance, a view based on the surmise that the availability of abortion since *Roe* has led to "two decades of economic and social developments" that would be undercut if the error of *Roe* were recognized. The joint opinion's assertion of this fact is undeveloped and totally conclusory. In fact, one can not be sure to what economic and social developments the opinion is referring. Surely it is dubious to suggest that women have reached their "places in society" in reliance upon *Roe,* rather than as a result of their determination to obtain higher education and compete with men in the job market, and of society's increasing recognition of their ability to fill positions that were previously thought to be reserved only for men.

In the end, having failed to put forth any evidence to prove any true reliance, the joint opinion's argument is based solely on generalized assertions about the national psyche, on a belief that the people of this country have grown accustomed to the *Roe* decision over the last 19 years and have "ordered their thinking and living around" it. As an initial matter, one might inquire how the joint opinion can view the "central holding" of *Roe* as so deeply rooted in our constitutional culture, when it so casually uproots and disposes of that same decision's trimester framework. Furthermore, at various points in the past, the same could have been said about this Court's erroneous decisions that the Constitution allowed "separate but equal" treatment of minorities or that "liberty" under the Due Process Clause protected "freedom of contract." The "separate but equal" doctrine lasted 58 years after *Plessy,* and *Lochner*'s protection of contractual freedom lasted 32 years. However, the simple fact that a generation or more had grown used to these major decisons did not prevent the Court from correcting its errors in those cases, nor should it prevent us from correctly interpreting the Constitution here.

Apparently realizing that conventional *stare decisis* principles do not support its position, the joint opinion advances a belief that retaining a portion of *Roe* is necessary to protect the "legitimacy" of this Court. Because the Court must take care to render decisions "grounded truly in principle," and not simply as political and social compromises, the joint opinion properly declares it to be this Court's duty to ignore the public criticism and protest that may arise as a result of a decision. Few would quarrel with this statement, although it may be doubted that Members of this Court, holding their tenure as they do during constitutional "good behavior," are at all likely to be intimidated by such public protests.

But the joint opinion goes on to state that when the Court "resolve[s] the sort of intensely divisive controversy reflected in *Roe* and those rare, comparable cases," its decision is exempt from reconsideration under established principles of *stare decisis* in constitutional cases. This is so, the joint opinion contends, because in those "intensely divisive" cases the Court has "call[ed] the contending sides of a national controversy to end their national division by accepting a common mandate rooted in the Constitution," and must therefore take special care not to be perceived as "surrender[ing] to political pressure" and continued opposition. This is a truly novel principle, one which is contrary to both the Court's historical practice and to the Court's traditional willingness to tolerate criticism of its opinions. Under this principle, when the Court has ruled on a divisive issue, it is apparently prevented from overruling that decision for the sole reason that it was incorrect, *unless opposition to the original decision has died away.*

The first difficulty with this principle lies in its assumption that cases which are "intensely divisive" can be readily distinguished from those that are not. The question of whether a particular issue is "intensely divisive" enough to qualify for special protection is entirely subjective and dependent on the individual assumptions of the Members of this Court. In addition, because the Court's duty is to ignore public opinion and criticism on issues that come before it, its members are in perhaps the worst position to judge whether a decision divides the Nation deeply enough to justify such uncommon protection. Although many of the Court's decisions divide the populace to a large degree, we have not previously on that account shied away from applying normal rules of *stare decisis* when urged to reconsider earlier decisions. Over the past 21 years, for example, the Court has overruled in whole or in part 34 of its previous constitutional decisions.

The joint opinion picks out and discusses two prior Court rulings that it believes are of the "intensely divisive" variety, and concludes that they are of comparable dimension to *Roe* [referring to the joint opinion's discussion of *Lochner* and *Plessy*]. It appears to us very odd indeed that the joint opinion chooses as benchmarks two cases in which the Court chose *not* to adhere to erroneous constitutional precedent, but instead enhanced its stature by acknowledging and correcting its error, apparently in violation of the joint opinion's "legitimacy" principle. One might also wonder how it is that the joint opinion puts these, and not others, in the "intensely divisive" category, and how it assumes that these are the only two lines of cases of comparable dimension to *Roe.* There is no reason to think that either *Plessy* or *Lochner* produced the sort of public protest when they were decided that *Roe* did. There were undoubtedly large segments of the bench and bar who agreed with the dissenting views in those cases, but surely that cannot be what the Court means when it uses the term "intensely divisive," or many other cases would have to be added to the list.

In terms of public protest, however, *Roe,* so far as we know, was unique. But just as the Court should not respond to that sort of protest by retreating from the decision simply to allay the concerns of the protesters, it should likewise not respond by determining to adhere to the decision at all costs lest it *seem* to be retreating under fire. Public protests should not alter the normal application of *stare decisis,* lest perfectly lawful protest activity be penalized by the Court itself.

Taking the joint opinion on its own terms, we doubt that its distinction between *Roe,* on the one hand, and *Plessy* and *Lochner,* on the other, withstands analysis. The joint opinion acknowledges that the Court improved its stature by overruling *Plessy* in *Brown* on a deeply divisive issue. And [the overruling of *Adkins* and *Lochner* occurred] at a time when Congress was considering President Franklin Roosevelt's proposal to "reorganize" this Court and enable him to name six additional Justices in the event that any member of the Court over the age of 70 did not elect to retire. It is difficult to imagine a situation in which the Court would face more intense opposition to a prior ruling than it did at that time, and, under the general principle proclaimed in the joint opinion, the Court seemingly should have responded to this opposition by stubbornly refusing to reexamine the *Lochner* rationale, lest it lose legitimacy by appearing to "overrule under fire."

The joint opinion agrees that the Court's stature would have been seriously damaged if in *Brown* and *West Coast Hotel* it had dug in its heels and refused to apply normal principles of *stare decisis* to the earlier decisions. But the opinion contends that the Court was entitled to overrule *Plessy* and *Lochner* in those cases, despite the existence of opposition to the original decisions, only because both the Nation and the Court had learned new lessons in the interim. This is at best a feebly supported, *post hoc* rationalization for those decisions.

For example, the opinion asserts that the Court could justifiably overrule its decision in *Lochner* only because the Depression had convinced "most people" that constitutional protection of contractual freedom contributed to an economy that failed to protect the welfare of all. Surely the joint opinion does not mean to suggest that people saw this Court's failure to uphold minimum wage statutes as the cause of the Great Depression! In any event, the *Lochner* Court did not base its rule upon the policy judgment that an unregulated market was fundamental to a stable economy; it simply believed, erroneously, that "liberty" under the Due Process Clause protected the "right to make a contract." Nor is it the case that the people of this Nation only discovered the dangers of extreme laissez faire economics because of the Depression. State laws regulating maximum hours and minimum wages were in existence well before that time.

[When] the Court finally recognized its error in *West Coast Hotel,* it did not engage in the *post hoc* rationalization that the joint opinion attributes to it today; it did not state that *Lochner* had been based on an economic view that had fallen into disfavor, and that it therefore should be overruled. Chief Justice Hughes in his opinion for the Court simply recognized what Justice Holmes had previously recognized in his *Lochner* dissent, that "[t]he Constitution does not speak of freedom of contract."

[The] joint opinion also agrees that the Court acted properly in rejecting the doctrine of "separate but equal" in *Brown.* In fact, the opinion lauds *Brown* in comparing it to *Roe.* This is strange, in that under the opinion's "legitimacy" principle the Court would seemingly have been forced to adhere to its erroneous decision in *Plessy* because of its "intensely divisive" character. To us, adherence to *Roe* today under the guise of "legitimacy" would seem to resemble more closely adherence to *Plessy* on the same ground. Fortunately, the Court did not choose that option in *Brown,* and instead frankly repudiated *Plessy.* The joint opinion concludes that such repudiation was justified only because of newly discovered evidence that segregation had the effect of treating one race as inferior to another. But it can hardly be argued that this was not urged upon those who decided *Plessy,* as Justice Harlan observed in his dissent that the law at issue "puts the brand of servitude and degradation upon a large class of our fellow-citizens, our equals before the law." It is clear that the same arguments made before the Court in *Brown* were made in *Plessy* as well. The Court in *Brown* simply recognized, as Justice Harlan had recognized beforehand, that the Fourteenth Amendment does not permit racial segregation. The rule of *Brown* is not tied to popular opinion about the evils of segregation; it is a judgment that the Equal Protection Clause does not permit racial segregation, no matter whether the public might come to believe that it is beneficial. On that ground it stands, and on that ground alone the Court was justified in properly concluding that the *Plessy* Court had erred.

There is also a suggestion in the joint opinion that the propriety of overruling a "divisive" decision depends in part on whether "most people" would now agree that it should be overruled. Either the demise of opposition or its progression to substantial popular agreement apparently is required to allow the Court to reconsider a divisive decision. How such agreement would be ascertained, short of a public opinion poll, the joint opinion does not say. But surely even the suggestion is totally at war with the idea of "legitimacy" in whose name it is invoked. The Judicial Branch derives its legitimacy, not from following public opinion, but from deciding by its best lights whether legislative enactments of the popular branches of Government comport with the Constitution. The doctrine of *stare decisis* is an adjunct of this duty, and should be no more subject to the vagaries of public opinion than is the basic judicial task.

There are other reasons why the joint opinion's discussion of legitimacy is unconvincing as well. In assuming that the Court is perceived as "surrender[ing] to political pressure" when it overrules a controversial decision, the joint opinion forgets that there are two sides to any controversy. The joint opinion asserts that, in order to protect its legitimacy, the Court must refrain from overruling a controversial decision lest it be viewed as favoring those who oppose the decision. But a decision to *adhere* to prior precedent is subject to the same criticism, for in such a case one can easily argue that the Court is responding to those who have demonstrated in favor of the original decision. The decision in *Roe* has engendered large demonstrations, including repeated marches on this Court and on Congress, both in opposition to and in support of that opinion. A decision either way on *Roe* can therefore be perceived as favoring one group or the other. But this perceived dilemma arises only if one assumes, as the joint opinion does, that the Court should make its decisions with a view toward speculative public perceptions. If one assumes instead, as the Court surely did in both *Brown* and *West Coast Hotel,* that the Court's legitimacy is enhanced by faithful interpretation of the Constitution irrespective of public opposition, such self-engendered difficulties may be put to one side.

Roe is not this Court's only decision to generate conflict. Our decisions in some recent capital cases, and in *Bowers v. Hardwick* (1986), have also engendered demonstrations in opposition. The joint opinion's message to such protesters appears to be that they must cease their activities in order to serve their cause, because their protests will only cement in place a decision which by normal standards of *stare decisis* should be reconsidered. * * * Strong and often misguided criticism of a decision should not render the decision immune from reconsideration, lest a fetish for legitimacy penalize freedom of expression.

The end result of the joint opinion's paeans of praise for legitimacy is the enunciation of a brand new standard for evaluating state regulation of a woman's right to abortion—the "undue burden" standard. As indicated above, *Roe* adopted a "fundamental right" standard under which state regulations could survive only if they met the requirement of "strict scrutiny." While we disagree with that standard, it at least had a recognized basis in constitutional law at the time *Roe* was decided. The same cannot be said for the "undue burden" standard, which is created largely out of whole cloth by the authors of the joint opinion. It is a standard which even today does not command the support of a majority of this Court. And it will not, we believe, result in the sort of "simple limitation," easily applied, which the joint opinion anticipates. In sum, it is a standard which is not built to last.

In evaluating abortion regulations under that standard, judges will have to decide whether they place a "substantial obstacle" in the path of a woman seeking an abortion. In that this standard is based even more on a judge's subjective determinations than was the trimester framework, the standard will do nothing to prevent "judges from roaming at large in the constitutional field" guided only by their personal views. *Griswold* (Harlan, J., concurring in judgment). Because the undue burden standard is plucked from nowhere, the question of what is a "substantial obstacle" to abortion will undoubtedly engender a variety of conflicting views. For example, in the very matter before us now, the authors of the joint opinion would uphold Pennsylvania's 24-hour waiting period, concluding that a "particular burden" on some women is not a substantial obstacle. But the authors would at the same time strike down Pennsylvania's spousal notice provision, after finding that in a "large fraction" of cases the provision will be a substantial obstacle. And, while the authors conclude that the informed consent provisions do not constitute an "undue burden," Justice Stevens would hold that they do.

Furthermore, while striking down the spousal *notice* regulation, the joint opinion would uphold a parental *consent* restriction that certainly places very substantial obstacles in the path of a minor's abortion choice. The joint opinion is forthright in admitting that it draws this distinction based on a policy judgment that parents will have the best interests of their children at heart, while the same is not necessarily true of husbands as to their wives. This may or may not be a correct judgment, but it is quintessentially a legislative one. The "undue burden" inquiry does not in any way supply the distinction between parental consent and spousal consent which the joint opinion adopts. Despite the efforts of the joint opinion, the undue burden standard presents nothing more workable than the trimester framework which it discards today. Under the guise of the Constitution, this Court will still impart its own preferences on the States in the form of a complex abortion code.

The sum of the joint opinion's labors in the name of *stare decisis* and "legitimacy" is this: *Roe* stands as a sort of judicial Potemkin Village, which may be pointed out to passers by as a monument to the importance of adhering to precedent. But behind the facade, an entirely new method of analysis, without any roots in constitutional law, is imported to decide the constitutionality of state laws regulating abortion. Neither *stare decisis* nor "legitimacy" are truly served by such an effort.

We have stated above our belief that the Constitution does not subject state abortion regulations to heightened scrutiny. Accordingly, we think that the correct analysis is that set forth by the plurality opinion in *Webster.* A woman's interest in having an abortion is a form of liberty protected by the Due Process Clause, but States may regulate abortion procedures in ways rationally related to a legitimate state interest. With this rule in mind, we examine each of the challenged provisions.

[The Chief Justice then discussed each of the challenged provisions and concluded that each should be upheld. The Chief Justice's analysis of the spousal notification provision follows.]

Section 3209 of the Act [requires] that, before a physician may perform an abortion on a married woman, the woman must sign a statement indicating that she has notified her husband of her planned abortion. A woman is not required to notify her husband if (1) her husband is not the father, (2) her husband, after diligent effort, cannot be located, (3) the pregnancy is the result of a spousal sexual assault that has been reported to the authorities, or (4) the woman has reason to believe that notifying her husband is likely to result in the infliction of bodily injury upon her by him or by another individual. In addition, a woman is exempted from the notification requirement in the case of a medical emergency.

We first emphasize that Pennsylvania has not imposed a spousal *consent* requirement of the type the Court struck down in *Danforth.* [T]his case involves a much less intrusive requirement of spousal *notification,* not consent. * * * *Danforth* thus does not control our analysis. Petitioners contend that it should, however; they argue that the real effect of such a notice requirement is to give the power to husbands to veto a woman's abortion choice. [For] example, petitioners argue, many notified husbands will prevent abortions through physical force, psychological coercion, and other types of threats. But Pennsylvania has incorporated exceptions in the notice provision in an attempt to deal with these problems. For instance, a woman need not notify her husband if the pregnancy is a result of a reported sexual assault, or if she has reason to believe that she would suffer bodily injury as a result of the notification. Furthermore, because this is a facial challenge to the Act, it is insufficient for petitioners to show that the notification provision "might operate unconstitutionally under some conceivable set of circumstances." * * * Because they are making a facial challenge to the provision, they must "show that no set of circumstances exists under which the [provision] would be valid." This they have failed to do.[2]

2. The joint opinion of Justices O'Connor, Kennedy, and Souter appears to ignore this point in concluding that the spousal notice provision imposes an undue burden on the abortion decision. In most instances the notification requirement operates without difficulty. As the District Court found, the vast majority of wives seeking abortions notify and consult with their husbands, and thus suffer no burden as a result of the provision. In other instances where a woman does not want to notify her husband, the Act provides exceptions.

[The] joint opinion puts to one side these situations where the regulation imposes no obstacle at all, and instead focuses on the group of married women who would not otherwise notify their husbands and who do not qualify for one of the exceptions. Having narrowed the focus, the joint opinion concludes that in a "large fraction" of those cases, the notification provision operates as a substantial obstacle, and that the provision is therefore invalid. There are certainly instances where a woman would prefer not to notify her husband, and yet does not qualify for an exception. For example, there are the situations of battered women who fear psychological abuse or injury to their children as a result of notification; because in these situations the women do not fear bodily injury, they do not qualify for an exception. And there are situations where a woman has become pregnant as a result of an unreported spousal sexual assault; when such an assault is unreported, no exception is available. But, as the District Court found, there are also instances where the woman prefers not to

The question before us is therefore whether the spousal notification requirement rationally furthers any legitimate state interests. We conclude that it does. First, a husband's interests in procreation within marriage and in the potential life of his unborn child are certainly substantial ones. [The] State itself has legitimate interests both in protecting these interests of the father and in protecting the potential life of the fetus, and the spousal notification requirement is reasonably related to advancing those state interests. By providing that a husband will usually know of his spouse's intent to have an abortion, the provision makes it more likely that the husband will participate in deciding the fate of his unborn child, a possibility that might otherwise have been denied him. This participation might in some cases result in a decision to proceed with the pregnancy.

[The] State also has a legitimate interest in promoting "the integrity of the marital relationship." [In] our view, the spousal notice requirement is a rational attempt by the State to improve truthful communication between spouses and encourage collaborative decisionmaking, and thereby fosters marital integrity. Petitioners argue that the notification requirement does not further any such interest; they assert that the majority of wives already notify their husbands of their abortion decisions, and the remainder have excellent reasons for keeping their decisions a secret. In the first case, they argue, the law is unnecessary, and in the second case it will only serve to foster marital discord and threats of harm. Thus, petitioners see the law as a totally irrational means of furthering whatever legitimate interest the State might have. But, in our view, it is unrealistic to assume that every husband-wife relationship is either (1) so perfect that this type of truthful and important communication will take place as a matter of course, or (2) so imperfect that, upon notice, the husband will react selfishly, violently, or contrary to the best interests of his wife. [The] spousal notice provision will admittedly be unnecessary in some circumstances, and possibly harmful in others, but "the existence of particular cases in which a feature of a statute performs no function (or is even counterproductive) ordinarily does not render the statute unconstitutional or even constitutionally suspect." *Thornburgh* (White, J., dissenting). The Pennsylvania Legislature was in a position to weigh the likely benefits of the provision against its likely adverse effects, and presumably concluded, on balance, that the provision would be beneficial. Whether this was a wise decision or not, we cannot say that it was irrational. We therefore conclude that the spousal notice provision comports with the Constitution. * * *

For the reasons stated, we therefore would hold that each of the challenged provisions of the Pennsylvania statute is consistent with the Constitution. It bears emphasis that our conclusion in this regard does not carry with it any necessary approval of these regulations. Our task is, as always, to decide only whether the challenged provisions of a law comport with the United States

---

notify her husband for a variety of other reasons. For example, a woman might desire to obtain an abortion without her husband's knowledge because of perceived economic constraints or her husband's previously expressed opposition to abortion. The joint opinion concentrates on the situations involving battered women and unreported spousal assault, and assumes, without any support in the record, that these instances constitute a "large fraction" of those cases in which women prefer not to notify their husbands (and do not qualify for an exception). This assumption is not based on any hard evidence, however. And were it helpful to an attempt to reach a desired result, one could just as easily assume that the battered women situations form 100 percent of the cases where women desire not to notify, or that they constitute only 20 percent of those cases. But reliance on such speculation is the necessary result of adopting the undue burden standard.

Constitution. If, as we believe, these do, their wisdom as a matter of public policy is for the people of Pennsylvania to decide.

JUSTICE SCALIA, with whom THE CHIEF JUSTICE, JUSTICE WHITE, and JUSTICE THOMAS join, concurring in the judgment in part and dissenting in part.

My views on this matter are unchanged from those I set forth in my separate opinions in *Webster* and *Ohio v. Akron Center for Reproductive Health (Akron II)*. The States may, if they wish, permit abortion-on-demand, but the Constitution does not *require* them to do so. The permissibility of abortion, and the limitations upon it, are to be resolved like most important questions in our democracy: by citizens trying to persuade one another and then voting. As the Court acknowledges, "where reasonable people disagree the government can adopt one position or the other." The Court is correct in adding the qualification that this "assumes a state of affairs in which the choice does not intrude upon a protected liberty"—but the crucial part of that qualification is the penultimate word. A State's choice between two positions on which reasonable people can disagree is constitutional even when (as is often the case) it intrudes upon a "liberty" in the absolute sense. Laws against bigamy, for example—which entire societies of reasonable people disagree with—intrude upon men and women's liberty to marry and live with one another. But bigamy happens not to be a liberty specially "protected" by the Constitution.

That is, quite simply, the issue in this case: not whether the power of a woman to abort her unborn child is a "liberty" in the absolute sense; or even whether it is a liberty of great importance to many women. Of course it is both. The issue is whether it is a liberty protected by the Constitution of the United States. I am sure it is not. I reach that conclusion not because of anything so exalted as my views concerning the "concept of existence, of meaning, of the universe, and of the mystery of human life." Rather, I reach it for the same reason I reach the conclusion that bigamy is not constitutionally protected—because of two simple facts: (1) the Constitution says absolutely nothing about it, and (2) the longstanding traditions of American society have permitted it to be legally proscribed.[1]

The Court destroys the proposition, evidently meant to represent my position, that "liberty" includes "only those practices, defined at the most specific level, that were protected against government interference by other rules of law when the Fourteenth Amendment was ratified" (citing *Michael H. v. Gerald D.*) (opinion of Scalia, J.). That is not, however, what *Michael H.* says; it merely observes that, in defining "liberty," we may not disregard a specific, "relevant tradition protecting, or denying protection to, the asserted right." But the Court does not wish to be fettered by any such limitation on its preferences. The Court's statement that it is "tempting" to acknowledge the authoritativeness of tradition in order to "cur[b] the discretion of federal judges" is of course rhetoric

---

1. The Court's suggestion that adherence to tradition would require us to uphold laws against interracial marriage is entirely wrong. Any tradition in that case was contradicted *by a text*—an Equal Protection Clause that explicitly establishes racial equality as a constitutional value. [The] enterprise launched in *Roe,* by contrast, sought to *establish*—in the teeth of a clear, contrary tradition—a value found nowhere in the constitutional text.

There is, of course, no comparable tradition barring recognition of a "liberty interest" in carrying one's child to term free from state efforts to kill it. For that reason, it does not follow that the Constitution does not protect childbirth simply because it does not protect abortion. The Court's contention that the only way to protect childbirth is to protect abortion shows the utter bankruptcy of constitutional analysis deprived of tradition as a validating factor. It drives one to say that the only way to protect the right to eat is to acknowledge the constitutional right to starve oneself to death.

rather than reality; no government official is "tempted" to place restraints upon his own freedom of action, which is why Lord Acton did not say "Power tends to purify." The Court's temptation is in the quite opposite and more natural direction—towards systematically eliminating checks upon its own power; and it succumbs.

Beyond that brief summary of the essence of my position, I will not swell the United States Reports with repetition of what I have said before; and applying the rational basis test, I would uphold the Pennsylvania statute in its entirety. I must, however, respond to a few of the more outrageous arguments in today's opinion, which it is beyond human nature to leave unanswered. I shall discuss each of them under a quotation from the Court's opinion to which they pertain.

"The inescapable fact is that adjudication of substantive due process claims may call upon the Court in interpreting the Constitution to exercise that same capacity which by tradition courts always have exercised: reasoned judgment."

Assuming that the question before us is to be resolved at such a level of philosophical abstraction, in such isolation from the traditions of American society, as by simply applying "reasoned judgment," I do not see how that could possibly have produced the answer the Court arrived at in *Roe*. Today's opinion describes the methodology of *Roe*, quite accurately, as weighing against the woman's interest the State's " 'important and legitimate interest in protecting the potentiality of human life.' " But "reasoned judgment" does not begin by begging the question, as *Roe* and subsequent cases unquestionably did by assuming that what the State is protecting is the mere "potentiality of human life." The whole argument of abortion opponents is that what the Court calls the fetus and what others call the unborn child *is a human life*. Thus, whatever answer *Roe* came up with after conducting its "balancing" is bound to be wrong, unless it is correct that the human fetus is in some critical sense merely potentially human. There is of course no way to determine that as a legal matter; it is in fact a value judgment. Some societies have considered newborn children not yet human, or the incompetent elderly no longer so.

The authors of the joint opinion, of course, do not squarely contend that *Roe* was a *correct* application of "reasoned judgment"; merely that it must be followed, because of *stare decisis*. But in their exhaustive discussion of all the factors that go into the determination of when *stare decisis* should be observed and when disregarded, they never mention "how wrong was the decision on its face?" Surely, if "[t]he Court's power lies [in] its legitimacy, a product of substance and perception," the "substance" part of the equation demands that plain error be acknowledged and eliminated. *Roe* was plainly wrong—even on the Court's methodology of "reasoned judgment," and even more so (of course) if the proper criteria of text and tradition are applied.

The emptiness of the "reasoned judgment" that produced *Roe* is displayed in plain view by the fact that, after more than 19 years of effort by some of the brightest (and most determined) legal minds in the country, after more than 10 cases upholding abortion rights in this Court, and after dozens upon dozens of *amicus* briefs submitted in this and other cases, the best the Court can do to explain how it is that the word "liberty" *must* be thought to include the right to destroy human fetuses is to rattle off a collection of adjectives that simply decorate a value judgment and conceal a political choice. The right to abort, we are told, inheres in "liberty" because it is among "a person's most basic decisions," it involves a "most intimate and personal choic[e]," it is "central to personal dignity and autonomy," it "originate[s] within the zone of conscience and belief," it is "too intimate and personal" for state interference, it reflects "intimate views" of a "deep, personal character," it involves "intimate relationships," and notions of "personal autonomy and bodily integrity," and it concerns a particularly " 'important decisio[n].²' " But it is obvious to anyone applying "reasoned judgment" that the same adjectives can be applied to many forms of conduct that this Court (including one of the Justices in today's majority, see *Bowers v. Hardwick*) has held are *not* entitled to constitutional protection— because, like abortion, they are forms of conduct that have long been criminalized in American society. Those adjectives might be applied, for example, to homosexual sodomy, polygamy, adult incest, and suicide, all of which are equally "intimate" and "deep[ly] personal" decisions involving "personal autonomy and bodily integrity," and all of which can constitutionally be proscribed because it is our unquestionable constitutional tradition that they are proscribable. It is not reasoned judgment that supports the Court's decision; only personal predilection. Justice Curtis's warning is as timely today as it was 135 years ago:

> "[W]hen a strict interpretation of the Constitution, according to the fixed rules which govern the interpretation of laws, is abandoned, and the theoretical opinions of individuals are allowed to control its meaning, we have no longer a Constitution; we are under the government of individual men, who for the time being have power to declare what the Constitution is, according to their own views of what it ought to mean." *Dred Scott v. Sandford* (1857) (Curtis, J., dissenting).

"Liberty finds no refuge in a jurisprudence of doubt."

One might have feared to encounter this august and sonorous phrase in an opinion defending the real *Roe v. Wade*, rather than the revised version fabricated today by the authors of the joint opinion. The shortcomings of *Roe* did not include lack of clarity: Virtually all regulation of abortion before the third trimester was invalid. But to come across this phrase in the joint opinion—which calls upon federal district judges to apply an "undue burden" standard as doubtful in application as it is unprincipled in origin—is really more than one should have to bear.

The joint opinion frankly concedes that the amorphous concept of "undue burden" has been inconsistently applied by the Members of this Court in the few brief years since that "test" was first explicitly propounded by Justice O'Connor in her dissent in *Akron I*. Because the three Justices now wish to "set forth a standard of general application," the joint opinion announces that "it is important to clarify what is meant by an undue burden." I certainly agree with that, but I do not agree that the joint opinion succeeds in the announced endeavor. To the contrary, its efforts at clarification make clear only that the standard is inherently manipulable and will prove hopelessly unworkable in practice.

The joint opinion explains that a state regulation imposes an "undue burden" if it "has the purpose or effect of placing a substantial obstacle in the path of a woman seeking an abortion of a nonviable fetus." An obstacle is

---

2. Justice Blackmun's parade of adjectives is similarly empty: Abortion is among "the most intimate and personal choices," it is a matter "central to personal dignity and autonomy," and it involves "personal decisions that profoundly affect bodily integrity, identity, and destiny." Justice Stevens is not much less conclusory: The decision to choose abortion is a matter of "the highest privacy and the most personal nature," it involves a "difficult choice having serious and personal consequences of major importance to [a woman's] future," the authority to make this "traumatic and yet empowering decisio[n]" is "an element of basic human dignity," and it is "nothing less than a matter of conscience."

"substantial," we are told, if it is "calculated[,] [not] to inform the woman's free choice, [but to] hinder it."[4] This latter statement cannot possibly mean what it says. *Any* regulation of abortion that is intended to advance what the joint opinion concedes is the State's "substantial" interest in protecting unborn life will be "calculated [to] hinder" a decision to have an abortion. It thus seems more accurate to say that the joint opinion would uphold abortion regulations only if they do not *unduly* hinder the woman's decision. That, of course, brings us right back to square one: Defining an "undue burden" as an "undue hindrance" (or a "substantial obstacle") hardly "clarifies" the test. Consciously or not, the joint opinion's verbal shell game will conceal raw judicial policy choices concerning what is "appropriate" abortion legislation.

The ultimately standardless nature of the "undue burden" inquiry is a reflection of the underlying fact that the concept has no principled or coherent legal basis. As the Chief Justice points out, *Roe*'s strict-scrutiny standard "at least had a recognized basis in constitutional law at the time *Roe* was decided," while "[t]he same cannot be said for the 'undue burden' standard, which is created largely out of whole cloth by the authors of the joint opinion." The joint opinion is flatly wrong in asserting that "our jurisprudence relating to all liberties save perhaps abortion has recognized" the permissibility of laws that do not impose an "undue burden." It argues that the abortion right is similar to other rights in that a law "not designed to strike at the right itself, [but which] has the incidental effect of making it more difficult or more expensive to [exercise the right,]" is not invalid. I agree, indeed I have forcefully urged, that a law of general applicability which places only an incidental burden on a fundamental right does not infringe that right, but that principle does not establish the quite different (and quite dangerous) proposition that a law which *directly* regulates a fundamental right will not be found to violate the Constitution unless it imposes an "undue burden." It is that, of course, which is at issue here: Pennsylvania has *consciously and directly* regulated conduct that our cases have held is constitutionally protected. The appropriate analogy, therefore, is that of a state law requiring purchasers of religious books to endure a 24-hour waiting period, or to pay a nominal additional tax of 1¢. The joint opinion

---

4. The joint opinion further asserts that a law imposing an undue burden on abortion decisions is not a "permissible" means of serving "legitimate" state interests. This description of the undue burden standard in terms more commonly associated with the rational-basis test will come as a surprise even to those who have followed closely our wanderings in this forsaken wilderness. See, e.g., *Akron I* (O'Connor, J., dissenting) ("The 'undue burden' * * * represents the required threshold inquiry that must be conducted before this Court can require a State to justify its legislative actions under the exacting 'compelling state interest' standard"); see also *Hodgson* (O'Connor, J., concurring in part and concurring in judgment in part); *Thornburgh* (O'Connor, J., dissenting). This confusing equation of the two standards is apparently designed to explain how one of the Justices who joined the plurality opinion in *Webster*, which adopted the rational basis test, could join an opinion expressly adopting the undue burden test. [The] same motive also apparently underlies the joint opinion's erroneous citation of the plurality opinion in *Akron II* (opinion of Kennedy, J.), as applying the undue burden test. See joint opinion (using this citation to support the proposition that "two of us"—i.e., two of the authors of the joint opinion—have previously applied this test). In fact, *Akron II* does not mention the undue burden standard until the conclusion of the opinion, when it states that the statute at issue "does not impose an undue, *or otherwise unconstitutional,* burden." (Emphasis added). I fail to see how anyone can think that saying a statute does not impose an unconstitutional burden under *any* standard, including the undue burden test, amounts to adopting the undue burden test as the *exclusive* standard. The Court's citation of *Hodgson* as reflecting Justice Kennedy's and Justice O'Connor's "shared premises" is similarly inexplicable, since the word "undue" was never even used in the former's opinion in that case. I joined Justice Kennedy's opinions in both *Hodgson* and *Akron II;* I should be grateful, I suppose, that the joint opinion does not claim that I, too, have adopted the undue burden test.

cannot possibly be correct in suggesting that we would uphold such legislation on the ground that it does not impose a "substantial obstacle" to the exercise of First Amendment rights. The "undue burden" standard is not at all the generally applicable principle the joint opinion pretends it to be; rather, it is a unique concept created specially for this case, to preserve some judicial foothold in this ill-gotten territory. In claiming otherwise, the three Justices show their willingness to place all constitutional rights at risk in an effort to preserve what they deem the "central holding in *Roe*."

The rootless nature of the "undue burden" standard, a phrase plucked out of context from our earlier abortion decisions, is further reflected in the fact that the joint opinion finds it necessary expressly to repudiate the more narrow formulations used in Justice O'Connor's earlier opinions. Those opinions stated that a statute imposes an "undue burden" if it imposes "*absolute* obstacles or *severe* limitations on the abortion decision," *Akron I* (O'Connor, J., dissenting) (emphasis added). Those strong adjectives are conspicuously missing from the joint opinion, whose authors have for some unexplained reason now determined that a burden is "undue" if it merely imposes a "substantial" obstacle to abortion decisions. Justice O'Connor has also abandoned (again without explanation) the view she expressed in *Ashcroft* (dissenting opinion), that a medical regulation which imposes an "undue burden" could nevertheless be upheld if it "reasonably relate[s] to the preservation and protection of maternal health." In today's version, even health measures will be upheld only "*if they do not constitute an undue burden*," (emphasis added). Gone too is Justice O'Connor's statement that "the State possesses *compelling* interests in the protection of potential human life * * * throughout pregnancy," *Akron I* (emphasis added); instead, the State's interest in unborn human life is stealthily downgraded to a merely "substantial" or "profound" interest. (That had to be done, of course, since designating the interest as "compelling" throughout pregnancy would have been, shall we say, a "substantial obstacle" to the joint opinion's determined effort to reaffirm what it views as the "central holding" of *Roe*.) And "viability" is no longer the "arbitrary" dividing line previously decried by Justice O'Connor in *Akron I;* the Court now announces that "the attainment of viability may continue to serve as the critical fact."[5] It is difficult to maintain the illusion that we are interpreting a Constitution rather than inventing one, when we amend its provisions so breezily.

Because the portion of the joint opinion adopting and describing the undue-burden test provides no more useful guidance than the empty phrases discussed above, one must turn to the 23 pages applying that standard to the present facts for further guidance. In evaluating Pennsylvania's abortion law, the joint opinion relies extensively on the factual findings of the District Court, and repeatedly qualifies its conclusions by noting that they are contingent upon the record developed in this case. Thus, the joint opinion would uphold the 24-hour waiting period contained in the Pennsylvania statute's informed consent provision because "the record evidence shows that in the vast majority of cases, a 24-

---

5. Of course Justice O'Connor was correct in her former view. The arbitrariness of the viability line is confirmed by the Court's inability to offer any justification for it beyond the conclusory assertion that it is only at that point that the unborn child's life "can in reason and all fairness" be thought to override the interests of the mother. Precisely why is it that, at the magical second when machines currently in use (though not necessarily available to the particular woman) are able to keep an unborn child alive apart from its mother, the creature is suddenly able (under our Constitution) to be protected by law, whereas before that magical second it was not? That makes no more sense than according infants legal protection only after the point when they can feed themselves.

hour delay does not create any appreciable health risk." The three Justices therefore conclude that "on the record before us, * * * we are not convinced that the 24–hour waiting period constitutes an undue burden." The requirement that a doctor provide the information pertinent to informed consent would also be upheld because "there is no evidence on this record that [this requirement] would amount in practical terms to a substantial obstacle to a woman seeking an abortion." Similarly, the joint opinion would uphold the reporting requirements of the Act, §§ 3207, 3214, because "there is no * * * showing on the record before us" that these requirements constitute a "substantial obstacle" to abortion decisions. But at the same time the opinion pointedly observes that these reporting requirements may increase the costs of abortions and that "at some point [that fact] could become a substantial obstacle." Most significantly, the joint opinion's conclusion that the spousal notice requirement of the Act, see § 3209, imposes an "undue burden" is based in large measure on the District Court's "detailed findings of fact," which the joint opinion sets out at great length.

I do not, of course, have any objection to the notion that, in applying legal principles, one should rely only upon the facts that are contained in the record or that are properly subject to judicial notice.[6] But what is remarkable about the joint opinion's fact-intensive analysis is that it does not result in any measurable clarification of the "undue burden" standard. Rather, the approach of the joint opinion is, for the most part, simply to highlight certain facts in the record that apparently strike the three Justices as particularly significant in establishing (or refuting) the existence of an undue burden; after describing these facts, the opinion then simply announces that the provision either does or does not impose a "substantial obstacle" or an "undue burden." We do not know whether the same conclusions could have been reached on a different record, or in what respects the record would have had to differ before an opposite conclusion would have been appropriate. The inherently standardless nature of this inquiry invites the district judge to give effect to his personal preferences about abortion. By finding and relying upon the right facts, he can invalidate, it would seem, almost any abortion restriction that strikes him as "undue"—subject, of course, to the possibility of being reversed by a Circuit Court or Supreme Court that is as unconstrained in reviewing his decision as he was in making it.

To the extent I can discern *any* meaningful content in the "undue burden" standard as applied in the joint opinion, it appears to be that a State may not regulate abortion in such a way as to reduce significantly its incidence. The joint opinion repeatedly emphasizes that an important factor in the "undue burden" analysis is whether the regulation "prevent[s] a significant number of women from obtaining an abortion," whether a "significant number of women * * * are likely to be deterred from procuring an abortion," and whether the regulation often "deters" women from seeking abortions. We are not told, however, what forms of "deterrence" are impermissible or what degree of success

---

6. The joint opinion is not entirely faithful to this principle, however. In approving the District Court's factual findings with respect to the spousal notice provision, it relies extensively on nonrecord materials, and in reliance upon them adds a number of factual conclusions of its own. Because this additional factfinding pertains to matters that surely are "subject to reasonable dispute," Fed.Rule Evid. 201(b), the joint opinion must be operating on the premise that these are "legislative" rather than "adjudicative" facts, see Rule 201(a). But if a court can find an undue burden simply by selectively string-citing the right social science articles, I do not see the point of emphasizing or requiring "detailed factual findings" in the District Court.

in deterrence is too much to be tolerated. If, for example, a State required a woman to read a pamphlet describing, with illustrations, the facts of fetal development before she could obtain an abortion, the effect of such legislation might be to "deter" a "significant number of women" from procuring abortions, thereby seemingly allowing a district judge to invalidate it as an undue burden. Thus, despite flowery rhetoric about the State's "substantial" and "profound" interest in "potential human life," and criticism of *Roe* for undervaluing that interest, the joint opinion permits the State to pursue that interest only so long as it is not too successful. As Justice Blackmun recognizes (with evident hope), the "undue burden" standard may ultimately require the invalidation of each provision upheld today if it can be shown, on a better record, that the State is too effectively "express[ing] a preference for childbirth over abortion." Reason finds no refuge in this jurisprudence of confusion.

"While we appreciate the weight of the arguments * * * that *Roe* should be overruled, the reservations any of us may have in reaffirming the central holding of *Roe* are outweighed by the explication of individual liberty we have given combined with the force of *stare decisis*."

The Court's reliance upon *stare decisis* can best be described as contrived. It insists upon the necessity of adhering not to all of *Roe*, but only to what it calls the "central holding." It seems to me that *stare decisis* ought to be applied even to the doctrine of *stare decisis*, and I confess never to have heard of this new, keep-what-you-want-and-throw-away-the-rest version. I wonder whether, as applied to *Marbury v. Madison*, for example, the new version of *stare decisis* would be satisfied if we allowed courts to review the constitutionality of only those statutes that (like the one in *Marbury*) pertain to the jurisdiction of the courts.

I am certainly not in a good position to dispute that the Court *has saved* the "central holding" of *Roe*, since to do that effectively I would have to know what the Court has saved, which in turn would require me to understand (as I do not) what the "undue burden" test means. I must confess, however, that I have always thought, and I think a lot of other people have always thought, that the arbitrary trimester framework, which the Court today discards, was quite as central to *Roe* as the arbitrary viability test, which the Court today retains. It seems particularly ungrateful to carve the trimester framework out of the core of *Roe*, since its very rigidity (in sharp contrast to the utter indeterminability of the "undue burden" test) is probably the only reason the Court is able to say, in urging *stare decisis*, that *Roe* "has in no sense proven 'unworkable.' " I suppose the Court is entitled to call a "central holding" whatever it wants to call a "central holding"—which is, come to think of it, perhaps one of the difficulties with this modified version of *stare decisis*. I thought I might note, however, that the following portions of *Roe* have not been saved:

• Under *Roe*, requiring that a woman seeking an abortion be provided truthful information about abortion before giving informed written consent is unconstitutional, if the information is designed to influence her choice, *Thornburgh*. Under the joint opinion's "undue burden" regime (as applied today, at least) such a requirement is constitutional.

• Under *Roe*, requiring that information be provided by a doctor, rather than by nonphysician counselors, is unconstitutional, *Akron I*. Under the "undue burden" regime (as applied today, at least) it is not.

• Under *Roe*, requiring a 24–hour waiting period between the time the woman gives her informed consent and the time of the abortion is unconstitutional, *Akron I.* Under the "undue burden" regime (as applied today, at least) it is not.

• Under *Roe,* requiring detailed reports that include demographic data about each woman who seeks an abortion and various information about each abortion is unconstitutional, *Thornburgh.* Under the "undue burden" regime (as applied today, at least) it generally is not.

"Where, in the performance of its judicial duties, the Court decides a case in such a way as to resolve the sort of intensely divisive controversy reflected in *Roe* * * *, its decision has a dimension that the resolution of the normal case does not carry. It is the dimension present whenever the Court's interpretation of the Constitution calls the contending sides of a national controversy to end their national division by accepting a common mandate rooted in the Constitution."

The Court's description of the place of *Roe* in the social history of the United States is unrecognizable. Not only did *Roe* not, as the Court suggests, *resolve* the deeply divisive issue of abortion; it did more than anything else to nourish it, by elevating it to the national level where it is infinitely more difficult to resolve. National politics were not plagued by abortion protests, national abortion lobbying, or abortion marches on Congress, before *Roe* was decided. Profound disagreement existed among our citizens over the issue—as it does over other issues, such as the death penalty—but that disagreement was being worked out at the state level. As with many other issues, the division of sentiment within each State was not as closely balanced as it was among the population of the Nation as a whole, meaning not only that more people would be satisfied with the results of state-by-state resolution, but also that those results would be more stable. Pre–*Roe,* moreover, political compromise was possible.

Roe's mandate for abortion-on-demand destroyed the compromises of the past, rendered compromise impossible for the future, and required the entire issue to be resolved uniformly, at the national level. At the same time, *Roe* created a vast new class of abortion consumers and abortion proponents by eliminating the moral opprobrium that had attached to the act. ("If the Constitution *guarantees* abortion, how can it be bad?"—not an accurate line of thought, but a natural one.) Many favor all of those developments, and it is not for me to say that they are wrong. But to portray *Roe* as the statesmanlike "settlement" of a divisive issue, a jurisprudential Peace of Westphalia that is worth preserving, is nothing less than Orwellian. *Roe* fanned into life an issue that has inflamed our national politics in general, and has obscured with its smoke the selection of Justices to this Court in particular, ever since. And by keeping us in the abortion-umpiring business, it is the perpetuation of that disruption, rather than of any *pax Roeana,* that the Court's new majority decrees.

"[T]o overrule under fire * * * would subvert the Court's legitimacy * * *.

"To all those who will be * * * tested by following, the Court implicitly undertakes to remain steadfast * * *. The promise of constancy, once given, binds its maker for as long as the power to stand by the decision survives and * * * the commitment [is not] obsolete * * *.

"[The American people's] belief in themselves as * * * a people [who aspire to live according to the rule of law] is not readily separable from their understanding of the Court invested with the authority to decide their constitutional cases and speak before all others for their constitu-

tional ideals. If the Court's legitimacy should be undermined, then, so would the country be in its very ability to see itself through its constitutional ideals."

The Imperial Judiciary lives. It is instructive to compare this Nietzschean vision of us unelected, life-tenured judges—leading a Volk who will be "tested by following," and whose very "belief in themselves" is mystically bound up in their "understanding" of a Court that "speak[s] before all others for their constitutional ideals"—with the somewhat more modest role envisioned for these lawyers by the Founders.

> "The judiciary * * * has * * * no direction either of the strength or of the wealth of the society, and can take no active resolution whatever. It may truly be said to have neither FORCE nor WILL but merely judgment * * *." *The Federalist* No. 78, pp. 393–394 (G. Wills ed. 1982).

Or, again, to compare this ecstasy of a Supreme Court in which there is, especially on controversial matters, no shadow of change or hint of alteration ("There is a limit to the amount of error that can plausibly be imputed to prior courts"), with the more democratic views of a more humble man:

> "[T]he candid citizen must confess that if the policy of the Government upon vital questions affecting the whole people is to be irrevocably fixed by decisions of the Supreme Court, * * * the people will have ceased to be their own rulers, having to that extent practically resigned their Government into the hands of that eminent tribunal." A. Lincoln, *First Inaugural Address* (Mar. 4, 1861), reprinted in Inaugural Addresses of the Presidents of the United States, S.Doc. No. 101–10, p. 139 (1989).

It is particularly difficult, in the circumstances of the present decision, to sit still for the Court's lengthy lecture upon the virtues of "constancy," of "remain[ing] steadfast," of adhering to "principle." Among the five Justices who purportedly adhere to *Roe*, at most three agree upon the *principle* that constitutes adherence (the joint opinion's "undue burden" standard)—and that principle is inconsistent with *Roe*.[7] To make matters worse, two of the three, in order thus to remain steadfast, had to abandon previously stated positions. See n. 4 supra. It is beyond me how the Court expects these accommodations to be accepted "as grounded truly in principle, not as compromises with social and political pressures having, as such, no bearing on the principled choices that the Court is obliged to make." The only principle the Court "adheres" to, it seems to me, is the principle that the Court must be seen as standing by *Roe*. That is not a principle of law (which is what I thought the Court was talking about), but a principle of *Realpolitik* —and a wrong one at that.

I cannot agree with, indeed I am appalled by, the Court's suggestion that the decision whether to stand by an erroneous constitutional decision must be strongly influenced—*against* overruling, no less—by the substantial and continuing public opposition the decision has generated. The Court's judgment that any other course would "subvert the Court's legitimacy" must be another consequence of reading the error-filled history book that described the deeply divided country brought together by *Roe*. In my history-book, the Court was covered with dishonor and deprived of legitimacy by *Dred Scott,* an erroneous (and

---

7. Justice Blackmun's effort to preserve as much of *Roe* as possible leads him to read the joint opinion as more "constan[t]" and "steadfast" than can be believed. He contends that the joint opinion's "undue burden" standard requires the application of strict scrutiny to "all non-*de minimis* " abortion regulations, but that could only be true if a "substantial obstacle" (joint opinion), were the same thing as a non-*de minimis* obstacle— which it plainly is not.

widely opposed) opinion that it did not abandon, rather than by *West Coast Hotel,* which produced the famous "switch in time" from the Court's erroneous (and widely opposed) constitutional opposition to the social measures of the New Deal. (Both *Dred Scott* and one line of the cases resisting the New Deal rested upon the concept of "substantive due process" that the Court praises and employs today. Indeed, *Dred Scott* was "very possibly the first application of substantive due process in the Supreme Court, the original precedent for *Lochner* and *Roe.*" D. Currie, *The Constitution in the Supreme Court* 271 (1985).)

But whether it would "subvert the Court's legitimacy" or not, the notion that we would decide a case differently from the way we otherwise would have in order to show that we can stand firm against public disapproval is frightening. It is a bad enough idea, even in the head of someone like me, who believes that the text of the Constitution, and our traditions, say what they say and there is no fiddling with them. But when it is in the mind of a Court that believes the Constitution has an evolving meaning; that the Ninth Amendment's reference to "othe[r]" rights is not a disclaimer, but a charter for action; and that the function of this Court is to "speak before all others for [the people's] constitutional ideals" unrestrained by meaningful text or tradition—then the notion that the Court must adhere to a decision for as long as the decision faces "great opposition" and the Court is "under fire" acquires a character of almost czarist arrogance. We are offended by these marchers who descend upon us, every year on the anniversary of *Roe,* to protest our saying that the Constitution requires what our society has never thought the Constitution requires. These people who refuse to be "tested by following" must be taught a lesson. We have no Cossacks, but at least we can stubbornly refuse to abandon an erroneous opinion that we might otherwise change—to show how little they intimidate us.

Of course, as The Chief Justice points out, we have been subjected to what the Court calls "political pressure" by *both* sides of this issue. Maybe today's decision *not* to overrule *Roe* will be seen as buckling to pressure from *that* direction. Instead of engaging in the hopeless task of predicting public perception—a job not for lawyers but for political campaign managers—the Justices should do what is *legally* right by asking two questions: (1) Was *Roe* correctly decided? (2) Has *Roe* succeeded in producing a settled body of law? If the answer to both questions is no, *Roe* should undoubtedly be overruled.

In truth, I am as distressed as the Court is—and expressed my distress several years ago, see *Webster*—about the "political pressure" directed to the Court: the marches, the mail, the protests aimed at inducing us to change our opinions. How upsetting it is, that so many of our citizens (good people, not lawless ones, on both sides of this abortion issue, and on various sides of other issues as well) think that we Justices should properly take into account their views, as though we were engaged not in ascertaining an objective law but in determining some kind of social consensus. The Court would profit, I think, from giving less attention to the *fact* of this distressing phenomenon, and more attention to the *cause* of it. That cause permeates today's opinion: a new mode of constitutional adjudication that relies not upon text and traditional practice to determine the law, but upon what the Court calls "reasoned judgment," which turns out to be nothing but philosophical predilection and moral intuition. All manner of "liberties," the Court tells us, inhere in the Constitution and are enforceable by this Court—not just those mentioned in the text or established in the traditions of our society. Why even the Ninth Amendment—which says only that "[t]he enumeration in the Constitution of certain rights shall not be construed to deny or disparage others retained by the people"—is, despite our contrary understanding for almost 200 years, a literally boundless source of additional, unnamed, unhinted-at "rights," definable and enforceable by us, through "reasoned judgment."

What makes all this relevant to the bothersome application of "political pressure" against the Court are the twin facts that the American people love democracy and the American people are not fools. As long as this Court thought (and the people thought) that we Justices were doing essentially lawyers' work up here—reading text and discerning our society's traditional understanding of that text—the public pretty much left us alone. Texts and traditions are facts to study, not convictions to demonstrate about. But if in reality our process of constitutional adjudication consists primarily of making *value judgments;* if we can ignore a long and clear tradition clarifying an ambiguous text, as we did, for example, five days ago in declaring unconstitutional invocations and benedictions at public-high-school graduation ceremonies, *Lee v. Weisman* [p. ___ of this Supplement]; if, as I say, our pronouncement of constitutional law rests primarily on value judgments, then a free and intelligent people's attitude towards us can be expected to be (*ought* to be) quite different. The people know that their value judgments are quite as good as those taught in any law school—maybe better. If, indeed, the "liberties" protected by the Constitution are, as the Court says, undefined and unbounded, then the people *should* demonstrate, to protest that we do not implement *their* values instead of *ours.* Not only that, but confirmation hearings for new Justices *should* deteriorate into question-and-answer sessions in which Senators go through a list of their constituents' most favored and most disfavored alleged constitutional rights, and seek the nominee's commitment to support or oppose them. Value judgments, after all, should be voted on, not dictated; and if our Constitution has somehow accidently committed them to the Supreme Court, at least we can have a sort of plebiscite each time a new nominee to that body is put forward. Justice Blackmun not only regards this prospect with equanimity, he solicits it.

* * *

There is a poignant aspect to today's opinion. Its length, and what might be called its epic tone, suggest that its authors believe they are bringing to an end a troublesome era in the history of our Nation and of our Court. "It is the dimension" of authority, they say, to "cal[l] the contending sides of national controversy to end their national division by accepting a common mandate rooted in the Constitution."

There comes vividly to mind a portrait by Emanuel Leutze that hangs in the Harvard Law School: Roger Brooke Taney, painted in 1859, the 82d year of his life, the 24th of his Chief Justiceship, the second after his opinion in *Dred Scott.* He is all in black, sitting in a shadowed red armchair, left hand resting upon a pad of paper in his lap, right hand hanging limply, almost lifelessly, beside the inner arm of the chair. He sits facing the viewer, and staring straight out. There seems to be on his face, and in his deep-set eyes, an expression of profound sadness and disillusionment. Perhaps he always looked that way, even when dwelling upon the happiest of thoughts. But those of us who know how the lustre of his great Chief Justiceship came to be eclipsed by *Dred Scott* cannot help believing that he had that case—its already apparent consequences for the Court, and its soon-to-be-played-out consequences for the Nation—burning on his mind. I expect that two years earlier he, too, had thought himself "call[ing] the contending sides of national controversy to end their national division by accepting a common mandate rooted in the Constitution."

It is no more realistic for us in this case, than it was for him in that, to think that an issue of the sort they both involved—an issue involving life and death, freedom and subjugation—can be "speedily and finally settled" by the Supreme Court, as President James Buchanan in his inaugural address said the issue of slavery in the territories would be. Quite to the contrary, by foreclosing all democratic outlet for the deep passions this issue arouses, by banishing the issue from the political forum that gives all participants, even the losers, the satisfaction of a fair hearing and an honest fight, by continuing the imposition of a rigid national rule instead of allowing for regional differences, the Court merely prolongs and intensifies the anguish.

We should get out of this area, where we have no right to be, and where we do neither ourselves nor the country any good by remaining.

CRITICISM OF BOWERS v. HARDWICK

CON LAW: P. 538, after note 1 add new note

AMER CON: P. 378, after note 1 add new note

RTS & LIB: P. 267, after note 1 add new note

1(a). *Under the circumstances of the Hardwick case, was sexuality "an anatomical irrelevance"?* For former Solicitor General Charles Fried's criticism of what he calls "Justice White's stunningly harsh and dismissive opinion in *Bowers v. Hardwick*" see Fried, *Order and Law* 82–84 (1991). Comments Professor Fried, id. at 82–83:

" * * * Unless one takes the implausible line that people generally choose their sexual orientation, then to criminalize any enjoyment of the sexual powers by a whole category of persons is either an imposition of very great cruelty or an exercise in hypocrisy inviting arbitrary and abusive applications of the criminal law. *Poe [v. Ullman]* and *Griswold* did emphasize the sanctity of marital intimacy, so that a step beyond these cases would have had to be taken to reach the conclusion Justice Blackmun urged in a particularly moving dissent. But it is a short step, and one authorized by reason and tradition: Hardwick was threatened with prosecution for having consensual sex with another man behind a closed bedroom door in his own home. The police found out about it by an uninvited accident. Here the conduct was truly private. It concerned no one else except in the question-begging sense that some may be offended by the very knowledge that such conduct goes unpunished. What is left is an act of private association and communication. The fact that sexuality is implicated seems an anatomical irrelevance."

THE "RIGHT TO DIE"

CON LAW: P. 545, drop fn. a to discussion of *Washington v. Harper*

AMER CON: P. 385, drop fn. a to discussion of *Washington v. Harper*

RTS & LIB: P. 274, drop fn. a to discussion of *Washington v. Harper*

a. See also *Riggins v. Nevada*, ___ U.S. ___, 112 S.Ct. 1810, 118 L.Ed.2d 479 (1992), (per O'Connor, J.), overturning a murder conviction on the ground that, absent any determination of the need for this course of action or any findings about reasonable alternatives, the forced administration of antipsychotic medication during petitioner's trial to render him competent to stand trial created an unacceptably high risk that his constitutionally protected trial rights were violated: "Under *Harper*, forcing antipsychotic drugs on a convicted prisoner is impermissible absent a finding of overriding justification and a determination of medical appropriateness. The Fourteenth Amendment affords at least as much protection to persons the State detains for trial."

SECTION: THE DEATH PENALTY AND RELATED PROBLEMS: CRUEL AND UNUSUAL PUNISHMENT

OTHER CONSTITUTIONAL CHALLENGES TO CAPITAL (AND LIFE) SENTENCES

"GROSSLY DISPROPORTIONATE" PUNISHMENT

CON LAW: P. 600, add to note 6

AMER CON: P. 420, end of Part II

RTS & LIB: P. 329, add to note 6

Consider HARMELIN v. MICHIGAN, ___ U.S. ___, 111 S.Ct. 2680, 115 L.Ed. 2d 836 (1991): Michigan law provides a mandatory sentence of life imprisonment without the possibility of parole for possession of 650 grams or more of cocaine. Convicted and sentenced under this law, petitioner contended that his sentence was "cruel and unusual" within the meaning of the Eighth Amendment because (1) it was "significantly disproportionate" to the crime he committed and (2) the sentencing judge was statutorily required to impose the punishment without considering the particularized circumstances of the crime and of the criminal. The Court rejected both claims.

SCALIA, J., delivered the opinion of the Court with respect to petitioner's second contention, concluding that "this claim has no support in the text and history of the Eighth Amendment":

"Severe, mandatory penalties may be cruel, but they are not unusual in the constitutional sense, having been employed in various forms throughout our Nation's history. [M]andatory death sentences abounded in our first Penal Code. They were also common in the several States—both at the time of the founding and throughout the 19th century. There can be no serious contention, then, that a sentence which is not otherwise cruel and unusual becomes so simply because it is 'mandatory.'

"Petitioner's 'required mitigation' claim, like his proportionality claim, does find support in our death-penalty jurisprudence. We have held that a capital sentence is cruel and unusual under the Eighth Amendment if it is imposed without an individualized determination that that punishment is 'appropriate'—whether or not the sentence is 'grossly disproportionate.' Petitioner asks us to extend this so-called 'individualized capital-sentencing doctrine' to an 'individualized mandatory life in prison without parole sentencing doctrine.' We refuse to do so.

"Our cases creating and clarifying the 'individualized capital sentencing doctrine' have repeatedly suggested that there is no comparable requirement outside the capital context, because of the qualitative difference between death and all other penalties.

"[It] is true that petitioner's sentence is unique in that it is the second most severe known to the law; but life imprisonment *with* possibility of parole is also unique in that it is the third most severe. And if petitioner's sentence forecloses some 'flexible techniques' for later reducing his sentence, it does not foreclose all of them, since there remain the possibilities of retroactive legislative reduction and executive clemency. In some cases, moreover, there will be negligible difference between life without parole and other sentences of imprisonment—for example, a life sentence with eligibility for parole after 20 years, or even a lengthy term sentence without eligibility for parole, given to a 65-year-old man. But even where the difference is the greatest, it cannot be compared with death. We have drawn the line of required individualized sentencing at capital cases, and see no basis for extending it further."

Although five justices rejected petitioner's claim that his sentence was unconstitutionally "cruel and unusual" because it was "significantly disproportionate" to the crime he committed, there was no opinion of the Court. JUSTICE SCALIA, joined by the Chief Justice, concluded that because the Eighth Amendment contains no proportionality guarantee, petitioner's sentence could not be considered unconstitutionally disproportionate:

"According to its terms, by forbidding 'cruel *and unusual* punishments,' the Clause disables the Legislature from authorizing particular forms or 'modes' of punishment—specifically, cruel methods of punishment that are not regularly or customarily employed.

"The language bears the construction, however—and here we come to the point crucial to resolution of the present case—that 'cruelty and unusualness' are to be determined not solely with reference to the punishment at issue ('Is life imprisonment a cruel and unusual punishment?') but with reference to the crime for which it is imposed as well ('Is life imprisonment cruel and unusual punishment for possession of unlawful drugs?'). The latter interpretation would make the provision a form of proportionality guarantee. The arguments against it, however, seem to us conclusive.

"First of all, to use the phrase 'cruel and unusual punishment' to describe a requirement of proportionality would have been an exceedingly vague and oblique way of saying what Americans were well accustomed to saying more directly. * * *

"Secondly, it would seem quite peculiar to refer to cruelty and unusualness *for the offense in question,* in a provision having application only to a new government that had never before defined offenses, and that would be defining new and peculiarly national ones. Finally and most conclusively, [the] fact that what was 'cruel and unusual' under the Eighth Amendment was to be determined without reference to the particular offense is confirmed by all available evidence of contemporary understanding. * * *

"We think it enough that those who framed and approved the Federal Constitution chose, for whatever reason, not to include within it the guarantee against disproportionate sentences that some State Constitutions contained. It is worth noting, however, that there was good reason for that choice—a reason that reinforces the necessity of overruling *Solem.* While there are relatively clear historical guidelines and accepted practices that enable judges to determine which *modes* of punishment are 'cruel and unusual,' *proportionality* does not lend itself to such analysis. Neither Congress nor any state legislature has ever set out with the objective of crafting a penalty that is 'disproportionate,' [yet] many enacted dispositions seem to be so—because they were made for other times or other places, with different social attitudes, different criminal epidemics, different public fears, and different prevailing theories of penology.

"[The] first holding of this Court unqualifiedly applying a requirement of proportionality to criminal penalties was issued 185 years after the Eighth Amendment was adopted. In *Coker* the Court held that, because of the disproportionality, it was a violation of the Cruel and Unusual Punishments Clause to impose capital punishment for rape of an adult woman. Four years later, in

Enmund, we held that it violates the Eighth Amendment, because of disproportionality, to impose the death penalty upon a participant in a felony that results in murder, without any inquiry into the participant's intent to kill. *Rummel* treated this line of authority as an aspect of our death penalty jurisprudence, rather than a generalizable aspect of Eighth Amendment law. We think that is an accurate explanation, and we reassert it. Proportionality review is one of several respects in which we have held that "death is different," and have imposed protections that the Constitution nowhere else provides. We would leave it there, but will not extend it further."

In a separate opinion, JUSTICE KENNEDY, joined by O'Connor and Souter, JJ., noted that the Court's decisions "recognize that the Cruel and Unusual Punishments Clause encompasses a narrow proportionality principle [that] applies to noncapital sentences," but rejected petitioner's claim for the reason that his sentence was not "grossly disproportionate" to his crime:

"Petitioner's life sentence without parole is the second most severe penalty permitted by law. It is the same sentence received by the petitioner in *Solem*. Petitioner's crime, however, was far more grave than the crime at issue in *Solem.* * * *

"Petitioner was convicted of possession of more than 650 grams (over 1.5 pounds) of cocaine. This amount of pure cocaine has a potential yield of between 32,500 and 65,000 doses. From any standpoint, this crime falls in a different category from the relatively minor, nonviolent crime at issue in *Solem*. Possession, use, and distribution of illegal drugs represents 'one of the greatest problems affecting the health and welfare of our population.' Petitioner's suggestion that his crime was nonviolent and victimless, echoed by the dissent, is false to the point of absurdity. To the contrary, petitioner's crime threatened to cause grave harm to society.

"[Various] reports detailing the pernicious effects of the drug epidemic in this country do not establish that Michigan's penalty scheme is correct or the most just in any abstract sense. But they do demonstrate that the Michigan Legislature could with reason conclude that the threat posed to the individual and society by possession of this large an amount of cocaine—in terms of violence, crime, and social displacement—is momentous enough to warrant the deterence and retribution of a life sentence without parole. * * *

"Petitioner and *amici* contend that our proportionality decisions require a comparative analysis between petitioner's sentence and sentences imposed for other crimes in Michigan and sentences imposed for the same crime in other jurisdictions. Given the serious nature of petitioner's crime, no such comparative analysis is necessary.

"[The] proper role for comparative analysis of sentences, then, is to validate an initial judgment that a sentence is grossly disproportionate to a crime. [In] light of the gravity of petitioner's offense, a comparison of his crime with his sentence does not give rise to an inference of gross disproportionality, and comparative analysis of his sentence with others in Michigan and across the Nation need not be performed."

Dissenting JUSTICE WHITE, joined by Blackmun and Stevens, JJ., protested:

"Not only is it undeniable that our cases have construed the Eighth Amendment to embody a proportionality component, but it is also evident that none of the Court's cases suggest that such a construction is impermissible. Indeed, *Rummel,* the holding of which Justice Scalia does not question, itself recognized that the Eighth Amendment contains a proportionality requirement, for it did not question *Coker* and indicated that the proportionality principle would come into play in some extreme, nonfelony cases.

"[Justice Scalia's] position restricts the reach of the Eighth Amendment far more than did *Rummel*. It also ignores the generality of the Court's several pronouncements about the Eighth Amendment's proportionality component. And it fails to explain why the words 'cruel and unusual' include a proportionality requirement in some cases but not in others. Surely, it is no explanation to say only that such a requirement in death penalty cases is part of our capital punishment jurisprudence. That is true but the decisions requiring proportionality do so because of the Eighth Amendment's prohibition against cruel and unusual punishments. The Court's capital punishment cases requiring proportionality reject Justice Scalia's notion that the Amendment bars only cruel and unusual modes or methods of punishment. Under that view, capital punishment—a mode of punishment—would either be completely barred or left to the discretion of the legislature. Yet neither is true. The death penalty is appropriate in some cases and not in others. The same should be true of punishment by imprisonment. * * *

"Two dangers lurk in Justice Scalia's analysis. First, he provides no mechanism for addressing a situation such as that proposed in *Rummel,* in which a legislature makes overtime parking a felony punishable by life imprisonment. He concedes that 'one can imagine extreme examples'—perhaps such as the one described in *Rummel*—'that no rational person, in no time or place, could accept,' but attempts to offer reassurance by claiming that 'for the same reason these examples are easy to decide, they are certain never to occur.' This is cold comfort indeed, for absent a proportionality guarantee, there would be no basis for deciding such cases should they arise.

"Second, * * * Justice Scalia's position that the Eighth Amendment addresses only modes or methods of punishment is quite inconsistent with our capital punishment cases, which do not outlaw death as a mode or method of punishment, but instead put limits on its application. If the concept of proportionality is downgraded in the Eighth Amendment calculus, much of this Court's capital penalty jurisprudence will rest on quicksand. * * *

"Because there is no justification for overruling or limiting *Solem,* it remains to apply that case's proportionality analysis to the sentence imposed on petitioner. Application of the *Solem* factors to the statutorily mandated punishment at issue here reveals that the punishment fails muster under *Solem* and, consequently, under the Eighth Amendment to the Constitution.

"[To] be constitutionally proportionate, punishment must be tailored to a defendant's personal responsibility and moral guilt. Justice Kennedy attempts to justify the harsh mandatory sentence imposed on petitioner by focusing on the subsidiary effects of drug use, and thereby ignores this aspect of our Eighth Amendment jurisprudence. While the collateral consequences of drugs such as cocaine are indisputably severe, they are not unlike those which flow from the misuse of other, legal, substances. For example, in considering the effects of alcohol on society, the Court has stressed that '[n]o one can seriously dispute the magnitude of the drunken driving problem or the States' interest in eradicating it,' but at the same time has recognized that the severity of the problem 'cannot excuse the need for scrupulous adherence to our constitutional principles.' * * * Indeed, it is inconceivable that a State could rationally choose to penalize one who possesses large quantities of alcohol in a manner similar to that in which Michigan has chosen to punish petitioner for cocaine possession, because of the tangential effects which might ultimately be traced to the alcohol at issue.

"[The] 'absolute magnitude' of petitioner's crime is not exceptionally serious. Because possession is necessarily a lesser included offense of possession with intent to distribute, it is odd to punish the former as severely as the latter. Nor is the requisite intent for the crime sufficient to render it particularly grave. To convict someone under the possession statute, it is only necessary to prove that the defendant knowingly possessed a mixture containing narcotics which weighs at least 650 grams. There is no *mens rea* requirement of intent to distribute the drugs, as there is in the parallel statute. * * * Finally, this statute applies equally to first-time offenders, such as petitioner, and recidivists. Consequently, the particular concerns reflected in recidivist statutes such as those in *Rummel* and *Solem* are not at issue here.

"[The] second prong of the *Solem* analysis is an examination of 'the sentences imposed on other criminals in the same jurisdiction.' [T]here is no death penalty in Michigan; consequently, life without parole, the punishment mandated here, is the harshest penalty available. [It] is clear that petitioner 'has been treated in the same manner as, or more severely than, criminals who have committed far more serious crimes.'

"The third factor set forth in *Solem* examines 'the sentences imposed for commission of the same crime in other jurisdictions.' No other jurisdiction imposes a punishment nearly as severe as Michigan's for possession of the amount of drugs at issue here. * * * Even under the Federal Sentencing Guidelines, with all relevant enhancements, petitioner's sentence would barely exceed ten years. * * * Indeed, the fact that no other jurisdiction provides such a severe, mandatory penalty for possession of this quantity of drugs is enough to establish 'the degree of national consensus this Court has previously thought sufficient to label a particular punishment cruel and unusual.'

"Application of *Solem's* proportionality analysis leaves no doubt that the Michigan statute at issue fails constitutional muster.[8]" [a]

CON LAW: P. 611, end of section

AMER CON: P. 429, end of section

RTS & LIB: P. 339, end of section

"VICTIM IMPACT" EVIDENCE

In *Booth v. Maryland,* 482 U.S. 496, 107 S.Ct. 2529, 96 L.Ed.2d 440 (1987), a 5–4 majority, per Powell, J., held that the Eighth Amendment prohibits a capital sentencing jury from considering a "victim impact statement"—evidence describing the personal characteristics of the victim(s), the emotional impact of the crime(s) on the family, and the family members' opinions and characterizations of the crimes and the defendant. The Court pointed out that "victim impact" evidence "may be wholly unrelated to the blameworthiness of a particular

---

[8]. Because the statute under which petitioner was convicted is unconstitutional under *Solem,* there is no need to reach his remaining argument that imposition of a life sentence without the possibility of parole necessitates the sort of individualized sentencing determination heretofore reserved for defendants subject to the death penalty.

[a]. Dissenting Justice Marshall "agree[d] with Justice White's dissenting opinion, except insofar as it asserts that the Eighth Amendment's Cruel and Unusual Punishments Clause does not proscribe the death penalty." In a separate dissent, Justice Stevens, joined by Blackmun, J., "agree[d] wholeheartedly" with Justice White's dissent, but made some additional comments.

defendant" and "could divert the jury's attention away from the defendant's background and record, and the circumstances of the crime." "Certainly," observed the Court, "the degree to which a family is willing and able to express its grief is irrelevant to the decision whether a defendant, who may merit the death penalty, should live or die." Two years later, in *South Carolina v. Gathers* 490 U.S. 805, 109 S.Ct. 2207, 104 L.Ed.2d 876 (1989), another 5–4 majority, per Brennan, J., extended the *Booth* rule to statements made by a prosecutor to the capital sentencing jury regarding the personal qualities of the murder victim.

In PAYNE v. TENNESSEE, ___ U.S. ___, 111 S.Ct. 2597, 115 L.Ed.2d 720 (1991), a 6–3 majority, per REHNQUIST, C.J., overruled *Booth* and *Gathers* and held that "the Eighth Amendment erects no *per se* bar" prohibiting a capital sentencing jury from considering "victim impact" evidence and prosecutorial argument on that subject.

Payne arose as follows: Petitioner was convicted of the first-degree murders of a woman and her 2–year–old daughter. He was also convicted of first-degree assault, with intent to murder, upon the woman's 3–year–old son, Nicholas. During the sentencing phase of the trial, the state called Nicholas' grandmother, who testified that the child missed his mother and his baby sister. In arguing for the death penalty, the prosecutor commented on the continuing effects of the crimes upon the victims' family.[a] The jury sentenced Payne to death on each murder count. The state supreme court affirmed.

In overturning the *Booth* and *Gathers* precedents and ruling that "[a] State may legitimately conclude that evidence about the victim's and about the impact of the murder on the victim's family is relevant to the jury's decision as to whether or not the death penalty should be imposed," the Court, per REHNQUIST, C.J., observed:

"*Booth* and *Gathers* were based on two premises: that evidence relating to a particular victim or to the harm that a capital defendant causes a victim's family do not in general reflect on the defendant's 'blameworthiness,' and that only evidence relating to 'blameworthiness' is relevant to the capital sentencing decision. However, the assessment of harm caused by the defendant as a result of the crime charged has understandably been an important concern of the criminal law, both in determining the elements of the offense and in determining the appropriate punishment. Thus, two equally blameworthy criminal defendants may be guilty of different offenses solely because their acts cause differing amounts of harm. 'If a bank robber aims his gun at a guard, pulls the trigger, and kills his target, he may be put to death. If the gun unexpectedly misfires, he may not. His moral guilt in both cases is identical, but his responsibility in the former is greater.'

"[It] was never held or even suggested in any of our cases preceding *Booth* that the defendant, entitled as he was to individualized consideration, was to receive that consideration wholly apart from the crime which he had committed. [This] misreading of precedent in *Booth* has, we think, unfairly weighted the scales in a capital trial; while virtually no limits are placed on the relevant mitigating evidence a capital defendant may introduce concerning his own circumstances, the State is barred from either offering 'a glimpse of the life' which a defendant 'chose to extinguish,' or demonstrating the loss to the victim's

---

a. During the sentencing phase, Payne called his mother, his girlfriend, and a clinical psychologist, each of whom testified as to various mitigating aspects of his background and character, e.g., that Payne was a good son, had no history of alcohol or drug abuse, and that, based on his low I.Q., he was "mentally handicapped."

family and to society which have resulted from the defendant's homicide.
* * *

"Payne echoes the concern voiced in *Booth*'s case that the admission of victim impact evidence permits a jury to find that defendants whose victims were assets to their community are more deserving of punishment that those whose victims are perceived to be less worthy. As a general matter, however, victim impact evidence is not offered to encourage comparative judgments of this kind—for instance, that the killer of a hardworking, devoted parent deserves the death penalty, but that the murderer of a reprobate does not. It is designed to show instead *each* victim's 'uniqueness as an individual human being,' whatever the jury might think the loss to the community resulting from his death might be. The facts of *Gathers* are an excellent illustration of this: the evidence showed that the victim was an out of work, mentally handicapped individual, perhaps not, in the eyes of most, a significant contributor to society, but nonetheless a murdered human being.

"[The] States remain free, in capital cases, as well as others, to devise new procedures and new remedies to meet felt needs. Victim impact evidence is simply another form or method of informing the sentencing authority about the specific harm caused by the crime in question, evidence of a general type long considered by sentencing authorities. We think the *Booth* Court was wrong in stating that this kind of evidence leads to the arbitrary imposition of the death penalty. In the majority of cases, and in this case, victim impact evidence serves entirely legitimate purposes. In the event that evidence is introduced that is so unduly prejudicial that it renders the trial fundamentally unfair, the Due Process Clause of the Fourteenth Amendment provides a mechanism for relief. Courts have always taken into consideration the harm done by the defendant in imposing sentence, and the evidence adduced in this case was illustrative of the harm caused by Payne's double murder.

"We are now of the view that a State may properly conclude that for the jury to assess meaningfully the defendant's moral culpability and blameworthiness, it should have before it at the sentencing phase evidence of the specific harm caused by the defendant. [By] turning the victim into a 'faceless stranger at the penalty phase of a capital trial,' *Booth* deprives the State of the full moral force of its evidence and may prevent the jury from having before it all the information necessary to determine the proper punishment for a first-degree murder. * * *

"Payne and his *amicus* argue that despite [the] numerous infirmities in the rule created by *Booth* and *Gathers,* we should adhere to the doctrine of *stare decisis* and stop short of overruling those cases. *Stare decisis* is the preferred course because it promotes the evenhanded, predictable, and consistent development of legal principles, fosters reliance on judicial decisions, and contributes to the actual and perceived integrity of the judicial process. [Nevertheless], when governing decisions are unworkable or are badly reasoned, 'this Court has never felt constrained to follow precedent.' *Smith v. Allwright,* 321 U.S. 649, 665, 64 S.Ct. 757, 765, 88 L.Ed. 987 (1944). *Stare decisis* is not an inexorable command; rather, it 'is a principle of policy and not a mechanical formula of adherence to the latest decision.' This is particularly true in constitutional cases, because in such cases 'correction through legislative action is practically impossible.'
* * *

"Applying these general principles, the Court has during the past 20 Terms overruled in whole or in part 33 of its previous constitutional decisions. *Booth* and *Gathers* were decided by the narrowest of margins, over spirited dissents challenging the basic underpinnings of those decisions. They have been questioned by members of the Court in later decisions, and have defied consistent application by the lower courts. [W]e conclude [that] they were wrongly decided and should be, and now are, overruled.[2]" [b]

Writing his last opinion as a member of the Court, dissenting JUSTICE MARSHALL, joined by Blackmun, J., deplored the majority's disregard for *stare decisis:*

"Power, not reason, is the new currency of this Court's decisionmaking. * * * Neither the law nor the facts supporting *Booth* and *Gathers* underwent any change in the last four years. Only the personnel of this Court did.

"In dispatching *Booth* and *Gathers* to their graves, today's majority ominously suggests that an even more extensive upheaval of this Court's precedents may be in store. * * * [T]he majority declares itself free to discard any principle of constitutional liberty which was recognized or reaffirmed over the dissenting votes of four Justices and with which five or more Justices *now* disagree. The majority today sends a clear signal that scores of established constitutional liberties are now ripe for reconsideration, thereby inviting the very type of open defiance of our precedents that the majority rewards in this case."

In a separate dissent, JUSTICE STEVENS, joined by Blackmun, J., suggested that "the 'hydraulic pressure' of public opinion" had led the Court astray:

"Justice Marshall is properly concerned about the majority's trivialization of the doctrine of *stare decisis*. But even if *Booth* and *Gathers* had not been decided, today's decision would represent a sharp break with past decisions. Our cases provide no support whatsoever for the majority's conclusion that the prosecutor may introduce evidence that sheds no light on the defendant's guilt or moral culpability, and thus serves no purpose other than to encourage jurors to decide in favor of death rather than life on the basis of their emotions rather than their reason.

"Until today our capital punishment jurisprudence has required that any decision to impose the death penalty be based solely on evidence that tends to inform the jury about the character of the offense and the character of the defendant. Evidence that serves no purpose other than to appeal to the sympathies or emotions of the jurors has never been considered admissible. Thus, if a defendant, who had murdered a convenience store clerk in cold blood in the course of an armed robbery, offered evidence unknown to him at the time of the crime about the immoral character of his victim, all would recognize immediately that the evidence was irrelevant and inadmissible. Evenhanded justice requires that the same constraint be imposed on the advocate of the death penalty. * * *

"Today's majority has obviously been moved by an argument that has strong political appeal but no proper place in a reasoned judicial opinion. Because our

---

2. Our holding today is limited to the holdings of *Booth* and *Gathers,* that evidence and argument relating to the victim and the impact of the victim's death on the victim's family are inadmissible at a capital sentencing hearing. *Booth* also held that the admission of a victim's family members' characterizations and opinions about the crime, the defendant, and the appropriate sentence violates the Eighth Amendment. No evidence of the latter sort was presented at the trial in this case.

b. There were three concurring opinions: Justice O'Connor, joined by White and Kennedy, JJ.; Justice Scalia, joined in part by O'Connor and Kennedy, JJ.; and Justice Souter, joined by Kennedy, J.

decision in *Lockett* recognizes the defendant's right to introduce all mitigating evidence that may inform the jury about his character, the Court suggests that fairness requires that the State be allowed to respond with similar evidence about the *victim.* This argument is a classic non sequitur: The victim is not on trial; her character, whether good or bad, cannot therefore constitute either an aggravating or mitigating circumstance.

"[The] premise that a criminal prosecution requires an evenhanded balance between the State and the defendant is also incorrect. The Constitution grants certain rights to the criminal defendant and imposes special limitations on the State designed to protect the individual from overreaching by the disproportionately powerful State. Thus, the State must prove a defendant's guilt beyond a reasonable doubt. Rules of evidence are also weighted in the defendant's favor. For example, the prosecution generally cannot introduce evidence of the defendant's character to prove his propensity to commit a crime, but the defendant can introduce such reputation evidence to show his law-abiding nature. Even if balance were required or desirable, today's decision, by permitting both the defendant and the State to introduce irrelevant evidence for the sentencer's consideration without any guidance, surely does nothing to enhance parity in the sentencing process.

"Victim impact evidence, as used in this case, has two flaws, both related to the Eighth Amendment's command that the punishment of death may not be meted out arbitrarily or capriciously. First, aspects of the character of the victim unforeseeable to the defendant at the time of his crime are irrelevant to the defendant's 'personal responsibility and moral guilt' and therefore cannot justify a death sentence. * * *

"Second, the quantity and quality of victim impact evidence sufficient to turn a verdict of life in prison into a verdict of death is not defined until after the crime has been committed and therefore cannot possibly be applied consistently in different cases. * * * Open-ended reliance by a capital sentencer on victim impact evidence simply does not provide a 'principled way to distinguish [cases], in which the death penalty [i]s imposed, from the many cases in which it [i]s not.' * * *

"The notion that the inability to produce an ideal system of justice in which every punishment is precisely married to the defendant's blameworthiness somehow justifies a rule that completely divorces some capital sentencing determinations from moral culpability is incomprehensible to me. Also incomprehensible is the argument that such a rule is required for the jury to take into account that each murder victim is a 'unique' human being. The fact that each of us is unique is a proposition so obvious that it surely requires no evidentiary support. What is not obvious, however, is the way in which the character or reputation in one case may differ from that of other possible victims. Evidence offered to prove such differences can only be intended to identify some victims as more worthy of protection than others. Such proof risks decisions based on the same invidious motives as a prosecutor's decision to seek the death penalty if a victim is white but to accept a plea bargain if the victim is black.

"Given the current popularity of capital punishment in a crime-ridden society, the political appeal of arguments that assume that increasing the severity of sentences is the best cure for the cancer of crime, and the political strength of the 'victims' rights' movement, I recognize that today's decision will be greeted with enthusiasm by a large number of concerned and thoughtful citizens. The great tragedy of the decision, however, is the danger that the 'hydraulic pressure' of public opinion that Justice Holmes once described—and that properly influences the deliberations of democratic legislatures—has played a role not only in the Court's decision to hear this case, and in its decision to reach the constitutional question without pausing to consider affirming on the basis of the Tennessee Supreme Court's rationale, but even in its resolution of the constitutional issue involved. Today is a sad day for a great institution."

SECTION: PROCEDURAL DUE PROCESS IN NON-CRIMINAL CASES

DEPRIVATION OF "LIBERTY" AND "PROPERTY" INTERESTS

CON LAW: P. 628, addition to note 7(b)

RTS & LIB: P. 357, addition to note 7(b)

See also *Foucha v. Louisiana*, ___ U.S. ___, 112 S.Ct. 1780, 118 L.Ed.2d 437 (1992) (also discussed infra this Supplement), where a 5-4 majority, per White, J., invalidated on due process grounds, a state statute permitting an insanity acquitee who no longer suffers from a mental illness to be indefinitely committed to a mental institution until he is able to demonstrate that he is not dangerous to himself or to others. The Court rejected the state's contention that an insanity acquitee could be confined on the basis of his antisocial personality, a condition that is not a mental disease and that is untreatable:

"First, even if his continued confinement were constitutionally permissible, keeping Foucha against his will in a mental institution is improper absent a determination in civil commitment proceedings of current mental illness and dangerousness. * * * Due process requires that the nature of commitment bear some reasonable relation to the purpose for which the individual is committed. * * *

"Second, if Foucha can no longer be held as an insanity acquitee in a mental hospital, he is entitled to constitutionally adequate procedures to establish the grounds for his confinement. * * * Third, 'the Due Process Clause contains a substantive component that bars certain arbitrary, wrongful government actions "regardless of the fairness of the procedures used to implement them." '

"[A] State, pursuant to its police power, may of course imprison convicted criminals for the purpose of deterrence and retribution. But there are constitutional limitations on the conduct that a State may criminalize. Here, the State has no such punitive interest. As Foucha was not convicted, he may not be punished.

"[The] State may also confine a mentally ill person if it shows 'by clear and convincing evidence that the individual is mentally ill and dangerous,' *Jones v. United States*, 463 U.S. 354, 103 S.Ct. 3043, 77 L.Ed.2d 694 (1983). Here, the State has not carried that burden; indeed, the State does not claim that Foucha is now mentally ill."

Chapter

FREEDOM OF EXPRESSION AND ASSOCIATION

SECTION: WHAT SPEECH IS NOT PROTECTED?

REPUTATION AND PRIVACY

PRIVATE INDIVIDUALS AND PUBLIC FIGURES

CON LAW: P. 716, after note 4

AMER CON: P. 500, after note 4

RTS & LIB: P. 445, after note 4

MASSON v. NEW YORKER MAGAZINE, INC., ___ U.S. ___, 111 S.Ct. 2419, 115 L.Ed.2d 447 (1991), per KENNEDY, J., held "that a deliberate alteration of the words uttered by a plaintiff does not equate with knowledge of falsity for purposes of [*Sullivan* and *Gertz*] unless the alteration results in a material change of meaning conveyed by the statement." Masson argued and Malcolm denied that Malcolm had falsely attributed quotations to Masson. The Court held that the issues raised by the disputes over some of the quotations at issue could not be resolved at the summary judgment stage:

"[For example], (a) '*Intellectual Gigolo*.' Malcolm quoted a description by petitioner of his relationship with [Dr. Kurt] Eissler [head of the Sigmund Freud Archives] and [Dr.] Anna Freud [daughter of Sigmund Freud and a major psychoanalyst in her own right] as follows: ' "Then I met a rather attractive older graduate student and I had an affair with her. One day, she took me to some art event, and she was sorry afterward. She said, 'Well, it is very nice sleeping with you in your room, but you're the kind of person who should never leave the room—you're just a social embarrassment anywhere else, though you do fine in your own room.' And you know, in their way, if not in so many words, Eissler and Anna Freud told me the same thing. They like me well enough 'in my own room.' They loved to hear from me what creeps and dolts analysts are. I was like an intellectual gigolo—you get your pleasure from him, but you don't take him out in public. . . ."'

"The tape recordings contain the substance of petitioner's reference to his graduate student friend, but no suggestion that Eissler or Anna Freud considered him, or that he considered himself, an ' "intellectual gigolo." ' Instead, petitioner said: 'They felt, in a sense, I was a private asset but a public liability. . . . They liked me when I was alone in their living room, and I could talk and chat and tell them the truth about things and they would tell me. But that I was, in a sense, much too junior within the hierarchy of analysis, for these important training analysts to be caught dead with me.' * * *

"(c) *'It Sounded Better.'* Petitioner [also] spoke with Malcolm about the history of his family, including the reasons his grandfather changed the family name from Moussaieff to Masson, and why petitioner adopted the abandoned family name as his middle name. The article contains the passage: ' "My father is a gem merchant who doesn't like to stay in any one place too long. His father was a gem merchant, too—a Bessarabian gem merchant, named Moussaieff, who went to Paris in the twenties and adopted the name Masson. My parents named me Jeffrey Lloyd Masson, but in 1975 I decided to change my middle name to Moussaieff—it sounded better." '

"In the most similar tape recorded statement, Masson explained at considerable length that his grandfather had changed the family name from Moussaieff to Masson when living in France, '[j]ust to hide his Jewishness.' Petitioner had changed his last name back to Moussaieff, but his then-wife Terry objected that 'nobody could pronounce it and nobody knew how to spell it, and it wasn't the name that she knew me by.' Petitioner had changed his name to Moussaieff because he 'just liked it.' '[I]t was sort of part of analysis: a return to the roots, and your family tradition and so on.' In the end, he had agreed with Terry that 'it wasn't her name after all,' and used Moussaieff as a middle instead of a last name. * * *[a]

"A fabricated quotation may injure reputation in at least two senses, either giving rise to a conceivable claim of defamation. First, the quotation might injure because it attributes an untrue factual assertion to the speaker. An example would be a fabricated quotation of a public official admitting he had been convicted of a serious crime when in fact he had not.

"Second, regardless of the truth or falsity of the factual matters asserted within the quoted statement, the attribution may result in injury to reputation because the manner of expression or even the fact that the statement was made indicates a negative personal trait or an attitude the speaker does not hold. John Lennon once was quoted as saying of the Beatles, 'We're more popular than Jesus Christ now.' Supposing the quotation had been a fabrication, it appears California law could permit recovery for defamation because, even without regard to the truth of the underlying assertion, false attribution of the statement could have injured his reputation. Here, in like manner, one need not determine whether petitioner is or is not the greatest analyst who ever lived in order to determine that it might have injured his reputation to be reported as having so proclaimed. * * *

"Of course, quotations do not always convey that the speaker actually said or wrote the quoted material. 'Punctuation marks, like words, have many uses.

---

[a]. The Court considered four other examples. It interpreted one as allegedly falsely attributing to Masson a plan to turn the Freud house into a place of "sex, women, and fun" (the tapes reveal Masson talking about how well he got along with a London analyst "and we were going to stay with each other and [laughs] we were going to pass women on to each other, and we were going to have a great time together when I lived in the Freud house"); another passage allegedly falsely quoted Masson as saying he did not know why he added a controversial passage at the end of one of his scholarly papers; another passage allegedly falsely quoted Masson as saying his work would be recognized as that of the greatest analyst after Freud; another passage allegedly falsely quoted Masson as being "the wrong man" to do an honorable thing. Under the test set out infra, the Court found each of these passages potentially actionable.

Writers often use quotation marks, yet no reasonable reader would assume that such punctuation automatically implies the truth of the quoted material.' *Baker v. Los Angeles Examiner,* 42 Cal.3d [254, 721 P.2d 87 (1986)]. In *Baker,* a television reviewer printed a hypothetical conversation between a station vice president and writer/producer, and the court found that no reasonable reader would conclude the plaintiff in fact had made the statement attributed to him. Writers often use quotations as in *Baker,* and a reader will not reasonably understand the quotations to indicate reproduction of a conversation that took place. In other instances, an acknowledgement that the work is so-called docudrama or historical fiction, or that it recreates conversations from memory, not from recordings, might indicate that the quotations should not be interpreted as the actual statements of the speaker to whom they are attributed.

"The work at issue here, however, as with much journalistic writing, provides the reader no clue that the quotations are being used as a rhetorical device or to paraphrase the speaker's actual statements. To the contrary, the work purports to be nonfiction, the result of numerous interviews. At least a trier of fact could so conclude. * * *

"The constitutional question we must consider here is whether, in the framework of a summary judgment motion, the evidence suffices to show that respondents acted with the requisite knowledge of falsity or reckless disregard as to truth or falsity. This inquiry in turn requires us to consider the concept of falsity; for we cannot discuss the standards for knowledge or reckless disregard without some understanding of the acts required for liability. We must consider whether the requisite falsity inheres in the attribution of words to the petitioner which he did not speak.

"In some sense, any alteration of a verbatim quotation is false. But writers and reporters by necessity alter what people say, at the very least to eliminate grammatical and syntactical infelicities. If every alteration constituted the falsity required to prove actual malice, the practice of journalism, which the First Amendment standard is designed to protect, would require a radical change, one inconsistent with our precedents and First Amendment principles. Petitioner concedes this absolute definition of falsity in the quotation context is too stringent, and acknowledges that 'minor changes to correct for grammar or syntax' do not amount to falsity for purposes of proving actual malice. We agree, and must determine what, in addition to this technical falsity, proves falsity for purposes of the actual malice inquiry.

"Petitioner argues that, excepting correction of grammar or syntax, publication of a quotation with knowledge that it does not contain the words the public figure used demonstrates actual malice. The author will have published the quotation with knowledge of falsity, and no more need be shown. [We] reject the idea that any alteration beyond correction of grammar or syntax by itself proves falsity in the sense relevant to determining actual malice under the First Amendment. An interviewer who writes from notes often will engage in the task of attempting a reconstruction of the speaker's statement. That author would, we may assume, act with knowledge that at times she has attributed to her subject words other than those actually used. Under petitioner's proposed standard, an author in this situation would lack First Amendment protection if she reported as quotations the substance of a subject's derogatory statements about himself.

"Even if a journalist has tape recorded the spoken statement of a public figure, the full and exact statement will be reported in only rare circumstances.

The existence of both a speaker and a reporter; the translation between two media, speech and the printed word; the addition of punctuation; and the practical necessity to edit and make intelligible a speaker's perhaps rambling comments, all make it misleading to suggest that a quotation will be reconstructed with complete accuracy. The use or absence of punctuation may distort a speaker's meaning, for example, where that meaning turns upon a speaker's emphasis of a particular word. In other cases, if a speaker makes an obvious misstatement, for example by unconscious substitution of one name for another, a journalist might alter the speaker's words but preserve his intended meaning. And conversely, an exact quotation out of context can distort meaning, although the speaker did use each reported word.

"In all events, technical distinctions between correcting grammar and syntax and some greater level of alteration do not appear workable, for we can think of no method by which courts or juries would draw the line between cleaning up and other changes, except by reference to the meaning a statement conveys to a reasonable reader. To attempt narrow distinctions of this type would be an unnecessary departure from First Amendment principles of general applicability, and, just as important, a departure from the underlying purposes of the tort of libel as understood since the latter half of the 16th century. From then until now, the tort action for defamation has existed to redress injury to the plaintiff's reputation by a statement that is defamatory and false. As we have recognized, '[t]he legitimate state interest underlying the law of libel is the compensation of individuals for the harm inflicted on them by defamatory falsehood.' *Gertz*. If an author alters a speaker's words but effects no material change in meaning, including any meaning conveyed by the manner or fact of expression, the speaker suffers no injury to reputation that is compensable as a defamation.

"These essential principles of defamation law accommodate the special case of inaccurate quotations without the necessity for a discrete body of jurisprudence directed to this subject alone. * * *

"The common law of libel takes but one approach to the question of falsity, regardless of the form of the communication. It overlooks minor inaccuracies and concentrates upon substantial truth. [Put] another way, the statement is not considered false unless it 'would have a different effect on the mind of the reader from that which the pleaded truth would have produced.' R. Sack, *Libel, Slander, and Related Problems* 138 (1980); see generally R. Smolla, *Law of Defamation* § 5.08 (1991). Our definition of actual malice relies upon this historical understanding.

"We conclude that a deliberate alteration of the words uttered by a plaintiff does not equate with knowledge of falsity for purposes of *Sullivan* and *Gertz* unless the alteration results in a material change in the meaning conveyed by the statement. The use of quotations to attribute words not in fact spoken bears in a most important way on that inquiry, but it is not dispositive in every case. [I]f the alterations of petitioner's words gave a different meaning to the statements, bearing upon their defamatory character, then the device of quotations might well be critical in finding the words actionable. * * *

"The Court of Appeals applied a test of substantial truth which, in exposition if not in application, comports with much of the above discussion. The Court of Appeals, however, went one step beyond protection of quotations that convey the meaning of a speaker's statement with substantial accuracy and concluded that an altered quotation is protected so long as it is a 'rational interpretation' of an actual statement * * *.

"The protection for rational interpretation serves First Amendment principles by allowing an author the interpretive license that is necessary when relying upon ambiguous sources. Where, however, a writer uses a quotation, and where a reasonable reader would conclude that the quotation purports to be a verbatim repetition of a statement by the speaker, the quotation marks indicate that the author is not involved in an interpretation of the speaker's ambiguous statement, but attempting to convey what the speaker said. * * *

"The significance of the quotations at issue, absent any qualification, is to inform us that we are reading the statement of petitioner, not Malcolm's rational interpretation of what petitioner has said or thought. Were we to assess quotations under a rational interpretation standard, we would give journalists the freedom to place statements in their subjects' mouths without fear of liability. By eliminating any method of distinguishing between the statements of the subject and the interpretation of the author, we would diminish to a great degree the trustworthiness of the printed word, and eliminate the real meaning of quotations. Not only public figures but the press doubtless would suffer under such a rule. Newsworthy figures might become more wary of journalists, knowing that any comment could be transmuted and attributed to the subject, so long as some bounds of rational interpretation were not exceeded. We would ill serve the values of the First Amendment if we were to grant near absolute, constitutional protection for such a practice. We doubt the suggestion that as a general rule readers will assume that direct quotations are but a rational interpretation of the speaker's words, and we decline to adopt any such presumption in determining the permissible interpretations of the quotations in question here. * * *

"We must determine whether the published passages differ materially in meaning from the tape recorded statements so as to create an issue of fact for a jury as to falsity.

"(a) *'Intellectual Gigolo.'* We agree with the dissenting opinion in the Court of Appeals that '[f]airly read, intellectual gigolo suggests someone who forsakes intellectual integrity in exchange for pecuniary or other gain.' A reasonable jury could find a material difference between the meaning of this passage and petitioner's tape-recorded statement that he was considered 'much too junior within the hierarchy of analysis, for these important training analysts to be caught dead with [him].'

"The Court of Appeals majority found it difficult to perceive how the 'intellectual gigolo' quotation was defamatory, a determination supported not by any citation to California law, but only by the argument that the passage appears to be a report of Eissler's and Anna Freud's opinions of petitioner. We agree with the Court of Appeals that the most natural interpretation of this quotation is not an admission that petitioner considers himself an intellectual gigolo but a statement that Eissler and Anna Freud considered him so. It does not follow, though, that the statement is harmless. Petitioner is entitled to argue that the passage should be analyzed as if Malcolm had reported falsely that Eissler had given this assessment (with the added level of complexity that the quotation purports to represent petitioner's understanding of Eissler's view). An admission that two well-respected senior colleagues considered one an 'intellectual gigolo' could be as or more damaging than a similar self-appraisal. In all events, whether the 'intellectual gigolo' quotation is defamatory is a question of

California law. To the extent that the Court of Appeals based its conclusion in the First Amendment, it was mistaken. * * *

"(c) *'It Sounded Better.'* We agree with the District Court and the Court of Appeals that any difference between petitioner's tape-recorded statement that he 'just liked' the name Moussaieff, and the quotation that 'it sounded better' is, in context, immaterial. Although Malcolm did not include all of petitioner's lengthy explanation of his name change, she did convey the gist of that explanation: Petitioner took his abandoned family name as his middle name. We agree with the Court of Appeals that the words attributed to petitioner did not materially alter the meaning of his statement. * * *

"Because of the Court of Appeals' disposition with respect to Malcolm, it did not have occasion to address petitioner's argument that the District Court erred in granting summary judgment to The New Yorker Magazine, Inc., and Alfred A. Knopf, Inc. on the basis of their respective relations with Malcolm or the lack of any independent actual malice. These questions are best addressed in the first instance on remand."

WHITE, J., joined by Scalia, J., dissented: "My principal disagreement is with the holding that 'a deliberate alteration of the words uttered by a plaintiff does not equate with knowledge of falsity . . . unless the alteration results in a material change in the meaning conveyed by the statement.' [As] the Court recognizes, the use of quotation marks in reporting what a person said asserts that the person spoke the words as quoted. As this case comes to us, it is to be judged on the basis that in the instances identified by the Court, the reporter, Malcolm, wrote that Masson said certain things that she knew Masson did not say. By any definition of the term, this was 'knowing falsehood': Malcolm asserts that Masson said these very words, knowing that he did not. The issue, as the Court recognizes, is whether Masson spoke the words attributed to him, not whether the fact, if any, asserted by the attributed words is true or false. In my view, we need to go no further to conclude that the defendants in this case were not entitled to summary judgment on the issue of malice with respect to any of the six erroneous quotations.

"That there was at least an issue for the jury to decide on the question of deliberate or reckless falsehood, does not mean that plaintiffs were necessarily entitled to go to trial. If, as a matter of law, reasonable jurors could not conclude that attributing to Masson certain words that he did not say amounted to libel under California law, *i.e.*, 'expose[d] [Masson] to hatred, contempt, ridicule, or obloquy, or which causes him to be shunned or avoided, or which has a tendency to injure him in his occupation,' Cal.Civ.Code Ann. § 45 (West 1982), a motion for summary judgment on this ground would be justified. I would suppose, for example that if Malcolm wrote that Masson said that he wore contact lenses, when he said nothing about his eyes or his vision, the trial judge would grant summary judgment for the defendants and dismiss the case. The same would be true if Masson had said 'I was spoiled as a child by my Mother,' whereas, Malcolm reports that he said 'I was spoiled as a child by my parents.' But if reasonable jurors could conclude that the deliberate misquotation was libelous, the case should go to the jury.

"This seems to me to be the straightforward, traditional approach to deal with this case. Instead, the Court states that deliberate misquotation does not amount to *New York Times* malice unless it results in a material change in the meaning conveyed by the statement. [The] falsehood, apparently, must be substantial; the reporter may lie a little, but not too much. * * *

"The Court attempts to justify its holding in several ways, none of which is persuasive. First, it observes that an interviewer who takes notes of any interview will attempt to reconstruct what the speaker said and will often knowingly attribute to the subject words that were not used by the speaker. But this is nothing more than an assertion that authors may misrepresent because they cannot remember what the speaker actually said. This should be no dilemma for such authors, or they could report their story without purporting to quote when they are not sure, thereby leaving the reader to trust or doubt the author rather than believing that the subject actually said what he is claimed to have said. Moreover, this basis for the Court's rule has no application where there is a tape of the interview and the author is in no way at a loss to know what the speaker actually said. Second, the Court speculates that even with the benefit of a recording, the author will find it necessary at times to reconstruct, but again, in those cases why should the author be free to put his or her reconstruction in quotation marks, rather than report without them? Third, the Court suggests that misquotations that do not materially alter the meaning inflict no injury to reputation that is compensable as defamation. This may be true, but this is a question of defamation or not, and has nothing to do with whether the author deliberately put within quotation marks and attributed to the speaker words that the author knew the speaker did not utter.

"As I see it, the defendants' motion for summary judgment based on lack of malice should not have been granted on any of the six quotations considered by the Court; [I] therefore dissent from the result reached with respect to the 'It Sounded Better' [quotation], but agree with the Court's judgment on the other five misquotations."

SECTION: IS SOME PROTECTED SPEECH LESS EQUAL THAN OTHER PROTECTED SPEECH?

NEAR OBSCENE SPEECH

CON LAW: P. 838, after note 3

AMER CON: P. 621, after note 3

RTS & LIB: P. 567, after note 3

BARNES v. GLEN THEATRE, INC., ___ U.S. ___, 111 S.Ct. 2456, 115 L.Ed. 2d 504 (1991) held that an Indiana statute prohibiting the knowing or intentional appearing in a public place in a state of nudity could constitutionally be applied to require that female dancers at a minimum wear "pasties" and a "G-string" when they dance. REHNQUIST, C.J., delivered the judgment [a] of the Court in an opinion joined by O'Connor, J., and Kennedy, J.:" "Several of our cases contain language suggesting that nude dancing of the kind involved here is expressive conduct protected by the First Amendment. In *Doran v. Salem Inn, Inc.,* 422 U.S. 922, 95 S.Ct. 2561, 45 L.Ed.2d 648 (1975), we said: '[A]lthough the customary "barroom" type of nude dancing may involve only the barest minimum of protected expression, we recognized in *California v. LaRue,* 409 U.S. 109, 93 S.Ct. 390, 34 L.Ed.2d 342 (1972), that this form of entertainment might be entitled to First and Fourteenth Amendment protection under some circumstances.' In *Schad v. Borough of Mount Ephraim,* we said that '[f]urthermore, as the state

---

a. The initial release of the opinions erroneously stated that Rehnquist, C.J.'s opinion was the opinion of the Court, and that statement appears in U.S. Law Week and the Supreme Court Bulletin, but we are informed that the initial release will be corrected.

courts in this case recognized, nude dancing is not without its First Amendment protections from official regulation.' These statements support the conclusion [that] nude dancing of the kind sought to be performed here is expressive conduct within the outer perimeters of the First Amendment, though we view it as only marginally so. This, of course, does not end our inquiry. We must determine the level of protection to be afforded to the expressive conduct at issue, and must determine whether the Indiana statute is an impermissible infringement of that protected activity.

"Indiana, of course, has not banned nude dancing as such, but has proscribed public nudity across the board. The Supreme Court of Indiana has construed the Indiana statute to preclude nudity in what are essentially places of public accommodation such as the Glen Theatre and the Kitty Kat Lounge. In such places, respondents point out, minors are excluded and there are no non-consenting viewers. Respondents contend that while the state may license establishments such as the ones involved here, and limit the geographical area in which they do business, it may not in any way limit the performance of the dances within them without violating the First Amendment. The petitioner contends, on the other hand, that Indiana's restriction on nude dancing is a valid 'time, place or manner' restriction under cases such as *Clark v. Community for Creative Non-Violence.*

"The 'time, place, or manner' test was developed for evaluating restrictions on expression taking place on public property which had been dedicated as a 'public forum,' although we have on at least one occasion applied it to conduct occurring on private property. See *Renton.* In *Clark* we observed that this test has been interpreted to embody much the same standards as those set forth in *United States v. O'Brien,* and we turn, therefore, to the rule enunciated in *O'Brien.* '[W]hen "speech" and "nonspeech" elements are combined in the same course of conduct, a sufficiently important governmental interest in regulating the nonspeech element can justify incidental limitations on First Amendment freedoms. To characterize the quality of the governmental interest which must appear, the Court has employed a variety of descriptive terms: compelling; substantial; subordinating; paramount; cogent; strong. Whatever imprecision inheres in these terms, we think it clear that a government regulation is sufficiently justified if it is within the constitutional power of the Government; if it furthers an important or substantial governmental interest; if the governmental interest is unrelated to the suppression of free expression; and if the incidental restriction on alleged First Amendment freedoms is no greater than is essential to the furtherance of that interest.'

"Applying the four-part *O'Brien* test enunciated above, we find that Indiana's public indecency statute is justified despite its incidental limitations on some expressive activity. The public indecency statute is clearly within the constitutional power of the State and furthers substantial governmental interests. It is impossible to discern, other than from the text of the statute, exactly what governmental interest the Indiana legislators had in mind when they enacted this statute, for Indiana does not record legislative history, and the state's highest court has not shed additional light on the statute's purpose. Nonetheless, the statute's purpose of protecting societal order and morality is clear from its text and history. Public indecency statutes of this sort are of ancient origin, and presently exist in at least 47 States. * * * [They] reflect moral disapproval of people appearing in the nude among strangers in public places.

"This public indecency statute follows a long line of earlier Indiana statutes banning all public nudity. The history of Indiana's public indecency statute shows that it predates barroom nude dancing and was enacted as a general prohibition. * * *

"This and other public indecency statutes were designed to protect morals and public order. The traditional police power of the States is defined as the authority to provide for the public health, safety, and morals, and we have upheld such a basis for legislation. In *Paris Adult Theatre I v. Slaton,* we said: 'In deciding *Roth* [*v. United States*], this Court implicitly accepted that a legislature could legitimately act on such a conclusion to protect "the social interest in order and morality."' And in *Bowers v. Hardwick,* we said: 'The law, however, is constantly based on notions of morality, and if all laws representing essentially moral choices are to be invalidated under the Due Process Clause, the courts will be very busy indeed.'

"Thus, the public indecency statute furthers a substantial government interest in protecting order and morality.

"This interest is unrelated to the suppression of free expression. Some may view restricting nudity on moral grounds as necessarily related to expression. We disagree. It can be argued, of course, that almost limitless types of conduct—including appearing in the nude in public—are 'expressive,' and in one sense of the word this is true. People who go about in the nude in public may be expressing something about themselves by so doing. But the court rejected this expansive notion of 'expressive conduct' in *O'Brien,* saying: 'We cannot accept the view that an apparently limitless variety of conduct can be labelled "speech" whenever the person engaging in the conduct intends thereby to express an idea.'

"And in *Dallas v. Stanglin* we further observed: 'It is possible to find some kernel of expression in almost every activity a person undertakes—for example, walking down the street or meeting one's friends at a shopping mall—but such a kernel is not sufficient to bring the activity within the protection of the First Amendment. * * *'

"Respondents contend that even though prohibiting nudity in public generally may not be related to suppressing expression, prohibiting the performance of nude dancing is related to expression because the state seeks to prevent its erotic message. Therefore, they reason that the application of the Indiana statute to the nude dancing in this case violates the First Amendment, because it fails the third part of the *O'Brien* test, viz: the governmental interest must be unrelated to the suppression of free expression.

"But we do not think that when Indiana applies its statute to the nude dancing in these nightclubs it is proscribing nudity because of the erotic message conveyed by the dancers. Presumably numerous other erotic performances are presented at these establishments and similar clubs without any interference from the state, so long as the performers wear a scant amount of clothing. Likewise, the requirement that the dancers don pasties and a G-string does not deprive the dance of whatever erotic message it conveys; it simply makes the message slightly less graphic. The perceived evil that Indiana seeks to address is not erotic dancing, but public nudity. The appearance of people of all shapes, sizes and ages in the nude at a beach, for example, would convey little if any erotic message, yet the state still seeks to prevent it. Public nudity is the evil the state seeks to prevent, whether or not it is combined with expressive activity.

* * *

"The fourth part of the *O'Brien* test requires that the incidental restriction on First Amendment freedom be no greater than is essential to the furtherance of the governmental interest. As indicated in the discussion above, the governmental interest served by the text of the prohibition is societal disapproval of nudity in public places and among strangers. The statutory prohibition is not a means to some greater end, but an end in itself. It is without cavil that the public indecency statute is 'narrowly tailored;' Indiana's requirement that the dancers wear at least pasties and a G-string is modest, and the bare minimum necessary to achieve the state's purpose."

SCALIA, J., concurred in the judgment: "I agree that the judgment of the Court of Appeals must be reversed. In my view, however, the challenged regulation must be upheld, not because it survives some lower level of First-Amendment scrutiny, but because, as a general law regulating conduct and not specifically directed at expression, it is not subject to First-Amendment scrutiny at all.

"Were it the case that Indiana *in practice* targeted only expressive nudity, while turning a blind eye to nude beaches and unclothed purveyors of hot dogs and machine tools, it might be said that what posed as a regulation of conduct in general was in reality a regulation of only communicative conduct. Respondents have adduced no evidence of that. Indiana officials have brought many public indecency prosecutions for activities having no communicative element. * * *

"The dissent confidently asserts that the purpose of restricting nudity in public places in general is to protect nonconsenting parties from offense; and argues that since only consenting, admission-paying patrons see respondents dance, that purpose cannot apply and the only remaining purpose must relate to the communicative elements of the performance. Perhaps the dissenters believe that 'offense to others' *ought* to be the only reason for restricting nudity in public places generally, but there is no basis for thinking that our society has ever shared that Thoreauvian 'you-may-do-what-you-like-so-long-as-it-does-not-injure-someone-else' beau ideal—much less for thinking that it was written into the Constitution. The purpose of Indiana's nudity law would be violated, I think, if 60,000 fully consenting adults crowded into the Hoosierdome to display their genitals to one another, even if there were not an offended innocent in the crowd. Our society prohibits, and all human societies have prohibited, certain activities not because they harm others but because they are considered, in the traditional phrase, '*contra bonos mores,*' *i.e.,* immoral. In American society, such prohibitions have included, for example, sadomasochism, cockfighting, bestiality, suicide, drug use, prostitution, and sodomy. While there may be great diversity of view on whether various of these prohibitions should exist (though I have found few ready to abandon, in principle, all of them) there is no doubt that, absent specific constitutional protection for the conduct involved, the Constitution does not prohibit them simply because they regulate 'morality.' See *Bowers v. Hardwick* (upholding prohibition of private homosexual sodomy enacted solely on 'the presumed belief of a majority of the electorate in [the jurisdiction] that homosexual sodomy is immoral and unacceptable'). * * *

"Since the Indiana regulation is a general law not specifically targeted at expressive conduct, its application to such conduct does not in my view implicate the First Amendment.[3]

3. The dissent [misunderstands] what is meant by the term "general law." I do not mean that the law restricts the targeted conduct in all places at all times. A law is "general" for the present purposes if it regulates conduct without regard to whether that conduct is expressive. Concededly, Indiana bans nudity in public places, but not within

"The First Amendment explicitly protects 'the freedom of speech [and] of the press'—oral and written speech—not 'expressive conduct.' When any law restricts speech, even for a purpose that has nothing to do with the suppression of communication (for instance, to reduce noise, see *Saia v. New York,* 334 U.S. 558, 68 S.Ct. 1148, 92 L.Ed. 1574 (1948), to regulate election campaigns, see *Buckley,* or to prevent littering, see *Schneider,* we insist that it meet the high, First-Amendment standard of justification. But virtually *every* law restricts conduct, and virtually *any* prohibited conduct can be performed for an expressive purpose—if only expressive of the fact that the actor disagrees with the prohibition. It cannot reasonably be demanded, therefore, that every restriction of expression incidentally produced by a general law regulating conduct pass normal First-Amendment scrutiny, or even—as some of our cases have suggested, see *e.g., O'Brien*—that it be justified by an 'important or substantial' government interest. Nor do our holdings require such justification: we have never invalidated the application of a general law simply because the conduct that it reached was being engaged in for expressive purposes and the government could not demonstrate a sufficiently important state interest.

"This is not to say that the First Amendment affords no protection to expressive conduct. Where the government prohibits conduct *precisely because of its communicative attributes,* we hold the regulation unconstitutional. See, *e.g., United States v. Eichman* (burning flag); *Texas v. Johnson* (same); *Tinker v. Des Moines* (wearing black arm bands).[4] In each of the foregoing cases, we explicitly found that suppressing communication was the object of the regulation of conduct. Where that has not been the case, however—where suppression of communicative use of the conduct was merely the incidental effect of forbidding the conduct for other reasons—we have allowed the regulation to stand. * * *

"All our holdings (though admittedly not some of our discussion) support the conclusion that 'the only First Amendment analysis applicable to laws that do not directly or indirectly impede speech is the threshold inquiry of whether the purpose of the law is to suppress communication. If not, that is the end of the matter so far as First Amendment guarantees are concerned; if so, the court then proceeds to determine whether there is substantial justification for the proscription.' *Community for Creative Non-Violence v. Watt,* 703 F.2d 586 (D.C. Cir.1983) (en banc) (Scalia, J., dissenting), (emphasis omitted), rev'd *Clark v. Community for Creative Non-Violence.* Such a regime ensures that the government does not act to suppress communication, without requiring that all conduct-restricting regulation (which means in effect all regulation) survive an enhanced level of scrutiny."[b]

the privacy of the home. (That is not surprising, since the common law offense, and the traditional moral prohibition, runs against *public* nudity, not against all nudity. But that confirms, rather than refutes, the general nature of the law: one may not go nude in public, whether or not one intends thereby to convey a message, and similarly one *may* go nude in private, again whether or not that nudity is expressive.

4. It is easy to conclude that conduct has been forbidden because of its communicative attributes when the conduct in question is what the Court has called 'inherently expressive,' and what I would prefer to call 'conventionally expressive'—such as flying a red flag. I mean by that phrase (as I assume the Court means by 'inherently expressive') conduct that is normally engaged in for the purpose of communicating an idea, or perhaps an emotion, to someone else. I am not sure whether dancing fits that description, see *Dallas v. Stanglin* (social dance group 'do[es] not involve the sort of expressive association that the First Amendment has been held to protect'). But even if it does, this law is directed against nudity, not dancing. Nudity is *not* normally engaged in for the purpose of communicating an idea or an emotion.

b. Scalia, J., observed that his analysis was consistent with that in the peyote case, Employment Division v. Smith [CON LAW, p. 1170] which he described as holding that "general laws not specifically targeted at religious

SOUTER, J., concurred in the judgment: "Not all dancing is entitled to First Amendment protection as expressive activity. This Court has previously categorized ballroom dancing as beyond the Amendment's protection, [*City of Dallas v. Stanglin*], and dancing as aerobic exercise would likewise be outside the First Amendment's concern. But dancing as a performance directed to an actual or hypothetical audience gives expression at least to generalized emotion or feeling, and where the dancer is nude or nearly so the feeling expressed, in the absence of some contrary clue, is eroticism, carrying an endorsement of erotic experience. Such is the expressive content of the dances described in the record.

"Although such performance dancing is inherently expressive, nudity per se is not. It is a condition, not an activity, and the voluntary assumption of that condition, without more, apparently expresses nothing beyond the view that the condition is somehow appropriate to the circumstances. But every voluntary act implies some such idea, and the implication is thus so common and minimal that calling all voluntary activity expressive would reduce the concept of expression to the point of the meaningless. A search for some expression beyond the minimal in the choice to go nude will often yield nothing: a person may choose nudity, for example, for maximum sunbathing. But when nudity is combined with expressive activity, its stimulative and attractive value certainly can enhance the force of expression, and a dancer's acts in going from clothed to nude, as in a strip-tease, are integrated into the dance and its expressive function. Thus I agree with the plurality and the dissent that an interest in freely engaging in the nude dancing at issue here is subject to a degree of First Amendment protection.

"I also agree with the plurality that the appropriate analysis to determine the actual protection required by the First Amendment is the four-part enquiry described in *United States v. O'Brien* for judging the limits of appropriate state action burdening expressive acts as distinct from pure speech or representation. I nonetheless write separately to rest my concurrence in the judgment, not on the possible sufficiency of society's moral views to justify the limitations at issue, but on the State's substantial interest in combating the secondary effects of adult entertainment establishments of the sort typified by respondents' establishments.

"It is, of course, true that this justification has not been articulated by Indiana's legislature or by its courts. [I] think [we may] legitimately consider petitioners' assertion that the statute is applied to nude dancing because such dancing 'encourag[es] prostitution, increas[es] sexual assaults, and attract[s] other criminal activity.'

"This asserted justification for the statute may not be ignored merely because it is unclear to what extent this purpose motivated the Indiana Legislature in enacting the statute. Our appropriate focus is not an empirical enquiry into the actual intent of the enacting legislature, but rather the existence or not of a current governmental interest in the service of which the challenged application of the statute may be constitutional. In my view, the interest asserted by petitioners in preventing prostitution, sexual assault, and other criminal activity, although presumably not a justification for all applications of

practices did not require heightened First Amendment scrutiny even though they diminished some people's ability to practice their religion." Scalia, J., also argued that the plurality had overread the precedents involving state interests in morality. As he read the cases, they only stood for the proposition that such interests were rational, not important or substantial.

the statute, is sufficient under *O'Brien* to justify the State's enforcement of the statute against the type of adult entertainment at issue here. * * *

"The asserted state interest is plainly a substantial one; the only question is whether prohibiting nude dancing of the sort at issue here 'furthers' that interest. I believe that our cases have addressed this question sufficiently to establish that it does. * * *

"In light of *Renton*'s recognition that legislation seeking to combat the secondary effects of adult entertainment need not await localized proof of those effects, the State of Indiana could reasonably conclude that forbidding nude entertainment of the type offered at the Kitty Kat Lounge [furthers] its interest in preventing prostitution, sexual assault, and associated crimes. Given our recognition that 'society's interest in protecting this type of expression is of a wholly different, and lesser, magnitude than the interest in untrammeled political debate,' *American Mini Theatres,* I do not believe that a State is required affirmatively to undertake to litigate this issue repeatedly in every case. The statute as applied to nudity of the sort at issue here therefore satisfies the second prong of *O'Brien*.[2] * * *

"The dissent contends, however, that Indiana seeks to regulate nude dancing as its means of combating such secondary effects 'because . . . creating or emphasizing [the] thoughts and ideas [expressed by nude dancing] in the minds of the spectators may lead to increased prostitution' and that regulation of expressive conduct because of the fear that the expression will prove persuasive is inherently related to the suppression of free expression.

"The major premise of the dissent's reasoning may be correct, but its minor premise describing the causal theory of Indiana's regulatory justification is not. To say that pernicious secondary effects are associated with nude dancing establishments is not necessarily to say that such effects result from the persuasive effect of the expression inherent in nude dancing. It is to say, rather, only that the effects are correlated with the existence of establishments offering such dancing, without deciding what the precise causes of the correlation actually are. It is possible, for example, that the higher incidence of prostitution and sexual assault in the vicinity of adult entertainment locations results from the concentration of crowds of men predisposed to such activities, or from the simple viewing of nude bodies regardless of whether those bodies are engaged in expression or not. In neither case would the chain of causation run through the persuasive effect of the expressive component of nude dancing.

"Because the State's interest in banning nude dancing results from a simple correlation of such dancing with other evils, rather than from a relationship between the other evils and the expressive component of the dancing, the interest is unrelated to the suppression of free expression.[3]

---

2. Because there is no overbreadth challenge before us, we are not called upon to decide whether the application of the statute would be valid in other contexts. It is enough, then, to say that the secondary effects rationale on which I rely here would be open to question if the State were to seek to enforce the statute by barring expressive nudity in classes of productions that could not readily be analogized to the adult films at issue in *Renton*. It is difficult to see, for example, how the enforcement of Indiana's statute against nudity in a production of 'Hair' or 'Equus' somewhere other than an 'adult' theater would further the State's interest in avoiding harmful secondary effects, in the absence of evidence that expressive nudity outside the context of *Renton*-type adult entertainment was correlated with such secondary effects.

3. I reach this conclusion again mindful, as was the Court in *Renton*, that the protection of sexually explicit expression may be of lesser societal importance than the protection of other forms of expression. See *Renton* n. 2, citing *American Mini Theatres*.

"The fourth *O'Brien* condition, that the restriction be no greater than essential to further the governmental interest, requires little discussion. Pasties and a G-string moderate the expression to some degree, to be sure, but only to a degree. Dropping the final stitch is prohibited, but the limitation is minor when measured against the dancer's remaining capacity and opportunity to express the erotic message. Nor, so far as we are told, is the dancer or her employer limited by anything short of obscenity laws from expressing an erotic message by articulate speech or representational means; a pornographic movie featuring one of respondents, for example, was playing nearby without any interference from the authorities at the time these cases arose.

"Accordingly, I find *O'Brien* satisfied and concur in the judgment."

WHITE, J., joined by Marshall, Blackmun, and Stevens, JJ., dissented:

"The Court's analysis is erroneous in several respects. Both the Court and Justice Scalia in his concurring opinion overlook a fundamental and critical aspect of our cases upholding the States' exercise of their police powers. None of the cases they rely upon, including *O'Brien* and *Bowers v. Hardwick* involved anything less than truly *general* proscriptions on individual conduct. In *O'Brien*, for example, individuals were prohibited from destroying their draft cards at any time and in any place, even in completely private places such as the home. Likewise, in *Bowers*, the State prohibited sodomy, regardless of where the conduct might occur, including the home as was true in that case. By contrast, in this case Indiana does not suggest that its statute applies to, or could be applied to, nudity wherever it occurs, including the home. We do not understand the Court or Justice Scalia to be suggesting that Indiana could constitutionally enact such an intrusive prohibition, nor do we think such a suggestion would be tenable in light of our decision in *Stanley v. Georgia*, in which we held that States could not punish the mere possession of obscenity in the privacy of one's own home.

"We are told by the Attorney General of Indiana that, in *State v. Baysinger*, 272 Ind. 236, 397 N.E.2d 580 (1979), the Indiana Supreme Court held that the statute at issue here cannot and does not prohibit nudity as a part of some larger form of expression meriting protection when the communication of ideas is involved. Petitioners also state that the evils sought to be avoided by applying the statute in this case would not obtain in the case of theatrical productions, such as *Salome* or *Hair*. Neither is there any evidence that the State has attempted to apply the statute to nudity in performances such as plays, ballets or operas. 'No arrests have ever been made for nudity as part of a play or ballet.' ([A]ffidavit of Sgt. Timothy Corbett).

"Thus, the Indiana statute is not a *general* prohibition of the type we have upheld in prior cases. As a result, the Court's and Justice Scalia's simple references to the State's general interest in promoting societal order and morality is not sufficient justification for a statute which concededly reaches a significant amount of protected expressive activity. Instead, in applying the *O'Brien* test, we are obligated to carefully examine the reasons the State has chosen to regulate this expressive conduct in a less than general statute. In other words, when the State enacts a law which draws a line between expressive conduct which is regulated and nonexpressive conduct of the same type which is not regulated, *O'Brien* places the burden on the State to justify the distinctions it has made. Closer inquiry as to the purpose of the statute is surely appropriate.

"Legislators do not just randomly select certain conduct for proscription; they have reasons for doing so and those reasons illuminate the purpose of the law that is passed. Indeed, a law may have multiple purposes. The purpose of forbidding people from appearing nude in parks, beaches, hot dog stands, and like public places is to protect others from offense. But that could not possibly be the purpose of preventing nude dancing in theaters and barrooms since the viewers are exclusively consenting adults who pay money to see these dances. The purpose of the proscription in these contexts is to protect the viewers from what the State believes is the harmful message that nude dancing communicates. * * * As the State now tells us, and as Justice Souter agrees, the State's goal in applying what it describes as its 'content neutral' statute to the nude dancing in this case is 'deterrence of prostitution, sexual assaults, criminal activity, degradation of women, and other activities which break down family structure.' The attainment of these goals, however, depends on preventing an expressive activity.

"The Court nevertheless holds that the third requirement of the *O'Brien* test, that the governmental interest be unrelated to the suppression of free expression, is satisfied because in applying the statute to nude dancing, the State is not 'proscribing nudity because of the erotic message conveyed by the dancers.' The Court suggests that this is so because the State does not ban dancing that sends an erotic message; it is only nude erotic dancing that is forbidden. The perceived evil is not erotic dancing but public nudity, which may be prohibited despite any incidental impact on expressive activity. This analysis is transparently erroneous.

"In arriving at its conclusion, the Court concedes that nude dancing conveys an erotic message and concedes that the message would be muted if the dancers wore pasties and G-strings. Indeed, the emotional or erotic impact of the dance is intensified by the nudity of the performers. As Judge Posner argued in his thoughtful concurring opinion in the Court of Appeals, the nudity of the dancer is an integral part of the emotions and thoughts that a nude dancing performance evokes. The sight of a fully clothed, or even a partially clothed, dancer generally will have a far different impact on a spectator than that of a nude dancer, even if the same dance is performed. The nudity is itself an expressive component of the dance, not merely incidental 'conduct.'

"This being the case, it cannot be that the statutory prohibition is unrelated to expressive conduct. Since the State permits the dancers to perform if they wear pasties and G-strings but forbids nude dancing, it is precisely because of the distinctive, expressive content of the nude dancing performances at issue in this case that the State seeks to apply the statutory prohibition. It is only because nude dancing performances may generate emotions and feelings of eroticism and sensuality among the spectators that the State seeks to regulate such expressive activity, apparently on the assumption that creating or emphasizing such thoughts and ideas in the minds of the spectators may lead to increased prostitution and the degradation of women. But generating thoughts, ideas, and emotions is the essence of communication. The nudity element of nude dancing performances cannot be neatly pigeonholed as mere 'conduct' independent of any expressive component of the dance.[2] * * *

2. Justice Souter agrees with the Court that the third requirement of the *O'Brien* test is satisfied, but only because he is not certain that there is a causal connection between the message conveyed by nude dancing and the evils which the State is seeking to prevent. Justice Souter's analysis is at least as flawed as that of the Court. If Justice Souter is correct that there is no causal connection between the message conveyed by the nude dancing at issue here and the negative secondary effects that the State desires to regulate, the State does not have even a rational basis for its absolute prohibition on nude dancing that is admittedly expressive. Furthermore, if the real problem is the 'concentration of

"That the performances in the Kitty Kat Lounge may not be high art, to say the least, and may not appeal to the Court, is hardly an excuse for distorting and ignoring settled doctrine. The Court's assessment of the artistic merits of nude dancing performances should not be the determining factor in deciding this case.
* * *

"The Court and Justice Souter do not go beyond saying that the state interests asserted here are important and substantial. But even if there were compelling interests, the Indiana statute is not narrowly drawn. If the State is genuinely concerned with prostitution and associated evils, as Justice Souter seems to think, [it] can adopt restrictions that do not interfere with the expressiveness of nonobscene nude dancing performances. For instance, the State could perhaps require that, while performing, nude performers remain at all times a certain minimum distance from spectators, that nude entertainment be limited to certain hours, or even that establishments providing such entertainment be dispersed throughout the city. Cf. *Renton*. Likewise, the State clearly has the authority to criminalize prostitution and obscene behavior. Banning an entire category of expressive activity, however, generally does not satisfy the narrow tailoring requirement of strict First Amendment scrutiny. Furthermore, if nude dancing in barrooms, as compared with other establishments, is the most worrisome problem, the State could invoke its Twenty-first Amendment powers and impose appropriate regulation.

"As I see it, our cases require us to affirm absent a compelling state interest supporting the statute. Neither the Court nor the State suggest that the statute could withstand scrutiny under that standard.

"Justice Scalia's views are similar to those of the Court and suffer from the same defects. The Justice asserts that a general law barring specified conduct does not implicate the First Amendment unless the purpose of the law is to suppress the expressive quality of the forbidden conduct, and that, absent such purpose, First Amendment protections are not triggered simply because the incidental effect of the law is to proscribe conduct that is unquestionably expressive. Cf. *Community for Creative Non–Violence v. Watt*, 703 F.2d 586, 622–623 (D.C.Cir.1983) (Scalia, J., dissenting). The application of the Justice's proposition to this case is simple to state: The statute at issue is a general law banning nude appearances in public places, including barrooms and theaters. There is no showing that the purpose of this general law was to regulate expressive conduct; hence, the First Amendment is irrelevant and nude dancing in theaters and barrooms may be forbidden, irrespective of the expressiveness of the dancing. * * *

"[T]he premise for the Justice's position—that the statute is a *general* law of the type our cases contemplate—is nonexistent in this case. Reference to Justice Scalia's own hypothetical makes this clear. We agree with Justice Scalia that the Indiana statute would not permit 60,000 consenting Hoosiers to expose themselves to each other in the Hoosierdome. No one can doubt, however, that those same 60,000 Hoosiers would be perfectly free to drive to their respective homes all across Indiana and, once there, to parade around, cavort, and revel in the nude for hours in front of relatives and friends. It is difficult to see why the State's interest in morality is any less in that situation, especially if, as Justice Scalia seems to suggest, nudity is inherently evil, but clearly the statute does not

crowds of men predisposed to the' designated evils, then the First Amendment requires that the State address that problem in a fashion that does not include banning an entire category of expressive activity. See *Renton*.

reach such activity. As we pointed out earlier, the State's failure to enact a truly general proscription requires closer scrutiny of the reasons for the distinctions the State has drawn."

[NEW SECTION]: CONCEIVING AND RECONCEIVING THE STRUCTURE OF FIRST AMENDMENT DOCTRINE: HATE SPEECH REVISITED—AGAIN

CON LAW: P. 869, after note 3

AMER CON: P. 650, after note 3

RTS & LIB: P. 598, after note 3

R.A.V. v. ST. PAUL
___ U.S. ___, 112 S.Ct. 2538, ___ L.Ed.2d ___ (1992).

JUSTICE SCALIA delivered the opinion of the Court.

In the predawn hours of June 21, 1990, petitioner and several other teenagers allegedly assembled a crudely-made cross by taping together broken chair legs. They then allegedly burned the cross inside the fenced yard of a black family that lived across the street from the house where petitioner was staying. Although this conduct could have been punished under any of a number of laws, one of the two provisions under which respondent city of St. Paul chose to charge petitioner (then a juvenile) was the St. Paul Bias-Motivated Crime Ordinance, St. Paul, Minn.Legis.Code § 292.02 (1990), which provides:

"Whoever places on public or private property a symbol, object, appellation, characterization or graffiti, including, but not limited to, a burning cross or Nazi swastika, which one knows or has reasonable grounds to know arouses anger, alarm or resentment in others on the basis of race, color, creed, religion or gender commits disorderly conduct and shall be guilty of a misdemeanor." * * *

I

In construing the St. Paul ordinance, we are bound by the construction given to it by the Minnesota court. Accordingly, we accept the Minnesota Supreme Court's authoritative statement that the ordinance reaches only those expressions that constitute "fighting words" within the meaning of *Chaplinsky*. Petitioner and his *amici* urge us to modify the scope of the *Chaplinsky* formulation, thereby invalidating the ordinance as "substantially overbroad," *Broadrick v. Oklahoma*. We find it unnecessary to consider this issue. Assuming, *arguendo*, that all of the expression reached by the ordinance is proscribable under the "fighting words" doctrine, we nonetheless conclude that the ordinance is facially unconstitutional in that it prohibits otherwise permitted speech solely on the basis of the subjects the speech addresses.

[From] 1791 to the present, our society, like other free but civilized societies, has permitted restrictions upon the content of speech in a few limited areas, which are "of such slight social value as a step to truth that any benefit that may be derived from them is clearly outweighed by the social interest in order and morality." *Chaplinsky*. * * *

We have sometimes said that these categories of expression are "not within the area of constitutionally protected speech," *Roth; Beauharnais; Chaplinsky;* or that the "protection of the First Amendment does not extend" to them, *Bose*

Corp. v. Consumers Union of United States, Inc.; Sable Communications of Cal., Inc. v. FCC. Such statements must be taken in context, however, and are no more literally true than is the occasionally repeated shorthand characterizing obscenity "as not being speech at all," Sunstein, *Pornography and the First Amendment,* 1986 Duke L.J. 589, 615, n. 146. What they mean is that these areas of speech can, consistently with the First Amendment, be regulated *because of their constitutionally proscribable content* (obscenity, defamation, etc.)—not that they are categories of speech entirely invisible to the Constitution, so that they may be made the vehicles for content discrimination unrelated to their distinctively proscribable content. Thus, the government may proscribe libel; but it may not make the further content discrimination of proscribing *only* libel critical of the government. * * *

Our cases surely do not establish the proposition that the First Amendment imposes no obstacle whatsoever to regulation of particular instances of such proscribable expression, so that the government "may regulate [them] freely," (White, J., concurring in judgment). That would mean that a city council could enact an ordinance prohibiting only those legally obscene works that contain criticism of the city government or, indeed, that do not include endorsement of the city government. Such a simplistic, all-or-nothing-at-all approach to First Amendment protection is at odds with common sense and with our jurisprudence as well.[4] It is not true that "fighting words" have at most a *"de minimis"* expressive content or that their content is *in all respects* "worthless and undeserving of constitutional protection"; sometimes they are quite expressive indeed. We have not said that they constitute *"no* part of the expression of ideas," but only that they constitute "no *essential* part of any exposition of ideas." *Chaplinsky.*

The proposition that a particular instance of speech can be proscribable on the basis of one feature (*e.g.,* obscenity) but not on the basis of another (*e.g.,* opposition to the city government) is commonplace, and has found application in many contexts. We have long held, for example, that nonverbal expressive activity can be banned because of the action it entails, but not because of the ideas it expresses—so that burning a flag in violation of an ordinance against outdoor fires could be punishable, whereas burning a flag in violation of an ordinance against dishonoring the flag is not. See *Johnson.* See also *Barnes v. Glen Theatre, Inc.* (Scalia, J., concurring in judgment) (Souter, J., concurring in judgment); *United States v. O'Brien.* Similarly, we have upheld reasonable "time, place, or manner" restrictions, but only if they are "justified without reference to the content of the regulated speech." *Ward v. Rock Against Racism;* see also *Clark v. Community for Creative Non–Violence* (noting that the *O'Brien* test differs little from the standard applied to time, place, or manner restrictions). And just as the power to proscribe particular speech on the basis of a noncontent element (*e.g.,* noise) does not entail the power to proscribe the same speech on the basis of a content element; so also, the power to proscribe it

---

4. Justice White concedes that a city council cannot prohibit only those legally obscene works that contain criticism of the city government, but asserts that to be the consequence, not of the First Amendment, but of the Equal Protection Clause. Such content-based discrimination would not, he asserts, "be rationally related to a legitimate government interest." But of course the only *reason* that government interest is not a "legitimate" one is that it violates the First Amendment. This Court itself has occasionally fused the First Amendment into the Equal Protection Clause in this fashion, but at least with the acknowledgment (which Justice White cannot afford to make) that the First Amendment underlies its analysis. * * *

on the basis of *one* content element (*e.g.,* obscenity) does not entail the power to proscribe it on the basis of *other* content elements.

In other words, the exclusion of "fighting words" from the scope of the First Amendment simply means that, for purposes of that Amendment, the unprotected features of the words are, despite their verbal character, essentially a "nonspeech" element of communication. Fighting words are thus analogous to a noisy sound truck: Each is, as Justice Frankfurter recognized, a "mode of speech," *Niemotko v. Maryland,* 340 U.S. 268, 71 S.Ct. 325, 95 L.Ed. 267 (1951) (Frankfurter, J., concurring in result); both can be used to convey an idea; but neither has, in and of itself, a claim upon the First Amendment. As with the sound truck, however, so also with fighting words: The government may not regulate use based on hostility—or favoritism—towards the underlying message expressed.

The concurrences describe us as setting forth a new First Amendment principle that prohibition of constitutionally proscribable speech cannot be "underinclusiv[e]" (White, J., concurring in judgment)—a First Amendment "absolutism" whereby "within a particular 'proscribable' category of expression, * * * a government must either proscribe *all* speech or no speech at all" (Stevens, J., concurring in judgment). That easy target is of the concurrences' own invention. In our view, the First Amendment imposes not an "underinclusiveness" limitation but a "content discrimination" limitation upon a State's prohibition of proscribable speech. There is no problem whatever, for example, with a State's prohibiting obscenity (and other forms of proscribable expression) only in certain media or markets, for although that prohibition would be "underinclusive," it would not discriminate on the basis of content. See, *e.g., Sable Communications* (upholding 47 U.S.C. § 223(b)(1) (1988), which prohibits obscene *telephone* communications).

Even the prohibition against content discrimination that we assert the First Amendment requires is not absolute. It applies differently in the context of proscribable speech than in the area of fully protected speech. The rationale of the general prohibition, after all, is that content discrimination "rais[es] the specter that the Government may effectively drive certain ideas or viewpoints from the marketplace," *Simon & Schuster.* But content discrimination among various instances of a class of proscribable speech often does not pose this threat.

When the basis for the content discrimination consists entirely of the very reason the entire class of speech at issue is proscribable, no significant danger of idea or viewpoint discrimination exists. Such a reason, having been adjudged neutral enough to support exclusion of the entire class of speech from First Amendment protection, is also neutral enough to form the basis of distinction within the class. To illustrate: A State might choose to prohibit only that obscenity which is the most patently offensive *in its prurience*—*i.e.,* that which involves the most lascivious displays of sexual activity. But it may not prohibit, for example, only that obscenity which includes offensive *political* messages. And the Federal Government can criminalize only those threats of violence that are directed against the President, see 18 U.S.C. § 871—since the reasons why threats of violence are outside the First Amendment (protecting individuals from the fear of violence, from the disruption that fear engenders, and from the possibility that the threatened violence will occur) have special force when applied to the person of the President. See *Watts v. United States* (upholding the facial validity of § 871 because of the "overwhelmin[g] interest in protecting the safety of [the] Chief Executive and in allowing him to perform his duties without interference from threats of physical violence"). But the Federal

Government may not criminalize only those threats against the President that mention his policy on aid to inner cities. And to take a final example (one mentioned by Justice Stevens), a State may choose to regulate price advertising in one industry but not in others, because the risk of fraud (one of the characteristics of commercial speech that justifies depriving it of full First Amendment protection) is in its view greater there. Cf. *Morales v. Trans World Airlines, Inc.,* ___ U.S. ___, 112 S.Ct. 2031, ___ L.Ed.2d ___ (1992) (state regulation of airline advertising); *Ohralik v. Ohio State Bar Assn.* (state regulation of lawyer advertising). But a State may not prohibit only that commercial advertising that depicts men in a demeaning fashion, see, *e.g.,* L.A. Times, Aug. 8, 1989, section 4, p. 6, col. 1.

Another valid basis for according differential treatment to even a content-defined subclass of proscribable speech is that the subclass happens to be associated with particular "secondary effects" of the speech, so that the regulation is "*justified* without reference to the content of the * * * speech," *Renton v. Playtime Theatres, Inc.* A State could, for example, permit all obscene live performances except those involving minors. Moreover, since words can in some circumstances violate laws directed not against speech but against conduct (a law against treason, for example, is violated by telling the enemy the nation's defense secrets), a particular content-based subcategory of a proscribable class of speech can be swept up incidentally within the reach of a statute directed at conduct rather than speech. Thus, for example, sexually derogatory "fighting words," among other words, may produce a violation of Title VII's general prohibition against sexual discrimination in employment practices. Where the government does not target conduct on the basis of its expressive content, acts are not shielded from regulation merely because they express a discriminatory idea or philosophy.

These bases for distinction refute the proposition that the selectivity of the restriction is "even arguably 'conditioned upon the sovereign's agreement with what a speaker may intend to say.'" There may be other such bases as well. Indeed, to validate such selectivity (where totally proscribable speech is at issue) it may not even be necessary to identify any particular "neutral" basis, so long as the nature of the content discrimination is such that there is no realistic possibility that official suppression of ideas is afoot. (We cannot think of any First Amendment interest that would stand in the way of a State's prohibiting only those obscene motion pictures with blue-eyed actresses.) Save for that limitation, the regulation of "fighting words," like the regulation of noisy speech, may address some offensive instances and leave other, equally offensive, instances alone. See *Posadas de Puerto Rico.*[6]

II

Applying these principles to the St. Paul ordinance, we conclude that, even as narrowly construed by the Minnesota Supreme Court, the ordinance is facially unconstitutional. Although the phrase in the ordinance, "arouses anger, alarm or resentment in others," has been limited by the Minnesota Supreme Court's construction to reach only those symbols or displays that amount to "fighting words," the remaining, unmodified terms make clear that the ordi-

---

6. Justice Stevens cites a string of opinions as supporting his assertion that "selective regulation of speech based on content" is not presumptively invalid. [A]ll that their contents establish is what we readily concede: that presumptive invalidity does not mean invariable invalidity, leaving room for such exceptions as reasonable and viewpoint-neutral content-based discrimination in nonpublic forums, or with respect to certain speech by government employees.

nance applies only to "fighting words" that insult, or provoke violence, "on the basis of race, color, creed, religion or gender." Displays containing abusive invective, no matter how vicious or severe, are permissible unless they are addressed to one of the specified disfavored topics. Those who wish to use "fighting words" in connection with other ideas—to express hostility, for example, on the basis of political affiliation, union membership, or homosexuality—are not covered. The First Amendment does not permit St. Paul to impose special prohibitions on those speakers who express views on disfavored subjects.

In its practical operation, moreover, the ordinance goes even beyond mere content discrimination, to actual viewpoint discrimination. Displays containing some words—odious racial epithets, for example—would be prohibited to proponents of all views. But "fighting words" that do not themselves invoke race, color, creed, religion, or gender—aspersions upon a person's mother, for example—would seemingly be usable *ad libitum* in the placards of those arguing *in favor* of racial, color, etc. tolerance and equality, but could not be used by that speaker's opponents. One could hold up a sign saying, for example, that all "anti-Catholic bigots" are misbegotten; but not that all "papists" are, for that would insult and provoke violence "on the basis of religion." St. Paul has no such authority to license one side of a debate to fight freestyle, while requiring the other to follow Marquis of Queensbury Rules.

What we have here, it must be emphasized, is not a prohibition of fighting words that are directed at certain persons or groups (which would be *facially* valid if it met the requirements of the Equal Protection Clause); but rather, a prohibition of fighting words that contain (as the Minnesota Supreme Court repeatedly emphasized) messages of "bias-motivated" hatred and in particular, as applied to this case, messages "based on virulent notions of racial supremacy." One must wholeheartedly agree with the Minnesota Supreme Court that "[i]t is the responsibility, even the obligation, of diverse communities to confront such notions in whatever form they appear," but the manner of that confrontation cannot consist of selective limitations upon speech. St. Paul's brief asserts that a general "fighting words" law would not meet the city's needs because only a content-specific measure can communicate to minority groups that the "group hatred" aspect of such speech "is not condoned by the majority." The point of the First Amendment is that majority preferences must be expressed in some fashion other than silencing speech on the basis of its content. * * *

[T]he reason why fighting words are categorically excluded from the protection of the First Amendment is not that their content communicates any particular idea, but that their content embodies a particularly intolerable (and socially unnecessary) *mode* of expressing *whatever* idea the speaker wishes to convey. St. Paul has not singled out an especially offensive mode of expression—it has not, for example, selected for prohibition only those fighting words that communicate ideas in a threatening (as opposed to a merely obnoxious) manner. Rather, it has proscribed fighting words of whatever manner that communicate messages of racial, gender, or religious intolerance. Selectivity of this sort creates the possibility that the city is seeking to handicap the expression of particular ideas.

[St.] Paul argues that the ordinance comes within another of the specific exceptions we mentioned, the one that allows content discrimination aimed only at the "secondary effects" of the speech, see *Renton v. Playtime Theatres, Inc.* According to St. Paul, the ordinance is intended, "not to impact on *[sic]* the right of free expression of the accused," but rather to "protect against the victimization of a person or persons who are particularly vulnerable because of their membership in a group that historically has been discriminated against." Even assuming that an ordinance that completely proscribes, rather than merely regulates, a specified category of speech can ever be considered to be directed only to the secondary effects of such speech, it is clear that the St. Paul ordinance is not directed to secondary effects within the meaning of *Renton*. As we said in *Boos v. Barry*, "[l]isteners' reactions to speech are not the type of 'secondary effects' we referred to in *Renton*." * * *[7]

Finally, St. Paul and its *amici* defend the conclusion of the Minnesota Supreme Court that, even if the ordinance regulates expression based on hostility towards its protected ideological content, this discrimination is nonetheless justified because it is narrowly tailored to serve compelling state interests. Specifically, they assert that the ordinance helps to ensure the basic human rights of members of groups that have historically been subjected to discrimination, including the right of such group members to live in peace where they wish. We do not doubt that these interests are compelling, and that the ordinance can be said to promote them. But the "danger of censorship" presented by a facially content-based statute requires that that weapon be employed only where it is "*necessary* to serve the asserted [compelling] interest,". The existence of adequate content-neutral alternatives thus "undercut[s] significantly" any defense of such a statute, casting considerable doubt on the government's protestations that "the asserted justification is in fact an accurate description of the purpose and effect of the law." The dispositive question in this case, therefore, is whether content discrimination is reasonably necessary to achieve St. Paul's compelling interests; it plainly is not. An ordinance not limited to the favored topics, for example, would have precisely the same beneficial effect. In fact the only interest distinctively served by the content limitation is that of displaying the city council's special hostility towards the particular biases thus singled out. That is precisely what the First Amendment forbids. The politicians of St. Paul are entitled to express that hostility—but not through the means of imposing unique limitations upon speakers who (however benightedly) disagree.

* * *

Let there be no mistake about our belief that burning a cross in someone's front yard is reprehensible. But St. Paul has sufficient means at its disposal to prevent such behavior without adding the First Amendment to the fire. * * *

JUSTICE WHITE, with whom JUSTICE BLACKMUN and JUSTICE O'CONNOR join, and with whom JUSTICE STEVENS joins except as to Part I(A), concurring in the judgment. * * *

Today [the] Court announces that earlier Courts did not mean their repeated statements that certain categories of expression are "not within the area of constitutionally protected speech." *Roth*. The present Court submits that such clear statements "must be taken in context" and are not "literally true."

To the contrary, those statements meant precisely what they said: The categorical approach is a firmly entrenched part of our First Amendment jurisprudence. * * * Nevertheless, the majority holds that the First Amend-

---

7. St. Paul has not argued in this case that the ordinance merely regulates that subclass of fighting words which is most likely to provoke a violent response. But even if one assumes (as appears unlikely) that the categories selected may be so described, that would not justify selective regulation under a "secondary effects" theory. The only reason why such expressive conduct would be especially correlated with violence is that it conveys a particularly odious message; because the "chain of causation" thus *necessarily* "run[s] through the persuasive effect of the expressive component" of the conduct, it is clear that the St. Paul ordinance regulates on the basis of the "primary" effect of the speech—*i.e.*, its persuasive (or repellant) force.

ment protects those narrow categories of expression long held to be undeserving of First Amendment protection—at least to the extent that lawmakers may not regulate some fighting words more strictly than others because of their content. The Court announces that such content-based distinctions violate the First Amendment because "the government may not regulate use based on hostility—or favoritism—towards the underlying message expressed." Should the government want to criminalize certain fighting words, the Court now requires it to criminalize all fighting words.

To borrow a phrase, "Such a simplistic, all-or-nothing-at-all approach to First Amendment protection is at odds with common sense and with our jurisprudence as well." It is inconsistent to hold that the government may proscribe an entire category of speech because the content of that speech is evil, but that the government may not treat a subset of that category differently without violating the First Amendment; the content of the subset is by definition worthless and undeserving of constitutional protection.

The majority's observation that fighting words are "quite expressive indeed," is no answer. Fighting words are not a means of exchanging views, rallying supporters, or registering a protest; they are directed against individuals to provoke violence or to inflict injury. Therefore, a ban on all fighting words or on a subset of the fighting words category would restrict only the social evil of hate speech, without creating the danger of driving viewpoints from the marketplace.

Therefore, the Court's insistence on inventing its brand of First Amendment underinclusiveness puzzles me.[3] [T]he Court's new "underbreadth" creation serves no desirable function. Instead, it permits, indeed invites, the continuation of expressive conduct that in this case is evil and worthless in First Amendment terms until the city of St. Paul cures the underbreadth by adding to its ordinance a catch-all phrase such as "and all other fighting words that may constitutionally be subject to this ordinance."

Any contribution of this holding to First Amendment jurisprudence is surely a negative one, since it necessarily signals that expressions of violence, such as the message of intimidation and racial hatred conveyed by burning a cross on someone's lawn, are of sufficient value to outweigh the social interest in order and morality that has traditionally placed such fighting words outside the First Amendment.[4] Indeed, by characterizing fighting words as a form of "debate" the majority legitimates hate speech as a form of public discussion. * * *

B

* * * The majority appears to believe that its doctrinal revisionism is necessary to prevent our elected lawmakers from prohibiting libel against members of one political party but not another and from enacting similarly preposterous laws. The majority is misguided.

Although the First Amendment does not apply to categories of unprotected speech, such as fighting words, the Equal Protection Clause requires that the regulation of unprotected speech be rationally related to a legitimate govern-

---

3. The assortment of exceptions the Court attaches to its rule belies the majority's claim that its new theory is truly concerned with content discrimination. See Part I(C), infra (discussing the exceptions).

4. This does not suggest, of course, that cross burning is always unprotected. Burning a cross at a political rally would almost certainly be protected expression. Cf. *Brandenburg v. Ohio*. But in such a context, the cross burning could not be characterized as a "direct personal insult or an invitation to exchange fisticuffs," *Texas v. Johnson*, to which the fighting words doctrine, see Part II, infra, applies.

ment interest. A defamation statute that drew distinctions on the basis of political affiliation or "an ordinance prohibiting only those legally obscene works that contain criticism of the city government" would unquestionably fail rational basis review.[9]

Turning to the St. Paul ordinance and assuming *arguendo,* as the majority does, that the ordinance is not constitutionally overbroad (but see Part II, *infra*), there is no question that it would pass equal protection review. The ordinance proscribes a subset of "fighting words," those that injure "on the basis of race, color, creed, religion or gender." This selective regulation reflects the City's judgment that harms based on race, color, creed, religion, or gender are more pressing public concerns than the harms caused by other fighting words. In light of our Nation's long and painful experience with discrimination, this determination is plainly reasonable. Indeed, as the majority concedes, the interest is compelling.

C

The Court has patched up its argument with an apparently nonexhaustive list of ad hoc exceptions, in what can be viewed either as an attempt to confine the effects of its decision to the facts of this case, or as an effort to anticipate some of the questions that will arise from its radical revision of First Amendment law.

For instance, if the majority were to give general application to the rule on which it decides this case, today's decision would call into question the constitutionality of the statute making it illegal to threaten the life of the President. Surely, this statute, by singling out certain threats, incorporates a content-based distinction; it indicates that the Government especially disfavors threats against the President as opposed to threats against all others.[10] But because the Government could prohibit all threats and not just those directed against the President, under the Court's theory, the compelling reasons justifying the enactment of special legislation to safeguard the President would be irrelevant, and the statute would fail First Amendment review.

To save the statute, the majority has engrafted the following exception onto its newly announced First Amendment rule: Content-based distinctions may be drawn within an unprotected category of speech if the basis for the distinctions is "the very reason the entire class of speech at issue is proscribable." Thus, the argument goes, the statute making it illegal to threaten the life of the President is constitutional, "since the reasons why threats of violence are outside the First Amendment (protecting individuals from the fear of violence, from the disruption that fear engenders, and from the possibility that the threatened violence will occur) have special force when applied to the person of the President."

The exception swallows the majority's rule. Certainly, it should apply to the St. Paul ordinance, since "the reasons why [fighting words] are outside the First

---

9. The majority is mistaken in stating that a ban on obscene works critical of government would fail equal protection review only because the ban would violate the First Amendment. While decisions such as *Police Dept. of Chicago v. Mosley,* 408 U.S. 92 (1972), recognize that First Amendment principles may be relevant to an equal protection claim challenging distinctions that impact on protected expression, there is no basis for linking First and Fourteenth Amendment analysis in a case involving unprotected expression. Certainly, one need not resort to First Amendment principles to conclude that the sort of improbable legislation the majority hypothesizes is based on senseless distinctions.

10. Indeed, such a law is content-based in and of itself because it distinguishes between threatening and nonthreatening speech.

Amendment * * * have special force when applied to [groups that have historically been subjected to discrimination]."

To avoid the result of its own analysis, the Court suggests that fighting words are simply a mode of communication, rather than a content-based category, and that the St. Paul ordinance has not singled out a particularly objectionable mode of communication. Again, the majority confuses the issue. A prohibition on fighting words is not a time, place, or manner restriction; it is a ban on a class of speech that conveys an overriding message of personal injury and imminent violence, a message that is at its ugliest when directed against groups that have long been the targets of discrimination. Accordingly, the ordinance falls within the first exception to the majority's theory.

As its second exception, the Court posits that certain content-based regulations will survive under the new regime if the regulated subclass "happens to be associated with particular 'secondary effects' of the speech * * *" which the majority treats as encompassing instances in which "words can * * * violate laws directed not against speech but against conduct * * *".[11] Again, there is a simple explanation for the Court's eagerness to craft an exception to its new First Amendment rule: Under the general rule the Court applies in this case, Title VII hostile work environment claims would suddenly be unconstitutional.

Title VII makes it unlawful to discriminate "because of [an] individual's race, color, religion, sex, or national origin," 42 U.S.C. § 2000e–2(a)(1), and the regulations covering hostile workplace claims forbid "sexual harassment," which includes "[u]nwelcome sexual advances, requests for sexual favors, and other verbal or physical conduct of a sexual nature" which creates "an intimidating, hostile, or offensive working environment." The regulation does not prohibit workplace harassment generally; it focuses on what the majority would characterize as the "disfavored topi[c]" of sexual harassment. In this way, Title VII is similar to the St. Paul ordinance that the majority condemns because it "impose[s] special prohibitions on those speakers who express views on disfavored subjects." Under the broad principle the Court uses to decide the present case, hostile work environment claims based on sexual harassment should fail First Amendment review; because a general ban on harassment in the workplace would cover the problem of sexual harassment, any attempt to proscribe the subcategory of sexually harassing expression would violate the First Amendment.

Hence, the majority's second exception, which the Court indicates would insulate a Title VII hostile work environment claim from an underinclusiveness challenge because "sexually derogatory 'fighting words' * * * may produce a violation of Title VII's general prohibition against sexual discrimination in employment practices." But application of this exception to a hostile work environment claim does not hold up under close examination.

First, the hostile work environment regulation is not keyed to the presence or absence of an economic *quid pro quo,* but to the impact of the speech on the victimized worker. Consequently, the regulation would no more fall within a secondary effects exception than does the St. Paul ordinance. Second, the majority's focus on the statute's general prohibition on discrimination glosses over the language of the specific regulation governing hostile working environment, which reaches beyond any "incidental" effect on speech. If the relation-

---

11. The consequences of the majority's conflation of the rarely-used secondary effects standard and the *O'Brien* test for conduct incorporating "speech" and "nonspeech" elements, see generally *United States v. O'Brien,* present another question that I fear will haunt us and the lower courts in the aftermath of the majority's opinion.

ship between the broader statute and specific regulation is sufficent to bring the Title VII regulation within *O'Brien,* then all St. Paul need do to bring its ordinance within this exception is to add some prefatory language concerning discrimination generally.

As the third exception to the Court's theory for deciding this case, the majority concocts a catchall exclusion to protect against unforeseen problems. * * * This final exception would apply in cases in which "there is no realistic possibility that official suppression of ideas is afoot." As I have demonstrated, this case does not concern the official suppression of ideas. The majority discards this notion out-of-hand.

As I see it, the Court's theory does not work and will do nothing more than confuse the law. Its selection of this case to rewrite First Amendment law is particularly inexplicable, because the whole problem could have been avoided by deciding this case under settled First Amendment principles.

II

Although I disagree with the Court's analysis, I do agree with its conclusion: The St. Paul ordinance is unconstitutional. However, I would decide the case on overbreadth grounds. * * *

In construing the St. Paul ordinance, the Minnesota Supreme Court drew upon the definition of fighting words that appears in *Chaplinsky*—words "which by their very utterance inflict injury or tend to incite an immediate breach of the peace." However, the Minnesota court was far from clear in identifying the "injur[ies]" inflicted by the expression that St. Paul sought to regulate. Indeed, the Minnesota court emphasized (tracking the language of the ordinance) that "the ordinance censors only those displays that one knows or should know will create anger, alarm or resentment based on racial, ethnic, gender or religious bias." I therefore understand the court to have ruled that St. Paul may constitutionally prohibit expression that "by its very utterance" causes "anger, alarm or resentment."

Our fighting words cases have made clear, however, that such generalized reactions are not sufficient to strip expression of its constitutional protection. The mere fact that expressive activity causes hurt feelings, offense, or resentment does not render the expression unprotected. See *United States v. Eichman,* 496 U.S. 310, 319 (1990); *Texas v. Johnson,* 491 U.S. 397, 409, 414 (1989); *Hustler Magazine, Inc. v. Falwell,* 485 U.S. 46, 55–56 (1988). * * * Although the ordinance reaches conduct that is unprotected, it also makes criminal expressive conduct that causes only hurt feelings, offense, or resentment, and is protected by the First Amendment. Cf. *Lewis, supra,* at 132.[13] The ordinance is therefore fatally overbroad and invalid on its face.

JUSTICE BLACKMUN, concurring in the judgment.

I regret what the Court has done in this case. The majority opinion signals one of two possibilities: it will serve as precedent for future cases, or it will not. Either result is disheartening.

In the first instance, by deciding that a State cannot regulate speech that causes great harm unless it also regulates speech that does not (setting law and

---

13. Although the First Amendment protects offensive speech, it does not require us to be subjected to such expression at all times, in all settings. We have held that such expression may be proscribed when it intrudes upon a "captive audience." And expression may be limited when it merges into conduct. *United States v. O'Brien,* 391 U.S. 367 (1968). However, because of the manner in which the Minnesota Supreme Court construed the St. Paul ordinance, those issues are not before us in this case.

logic on their heads), the Court seems to abandon the categorical approach, and inevitably to relax the level of scrutiny applicable to content-based laws. [T]his weakens the traditional protections of speech. If all expressive activity must be accorded the same protection, that protection will be scant. The simple reality is that the Court will never provide child pornography or cigarette advertising the level of protection customarily granted political speech. If we are forbidden from categorizing, as the Court has done here, we shall reduce protection across the board. It is sad that in its effort to reach a satisfying result in this case, the Court is willing to weaken First Amendment protections.

In the second instance is the possibility that this case will not significantly alter First Amendment jurisprudence, but, instead, will be regarded as an aberration—a case where the Court manipulated doctrine to strike down an ordinance whose premise it opposed, namely, that racial threats and verbal assaults are of greater harm than other fighting words. I fear that the Court has been distracted from its proper mission by the temptation to decide the issue over "politically correct speech" and "cultural diversity," neither of which is presented here. If this is the meaning of today's opinion, it is perhaps even more regrettable.

I see no First Amendment values that are compromised by a law that prohibits hoodlums from driving minorities out of their homes by burning crosses on their lawns, but I see great harm in preventing the people of Saint Paul from specifically punishing the race-based fighting words that so prejudice their community.

I concur in the judgment, however, because I agree with Justice White that this particular ordinance reaches beyond fighting words to speech protected by the First Amendment.

JUSTICE STEVENS, with whom JUSTICE WHITE and JUSTICE BLACKMUN join as to Part I, concurring in the judgment.

Conduct that creates special risks or causes special harms may be prohibited by special rules. Lighting a fire near an ammunition dump or a gasoline storage tank is especially dangerous; such behavior may be punished more severely than burning trash in a vacant lot. Threatening someone because of her race or religious beliefs may cause particularly severe trauma or touch off a riot, and threatening a high public official may cause substantial social disruption; such threats may be punished more severely than threats against someone based on, say, his support of a particular athletic team. There are legitimate, reasonable, and neutral justifications for such special rules.

This case involves the constitutionality of one such ordinance. * * *

I

* * * Our First Amendment decisions have created a rough hierarchy in the constitutional protection of speech. Core political speech occupies the highest, most protected position; commercial speech and nonobscene, sexually explicit speech are regarded as a sort of second-class expression; obscenity and fighting words receive the least protection of all. Assuming that the Court is correct that this last class of speech is not wholly "unprotected," it certainly does not follow that fighting words and obscenity receive the *same* sort of protection afforded core political speech. Yet in ruling that proscribable speech cannot be regulated based on subject matter, the Court does just that. Perversely, this gives fighting words *greater* protection than is afforded commercial speech. If Congress can prohibit false advertising directed at airline passengers without

also prohibiting false advertising directed at bus passengers and if a city can prohibit political advertisements in its buses while allowing other advertisements, it is ironic to hold that a city cannot regulate fighting words based on "race, color, creed, religion or gender" while leaving unregulated fighting words based on "union membership or homosexuality." The Court today turns First Amendment law on its head: Communication that was once entirely unprotected (and that still can be wholly proscribed) is now entitled to greater protection than commercial speech—and possibly greater protection than core political speech. See *Burson v. Freeman,* [in this Supplement infra].

Perhaps because the Court recognizes these perversities, it quickly offers some ad hoc limitations on its newly extended prohibition on content-based regulations.[a]

[T]he Court recognizes that a State may regulate advertising in one industry but not another because "the risk of fraud (one of the characteristics that justifies depriving [commercial speech] of full First Amendment protection . . .)" in the regulated industry is "greater" than in other industries. [T]he same reasoning demonstrates the constitutionality of St. Paul's ordinance. "[O]ne of the characteristics that justifies" the constitutional status of fighting words is that such words "by their very utterance inflict injury or tend to incite an immediate breach of the peace." *Chaplinsky.* Certainly a legislature that may determine that the risk of fraud is greater in the legal trade than in the medical trade may determine that the risk of injury or breach of peace created by race-based threats is greater than that created by other threats.

Similarly, it is impossible to reconcile the Court's analysis of the St. Paul ordinance with its recognition that "a prohibition of fighting words that are directed at certain persons or groups * * * would be facially valid." A selective proscription of unprotected expression designed to protect "certain persons or groups" (for example, a law proscribing threats directed at the elderly) would be constitutional if it were based on a legitimate determination that the harm created by the regulated expression differs from that created by the unregulated expression (that is, if the elderly are more severely injured by threats than are the nonelderly). Such selective protection is no different from a law prohibiting minors (and only minors) from obtaining obscene publications. St. Paul has determined—reasonably in my judgment—that fighting-word injuries "based on race, color, creed, religion or gender" are qualitatively different and more severe than fighting-word injuries based on other characteristics. Whether the selective proscription of proscribable speech is defined by the protected target ("certain persons or groups") or the basis of the harm (injuries "based on race, color, creed, religion or gender") makes no constitutional differ-

---

a. In an earlier passage and footnote of his opinion, Stevens, J., argued: "[W]hile the Court rejects the "all-or-nothing-at-all" nature of the categorical approach, it promptly embraces an absolutism of its own: within a particular "proscribable" category of expression, the Court holds, a government must either proscribe all speech or no speech at all. The Court disputes this characterization because it has crafted two exceptions, one for "certain media or markets" and the other for content discrimination based upon "the very reason that the entire class of speech at issue is proscribable." These exceptions are, at best, ill-defined. The Court does not tell us whether, with respect to the former, fighting words such as cross-burning could be proscribed only in certain neighborhoods where the threat of violence is particularly severe, or whether, with respect to the second category, fighting words that create a particular risk of harm (such as a race riot) would be proscribable. The hypothetical and illusory category of these two exceptions persuades me that either my description of the Court's analysis is accurate or that the Court does not in fact mean much of what it says in its opinion."

ence: what matters is whether the legislature's selection is based on a legitimate, neutral, and reasonable distinction.

In sum, the central premise of the Court's ruling—that "[c]ontent-based regulations are presumptively invalid"—has simplistic appeal, but lacks support in our First Amendment jurisprudence. To make matters worse, the Court today extends this overstated claim to reach categories of hitherto unprotected speech and, in doing so, wreaks havoc in an area of settled law. Finally, although the Court recognizes exceptions to its new principle, those exceptions undermine its very conclusion that the St. Paul ordinance is unconstitutional. Stated directly, the majority's position cannot withstand scrutiny. * * *

III

* * * Unlike the Court, I do not believe that all content-based regulations are equally infirm and presumptively invalid; unlike Justice White, I do not believe that fighting words are wholly unprotected by the First Amendment. To the contrary, I believe our decisions establish a more complex and subtle analysis, one that considers the content and context of the regulated speech, and the nature and scope of the restriction on speech. * * *

* * * Whatever the allure of absolute doctrines, it is just too simple to declare expression "protected" or "unprotected" or to proclaim a regulation "content-based" or "content-neutral."

In applying this analysis to the St. Paul ordinance, I assume *arguendo*—as the Court does—that the ordinance regulates *only* fighting words and therefore is *not* overbroad. Looking to the content and character of the regulated activity, two things are clear. First, by hypothesis the ordinance bars only low-value speech, namely, fighting words. By definition such expression constitutes "no essential part of any exposition of ideas, and [is] of such slight social value as a step to truth that any benefit that may be derived from [it] is clearly outweighed by the social interest in order and morality." *Chaplinsky*. Second, the ordinance regulates "expressive conduct [rather] than * * * the written or spoken word."

Looking to the context of the regulated activity, it is again significant that the statute (by hypothesis) regulates *only* fighting words. Whether words are fighting words is determined in part by their context. Fighting words are not words that merely cause offense; fighting words must be directed at individuals so as to "by their very utterance inflict injury." By hypothesis, then, the St. Paul ordinance restricts speech in confrontational and potentially violent situations. The case at hand is illustrative. The cross-burning in this case—directed as it was to a single African–American family trapped in their home—was nothing more than a crude form of physical intimidation. That this cross-burning sends a message of racial hostility does not automatically endow it with complete constitutional protection.

Significantly, the St. Paul ordinance regulates speech not on the basis of its subject matter or the viewpoint expressed, but rather on the basis of the *harm* the speech causes. * * * Contrary to the Court's suggestion, the ordinance regulates only a subcategory of expression that causes *injuries based on* "race, color, creed, religion or gender," not a subcategory that involves *discussions* that concern those characteristics.[9] The ordinance, as construed by the Court,

---

9. The Court contends that this distinction is "wordplay," reasoning that "[w]hat makes [the harms caused by race-based threats] distinct from [the harms] produced by other fighting words is * * * the fact that [the former are] caused by a *distinctive idea*." In this way, the Court concludes that regulating speech based on the injury it causes is no

criminalizes expression that "one knows * * * [by its very utterance inflicts injury on] others on the basis of race, color, creed, religion or gender." * * *

Finally, it is noteworthy that the St. Paul ordinance is, as construed by the Court today, quite narrow. The St. Paul ordinance does not ban all "hate speech," nor does it ban, say, all cross-burnings or all swastika displays. Rather it only bans a subcategory of the already narrow category of fighting words. Such a limited ordinance leaves open and protected a vast range of expression on the subjects of racial, religious, and gender equality. As construed by the Court today, the ordinance certainly does not "'raise the specter that the Government may effectively drive certain ideas or viewpoints from the marketplace.'" Petitioner is free to burn a cross to announce a rally or to express his views about racial supremacy, he may do so on private property or public land, at day or at night, so long as the burning is not so threatening and so directed at an individual as to "by its very [execution] inflict injury." Such a limited proscription scarcely offends the First Amendment.

In sum, the St. Paul ordinance (as construed by the Court) regulates expressive activity that is wholly proscribable and does so not on the basis of viewpoint, but rather in recognition of the different harms caused by such activity. Taken together, these several considerations persuade me that the St. Paul ordinance is not an unconstitutional content-based regulation of speech. Thus, were the ordinance not overbroad, I would vote to uphold it.

Notes and Questions

At the capital sentencing phase of a murder case, the prosecution sought to introduce evidence that the defendant was a member of the Aryan Brotherhood which was stipulated to be a "white racist gang." DAWSON v. DELAWARE, ___ U.S. ___, 112 S.Ct. 1093, 117 L.Ed.2d 309 (1992), per REHNQUIST, C.J., held that the admission of the evidence was irrelevant and concluded that its admission violated the first amendment: "Even if the Delaware group to which Dawson allegedly belongs is racist, those beliefs, so far as we can determine, had no relevance to the sentencing proceeding in this case. For example, the Aryan Brotherhood evidence was not tied in any way to the murder of Dawson's [white] victim. * * * Whatever label is given to the evidence presented, however, we conclude that Dawson's First Amendment rights were violated by the admission of the Aryan Brotherhood evidence in this case, because the evidence proved nothing more than Dawson's abstract beliefs. [Delaware] might have avoided this problem if it had presented evidence showing more than mere abstract beliefs on Dawson's part, but on the present record one is left with the feeling that the Aryan Brotherhood evidence was employed simply because the jury would find these beliefs morally reprehensible. Because Delaware failed to do more, we cannot find the evidence was properly admitted as relevant character evidence."

different from regulating speech based on its subject matter. This analysis fundamentally miscomprehends the role of "race, color, creed, religion [and] gender" in contemporary American society. One need look no further than the recent social unrest in the Nation's cities to see that race-based threats may cause more harm to society and to individuals than other threats. Just as the statute prohibiting threats against the President is justifiable because of the place of the President in our social and political order, so a statute prohibiting race-based threats is justifiable because of the place of race in our social and political order. Although it is regrettable that race occupies such a place and is so incendiary an issue, until the Nation matures beyond that condition, laws such as St. Paul's ordinance will remain reasonable and justifiable.

THOMAS, J., dissented: "Dawson introduced mitigating character evidence that he had acted kindly toward his family. The stipulation tended to undercut this showing by suggesting that Dawson's kindness did not extend to members of other racial groups. Although we do not sit in judgment of the morality of particular creeds, we cannot bend traditional concepts of relevance to exempt the antisocial."

SECTION: FAIR ADMINISTRATION OF JUSTICE AND THE FIRST AMENDMENT AS SWORD

JUSTICE AND THE FIRST AMENDMENT AS SHIELD

CON LAW: P. 901, after note 5

AMER CON: P. 672, after note 5

RTS & LIB: P. 630, after note 5

Nevada Supreme Court Rule 177(1) prohibits a lawyer from making extrajudicial statements to the press that he knows or reasonably should know will have a "substantial likelihood of materially prejudicing" an adjudicative proceeding. 177(2) lists a number of statements that are "ordinarily * * * likely" to result in material prejudice. 177(3) provides that: "Notwithstanding subsections 1 and [2], a lawyer involved in the investigation or litigation of a matter may state without elaboration * * * the general nature of the claim or defense."

Acting as an attorney for a client accused of stealing drugs, money, and traveler's checks, attorney Gentile stated: "I want to start this off by saying in clear terms that I think that this indictment is a significant event in the history of the evolution of sophistication of the City of Las Vegas, because things of this nature, of exactly this nature have happened in New York with the French connection case and in Miami with cases—at least two cases there—have happened in Chicago as well, but all three of those cities have been honest enough to indict the people who did it: the police department, crooked cops.

"When this case goes to trial, and as it develops, you're going to see that the evidence will prove not only that Grady Sanders is an innocent person and had nothing to do with any of the charges that are being leveled against him, but that the person that was in the most direct position to have stolen the drugs and money, the American Express Travelers' checks, is Detective Steve Scholl.

"There is far more evidence that will establish that Detective Scholl took these drugs and took these American Express Travelers' checks than any other living human being.

"And I have to say that I feel that Grady Sanders is being used as a scapegoat to try to cover up for what has to be obvious to people at Las Vegas Metropolitan Police Department and at the District Attorney's office."

The Disciplinary Board found that Gentile violated Rule 177 and recommended a private reprimand. The Nevada Supreme Court affirmed.

GENTILE v. STATE BAR, ___ U.S. ___, 111 S.Ct. 2720, 115 L.Ed.2d 888 (1991), per KENNEDY, J., reversed, holding that the Rule as interpreted by the Nevada Supreme Court was unconstitutionally vague.

In a portion of his opinion joined only by Marshall, Blackmun, and Stevens, JJ., Kennedy, J., also argued that "the substantial likelihood of material prejudice test" as interpreted by the Nevada Supreme Court did not meet first amendment standards: "The State Bar of Nevada reprimanded petitioner for his assertion, supported by a brief sketch of his client's defense, that the State sought the indictment and conviction of an innocent man as a 'scapegoat,' and had not 'been honest enough to indict the people who did it; the police department, crooked cops.' At issue here is the constitutionality of a ban on political speech critical of the government and its officials. * * *

"Unlike other First Amendment cases this Term in which speech is not the direct target of the regulation or statute in question, see, e.g., *Barnes v. Glen Theatre, Inc.,* [p. 26 of this Supplement] (ban on nude barroom dancing); *Leathers v. Medlock* [p. 42 of this Supplement] (sales tax on cable and satellite television), this case involves punishment of pure speech in the political forum. Petitioner engaged not in solicitation of clients or advertising for his practice, as in our precedents from which some of our colleagues would discern a standard of diminished First Amendment protection. His words were directed at public officials and their conduct in office.

"There is no question that speech critical of the exercise of the State's power lies at the very center of the first amendment. * * *

"A rule governing speech, even speech entitled to full constitutional protection, need not use the words 'clear and present danger' in order to pass constitutional muster. '[Properly] applied, the test requires a court to make its own inquiry into the imminence and magnitude of the danger said to flow from the particular utterance and then to balance the character of the evil, as well as its likelihood, against the need for free and unfettered expression. The possibility that other measures will serve the State's interests should also be weighed.' *Landmark Communications, Inc. v. Virginia.* * * *

The difference between the requirement of serious and imminent threat found in the disciplinary rules of some States and the more common formulation of substantial likelihood of material prejudice could prove mere semantics.[a] Each standard requires an assessment of proximity and degree of harm. Each may be capable of valid application. Under those principles, nothing inherent in Nevada's formulation fails first amendment review; but as this case demonstrates, Rule 177 has not been interpreted in conformance with those principles by the Nevada Supreme Court. * * *

"Even if one were to accept respondent's argument that lawyers participating in judicial proceedings may be subjected, consistent with the first amendment, to speech restrictions that could not be imposed on the press or general public, the judgment should not be upheld. The record does not support the conclusion that petitioner knew or reasonably should have known his remarks created a substantial likelihood of material prejudice, if the Rule's terms are given any meaningful content. * * * Our decision earlier this Term in *Mu'Min v. Virginia* [___ U.S. ___, 111 S.Ct. 1899, 114 L.Ed.2d 493 (1991)] provides a pointed contrast to respondent's contention in this case. There, the community had been subjected to a barrage of publicity prior to Mu'Min's trial for capital murder. News stories appeared over a course of several months and included, in addition to details of the crime itself, numerous items of prejudicial

---

a. In an earlier passage Kennedy, J., stated: "We are not called upon to determine the constitutionality of the ABA Model Rule of Professional Conduct 3.6 (1981), but only Rule 177 as it has been interpreted and applied by the State of Nevada. Model Rule 3.6's requirement of substantial likelihood of material prejudice is not necessarily flawed. The drafters of Model Rule 3.6 apparently thought the substantial likelihood of material prejudice formulation approximated the clear and present danger test. See ABA Annotated Model Rules of Professional Conduct 243 (1984) ('formulation in Model Rule 3.6 incorporates a standard approximating clear and present danger by focusing on the likelihood of injury and its [substantiality]')."

information inadmissible at trial. Eight of the twelve individuals seated on Mu'Min's jury admitted some exposure to pretrial publicity. We held that the publicity did not rise even to a level requiring questioning of individual jurors about the content of publicity. In light of that holding, the Nevada court's conclusion that petitioner's abbreviated, general comments six months before trial created a 'substantial likelihood of materially prejudicing' the proceeding is, to say the least, most unconvincing.

"[A]s petitioner explained to the disciplinary board, his primary motivation was the concern that, unless some of the weaknesses in the State's case were made public, a potential jury venire would be poisoned by repetition in the press of information being released by the police and prosecutors, in particular the repeated press reports about polygraph tests and the fact that the two police officers were no longer suspects. Respondent distorts Rule 177 when it suggests this explanation admits a purpose to prejudice the venire and so proves a violation of the Rule. Rule 177 only prohibits the dissemination of information that one knows or reasonably should know has a 'substantial likelihood of materially prejudicing an adjudicative proceeding.' * * * Petitioner did not indicate he thought he could sway the pool of potential jurors to form an opinion in advance of the trial, nor did he seek to discuss evidence that would be inadmissible at trial. He sought only to counter publicity already deemed prejudicial. * * * Far from an admission that he sought to 'materially prejudic[e] an adjudicative proceeding,' petitioner sought only to stop a wave of publicity he perceived as prejudicing potential jurors against his client and injuring his client's reputation in the community.

"Petitioner gave a second reason for holding the press conference, which demonstrates the additional value of his speech. Petitioner acted in part because the investigation had taken a serious toll on his client. Sanders was 'not a man in good health,' having suffered multiple open-heart surgeries prior to these events. And prior to indictment, the mere suspicion of wrongdoing had caused the [loss] of Sanders' ground lease on an Atlantic City, New Jersey property.

"An attorney's duties do not begin inside the courtroom door. He or she cannot ignore the practical implications of a legal proceeding for the client. Just as an attorney may recommend a plea bargain or civil settlement to avoid the adverse consequences of a possible loss after trial, so too an attorney may take reasonable steps to defend a client's reputation and reduce the adverse consequences of indictment, especially in the face of a prosecution deemed unjust or commenced with improper motives. * * *

"There is no support for the conclusion that petitioner's statement created a likelihood of material prejudice, or indeed of any harm of sufficient magnitude or imminence to support a punishment for speech."

Although the prior passages of Kennedy, J.'s opinion attracted only three of his colleagues, O'Connor, J., joined them on the vagueness issue, and this portion of Kennedy, J.'s opinion was designated as the Opinion of the Court: "As interpreted by the Nevada Supreme Court, the Rule is void for vagueness, in any event, for its safe harbor provision, Rule 177(3), misled petitioner into thinking that he could give his press conference without fear of discipline. Rule 177(3)(a) provides that a lawyer 'may state without elaboration . . . the general nature of the . . . defense.' Statements under this provision are protected '[n]otwithstanding subsection 1 and 2(a–f).' By necessary operation of the word 'notwithstanding,' the Rule contemplates that a lawyer describing the 'general nature of the * * * defense' 'without elaboration' need fear no discipline, even if he comments on '[t]he character, credibility, reputation or criminal record of a * * * witness,' and even if he 'knows or reasonably should know that [the statement] will have a substantial likelihood of materially prejudicing an adjudicative proceeding.' Given this grammatical structure, and absent any clarifying interpretation by the state court, the Rule fails to provide 'fair notice to those to whom [it] is directed.' A lawyer seeking to avail himself of Rule 177(3)'s protection must guess at its contours. The right to explain the 'general' nature of the defense without 'elaboration' provides insufficient guidance because 'general' and 'elaboration' are both classic terms of degree. In the context before us, these terms have no settled usage or tradition of interpretation in law. The lawyer has no principle for determining when his remarks pass from the safe harbor of the general to the forbidden sea of the elaborated.

"Petitioner testified he thought his statements were protected by Rule 177(3). A review of the press conference supports that claim. He gave only a brief opening statement and on numerous occasions declined to answer reporters' questions seeking more detailed comments. * * *

"The prohibition against vague regulations of speech is based in part on the need to eliminate the impermissible risk of discriminatory enforcement, for history shows that speech is suppressed when either the speaker or the message is critical of those who enforce the law. The question is not whether discriminatory enforcement occurred here, and we assume it did not, but whether the Rule is so imprecise that discriminatory enforcement is a real possibility. The inquiry is of particular relevance when one of the classes most affected by the regulation is the criminal defense bar, which has the professional mission to challenge actions of the State. Petitioner, for instance, succeeded in preventing the conviction of his client, and the speech in issue involved criticism of the government."

REHNQUIST, C.J., joined by White, Scalia, and Souter, JJ., dissented. But O'Connor, J., also joined two sections of Rehnquist, J.'s opinion and those sections were designated as the Opinion of the Court.[b] One of the sections recited the facts. The other dealt with the appropriate first amendment test under the circumstances. In the latter section, Rehnquist, C.J., *rejected* the contention that the "same stringent standard applied in *Nebraska Press Ass'n. v. Stuart* to restraints on press publication during the pendency of a criminal trial should be applied to speech by a lawyer whose client is a defendant in a criminal proceeding": "Lawyers representing clients in pending cases are key participants in the criminal justice system, and the State may demand some adherence to the precepts of that system in regulating their speech as well as their conduct. As noted by Justice Brennan in his concurring opinion in *Nebraska Press*, which was joined by Justices Stewart and Marshall, '[a]s officers of the court, court personnel and attorneys have a fiduciary responsibility not to engage in public debate that will redound to the detriment of the accused or that will obstruct the fair administration of justice.' Because lawyers have special access to information through discovery and client communications, their extrajudicial statements pose a threat to the fairness of a pending proceeding since lawyers' statements are likely to be received as especially authoritative.[5] We agree with the

b. The portion of Kennedy, J.'s opinion dealing with vagueness and the portion announcing the judgment were also designated as the Opinion of the Court.

[5.] The Nevada Supreme Court has consistently read all parts of Rule 177 as applying only to lawyers in pending cases, and not to other lawyers or nonlawyers. We express no opinion on the constitutionality of a rule regu-

majority of the States that the 'substantial likelihood of material prejudice' standard constitutes a constitutionally permissible balance between the first amendment rights of attorneys in pending cases and the state's interest in fair trials.c

"When a state regulation implicates first amendment rights, the Court must balance those interests against the State's legitimate interest in regulating the activity in question. The 'substantial likelihood' test embodied in Rule 177 is constitutional under this analysis, for it is designed to protect the integrity and fairness of a state's judicial system, and it imposes only narrow and necessary limitations on lawyers' speech. The limitations are aimed at two principal evils: (1) comments that are likely to influence the actual outcome of the trial, and (2) comments that are likely to prejudice the jury venire, even if an untainted panel can ultimately be found. Few, if any, interests under the Constitution are more fundamental than the right to a fair trial by 'impartial' jurors, and an outcome affected by extrajudicial statements would violate that fundamental right. Even if a fair trial can ultimately be ensured through voir dire, change of venue, or some other device, these measures entail serious costs to the system. Extensive voir dire may not be able to filter out all of the effects of pretrial publicity, and with increasingly widespread media coverage of criminal trials, a change of venue may not suffice to undo the effects of statements such as those made by petitioner. The State has a substantial interest in preventing officers of the court, such as lawyers, from imposing such costs on the judicial system and on the litigants.

"The restraint on speech is narrowly tailored to achieve those objectives. The regulation of attorneys' speech is limited—it applies only to speech that is substantially likely to have a materially prejudicial effect; it is neutral as to points of view, applying equally to all attorneys' participating in a pending case; and it merely postpones the attorney's comments until after the trial. While supported by the substantial state interest in preventing prejudice to an adjudicative proceeding by those who have a duty to protect its integrity, the rule is limited on its face to preventing only speech having a substantial likelihood of materially prejudicing that proceeding."

In the portion of his opinion joined by only three of his colleagues, Rehnquist, C.J., denied that Gentile was the victim of a vague rule: "Under the circumstances of his case, petitioner cannot complain about lack of notice, as he

lating the statements of a lawyer who is not participating in the pending case about which the statements are made. We note that of all the cases petitioner cites as supporting the use of the clear and present danger standard, the only one that even arguably involved a non-third party was *Wood v. Georgia,* where a county sheriff was held in contempt for publicly criticizing instructions given by a judge to a grand jury. Although the sheriff was technically an "officer of the court" by virtue of his position, the Court determined that his statements were made in his capacity as a private citizen, with no connection to his official duties. The same cannot be said about petitioner, whose statements were made in the course of and in furtherance of his role as defense counsel.

c. In an earlier footnote, joined by four members of the Court, Rehnquist, C.J., stated:

"We disagree with Justice Kennedy's statement that this case 'does not call into question the constitutionality of other states' prohibitions upon attorney speech that will have a "substantial likelihood of materially prejudicing an adjudicative proceeding," but is limited to Nevada's interpretation of that standard.' Petitioner challenged Rule 177 as being unconstitutional on its face in addition to as applied, contending that the 'substantial likelihood of material prejudice' test was unconstitutional, and that lawyer speech should be punished only if it violates the standard for clear and present danger set forth in Nebraska Press. The validity of the rules in the many states applying the 'substantial likelihood of material prejudice' test has, therefore, been called into question in this case.

has admitted that his primary objective in holding the press conference was the violation of Rule 177's core prohibition—to prejudice the upcoming trial by influencing potential jurors. * * * It is of course true, as the majority points out, that the word 'general' and the word 'elaboration' are both terms of degree. But combined as they are in the first sentence of [subsection] 3, they convey the very definite proposition that the authorized statements must not contain the sort of detailed allegations that petitioner made at his press conference. No sensible person could think that the following were 'general' statements of a claim or defense made 'without elaboration': 'the person that was in the most direct position to have stolen the drugs and the money . . . is Detective Steve Scholl'; 'there is far more evidence that will establish that Detective Scholl took these drugs and took these American Express travelers' checks than any other living human being'; '[Detective Scholl] either had a hell of a cold, or he should have seen a better doctor'; and 'the so-called other victims * * * one, two-four of them are known drug dealers and convicted money launderers.' [Subsection] 3, as an exception to the provisions of [subsections] 1 and 2, must be read in the light of the prohibitions and examples contained in the first two sections. It was obviously not intended to negate the prohibitions or the examples wholesale, but simply intended to provide a 'safe harbor' where there might be doubt as to whether one of the examples covered proposed conduct. These provisions were not vague as to the conduct for which petitioner was [disciplined] * * *.

"Petitioner's strongest arguments are that the statement was made well in advance of trial, and that the statements did not in fact taint the jury panel. But the Supreme Court of Nevada pointed out that petitioner's statements were not only highly inflammatory—they portrayed prospective government witnesses as drug users and dealers, and as money launderers—but the statements were timed to have maximum impact, when public interest in the case was at its height * * *. While there is evidence pro and con on that point, we find it persuasive that, by his own admission, petitioner called the press conference for the express purpose of influencing the venire. It is difficult to believe that he went to such trouble, and took such a risk, if there was no substantial likelihood that he would succeed.

"While in a case such as this we must review the record for ourselves, when the highest court of a state has reached a determination 'we give most respectful attention to its reasoning and conclusion.'"

O'CONNOR, J., concurred: "I agree with much of The Chief Justice's opinion. In particular, I agree that a State may regulate speech by lawyers representing clients in pending cases more readily than it may regulate the press. Lawyers are officers of the court and, as such, may legitimately be subject to ethical precepts that keep them from engaging in what otherwise might be constitutionally protected speech. This does not mean, of course, that lawyers forfeit their first amendment rights, only that a less demanding standard applies. I agree with The Chief Justice that the 'substantial likelihood of material prejudice' standard articulated in Rule 177 passes constitutional muster. * * *

"For the reasons set out in [Justice] Kennedy's opinion, however, I believe that Nevada's rule is void for vagueness. Subsection (3) of Rule 177 is a 'safe harbor' provision. It states that 'notwithstanding' the prohibitory language located elsewhere in the rule, 'a lawyer involved in the investigation or litigation may state without elaboration * * * [t]he general nature of the claim or defense.' Gentile made a conscious effort to stay within the boundaries of this 'safe harbor.' In his brief press conference, Gentile gave only a rough sketch of the defense that he intended to present at trial—i.e., that Detective Scholl, not

Grady Sanders, stole the cocaine and traveler's checks. When asked to provide more details, he declined, stating explicitly that the ethical rules compelled him to do so. Nevertheless, the disciplinary board sanctioned Gentile because, in its view, his remarks went beyond the scope of what was permitted by the rule. Both Gentile and the disciplinary board have valid arguments on their side, but this serves to support the view that the rule provides insufficient guidance. As Justice Kennedy correctly points out, a vague law offends the Constitution because it fails to give fair notice to those it is intended to deter and creates the possibility of discriminatory enforcement."

SECTION: GOVERNMENT PROPERTY AND THE PUBLIC FORUM

FOUNDATION CASES

CON LAW: P. 914, addition to note 4

AMER CON: P. 685, addition to note 4

RTS & LIB: P. 643, addition to note 4

A county ordinance required permits for private parades, assemblies, and other uses of public property. An applicant was required to pay a fee of no more than $1,000 per day of the property's use, the amount to be determined by the county administrator "in order to meet the expense incident to the administration of the Ordinance and to the maintenance of public order in the matter licensed."

FORSYTH COUNTY v. NATIONALIST MOVEMENT, ___ U.S. ___, 112 S.Ct. 2395, ___ L.Ed.2d ___ (1992), per BLACKMUN, J., overturned the ordinance: "There are no articulated standards either in the ordinance or in the county's established practice. The administrator is not required to rely on any objective factors.[11]

"The Forsyth County ordinance contains more than the possibility of censorship through uncontrolled discretion. As construed by the county, the ordinance often requires that the fee be based on the content of the speech.

"The county envisions that the administrator, in appropriate instances, will assess a fee to cover 'the cost of necessary and reasonable protection of persons participating in or observing said * * * activit[y].' In order to assess accurately the cost of security for parade participants, the administrator 'must necessarily examine the content of the message that is conveyed,' *Arkansas Writers' Project, Inc. v. Ragland,* estimate the response of others to that content, and judge the number of police necessary to meet that response. The fee assessed will depend on the administrator's measure of the amount of hostility likely to be created by the speech based on its content. Those wishing to express views unpopular with bottle-throwers, for example, may have to pay more for their permit.

"Although petitioner agrees that the cost of policing relates to content, it contends that the ordinance is content-neutral because it is aimed only at a

---

[11]. Petitioner [claims] that *Cox v. New Hampshire* excuses the administrator's discretion in setting the fee. Reliance on *Cox* is misplaced. Although the discretion granted to the administrator under the language in this ordinance is the same as in the statute at issue in *Cox*, the interpretation and application of that language are different. Unlike this case, there was in *Cox* no testimony or evidence that the statute granted unfettered discretion to the licensing authority.

secondary effect—the cost of maintaining public order. It is clear, however, that, in this case, it cannot be said that the fee's justification 'ha[s] nothing to do with content.'

"The costs to which petitioner refers are those associated with the public's reaction to the speech. Listeners' reaction to speech is not a content-neutral basis for regulation. * * *

"Petitioner insists that its ordinance cannot be unconstitutionally content-based because it contains much of the same language as did the state statute upheld in *Cox v. New Hampshire*. Although the Supreme Court of New Hampshire had interpreted the statute at issue in *Cox* to authorize the municipality to charge a permit fee for the maintenance of public order,' no fee was actually assessed. Nothing in this Court's opinion suggests that the statute, as interpreted by the New Hampshire Supreme Court, called for charging a premium in the case of a controversial political message delivered before a hostile audience. In light of the Court's subsequent First Amendment jurisprudence, we do not read *Cox* to permit such a premium.

"Petitioner, as well as the Court of Appeals and the District Court, all rely on the maximum allowable fee as the touchstone of constitutionality. Petitioner contends that the $1,000 cap on the fee ensures that the ordinance will not result in content-based discrimination. The ordinance was found unconstitutional by the Court of Appeals because the $1,000 cap was not sufficiently low to be "nominal." Neither the $1,000 cap on the fee charged, nor even some lower nominal cap, could save the ordinance because in this context, the level of the fee is irrelevant. A tax based on the content of speech does not become more constitutional because it is a small tax.

"The lower courts derived their requirement that the permit fee be 'nominal' from a sentence in the opinion in *Murdock v. Pennsylvania*. In *Murdock*, the Court invalidated a flat license fee levied on distributors of religious literature. In distinguishing the case from *Cox*, where the Court upheld a permit fee, the Court stated: 'And the fee is not a nominal one, imposed as a regulatory measure and calculated to defray the expense of protecting those on the streets and at home against the abuses of solicitors.' This sentence does not mean that an invalid fee can be saved if it is nominal, or that only nominal charges are constitutionally permissible. It reflects merely one distinction between the facts in *Murdock* and those in *Cox*.

"The tax at issue in *Murdock* was invalid because it was unrelated to any legitimate state interest, not because it was of a particular size. Similarly, the provision of the Forsyth County ordinance relating to fees is invalid because it unconstitutionally ties the amount of the fee to the content of the speech and lacks adequate procedural safeguards; no limit on such a fee can remedy these constitutional violations."

REHNQUIST, C.J., joined by White, Scalia, and Thomas, JJ., dissenting, observed that neither the discretion or scope of the licensing authority had been ruled upon by the lower courts, and argued that the majority should not have ruled on those issues. Instead, according to Rehnquist, C.J., the Court should have addressed the question and should have affirmatively decided that a locality can charge more than a nominal fee for the governmental expenses associated with a parade, assembly, or demonstration:

"The answer to this question seems to me quite simple, because it was authoritatively decided by this Court more than half a century ago in *Cox v. New Hampshire*. * * *

"In that case, the Court expressly recognized that the New Hampshire state statute allowed a city to levy much more than a nominal parade fee, as it stated that the fee provision 'had a permissible range from $300 to a nominal amount.' *Cox v. New Hampshire.* The use of the word 'nominal' in *Murdock* was thus unfortunate, as it represented a mistaken characterization of the fee statute in *Cox.* But a mistaken allusion in a later case to the facts of an earlier case does not by itself undermine the holding of the earlier case. The situations in *Cox* and *Murdock* were clearly different; the first involved a sliding fee to account for administrative and security costs incurred as a result of a parade on public property, while the second involved a flat tax on protected religious expression. I believe that the decision in *Cox* squarely controls the disposition of the question presented in this case, and I therefore would explicitly hold that the Constitution does not limit a parade license fee to a nominal amount." [a]

NEW FORUMS

CON LAW: P. 926, after note 5

AMER CON: P. 697, after note 5

RTS & LIB: P. 655, after note 5

INTERNATIONAL SOCIETY FOR KRISHNA CONSCIOUSNESS, INC. v. LEE

___ U.S. ___, 112 S.Ct. 2701, ___ L.Ed.2d ___ (1992).

CHIEF JUSTICE REHNQUIST delivered the opinion of the Court.

In this case we consider whether an airport terminal operated by a public authority is a public forum and whether a regulation prohibiting solicitation in the interior of an airport terminal violates the First Amendment.

The relevant facts in this case are not in dispute. Petitioner International Society for Krishna Consciousness, Inc. (ISKCON) is a not-for-profit religious corporation whose members perform a ritual known as *sankirtan.* The ritual consists of "'going into public places, disseminating religious literature and soliciting funds to support the religion.'" The primary purpose of this ritual is raising funds for the movement.

Respondent Walter Lee, now deceased, was the police superintendent of the Port Authority of New York and New Jersey and was charged with enforcing the regulation at issue. The Port Authority owns and operates three major airports in the greater New York City area: John F. Kennedy International Airport (Kennedy), La Guardia Airport (La Guardia), and Newark International Airport (Newark). The three airports collectively form one of the world's busiest metropolitan airport complexes. By decade's end they are expected to serve at least 110 million passengers annually. * * *

The Port Authority has adopted a regulation forbidding within the terminals the repetitive solicitation of money or distribution of literature. The regulation states: "1. The following conduct is prohibited within the interior areas of buildings or structures at an air terminal if conducted by a person to or with passers-by in a continuous or repetitive manner: "(a) The sale or distribution of any merchandise, including but not limited to jewelry, food stuffs,

---

[a] Rehnquist, C.J., also argued that nothing in the record supported the premise that the administrator would be permitted under the ordinance to take into account any expenses likely to be incurred as a result of opposition crowds. He would have remanded on that issue and on other questions relating to the administrator's discretion under the ordinance.

candles, flowers, badges and clothing. "(b) The sale or distribution of flyers, brochures, pamphlets, books or any other printed or written material. "(c) Solicitation and receipt of funds."

The regulation governs only the terminals; the Port Authority permits solicitation and distribution on the sidewalks outside the terminal buildings. The regulation effectively prohibits petitioner from performing *sankirtan* in the terminals. * * *

It is uncontested that the solicitation at issue in this case is a form of speech protected under the First Amendment.[3] But it is also well settled that the government need not permit all forms of speech on property that it owns and controls. * * *

[Our] precedents foreclose the conclusion that airport terminals are public fora. Reflecting the general growth of the air travel industry, airport terminals have only recently achieved their contemporary size and character. But given the lateness with which the modern air terminal has made its appearance, it hardly qualifies for the description of having "immemorially * * * time out of mind" been held in the public trust and used for purposes of expressive activity. Moreover, even within the rather short history of air transport, it is only "[i]n recent years [that] it has become a common practice for various religious and non-profit organizations to use commercial airports as a forum for the distribution of literature, the solicitation of funds, the proselytizing of new members, and other similar activities." 45 Fed.Reg. 35314 (1980). Thus, the tradition of airport activity does not demonstrate that airports have historically been made available for speech activity. Nor can we say that these particular terminals, or airport terminals generally, have been intentionally opened by their operators to such activity; the frequent and continuing litigation evidencing the operators' objections belies any such claim. In short, there can be no argument that society's time-tested judgment, expressed through acquiescence in a continuing practice, has resolved the issue in petitioner's favor.

Petitioner attempts to circumvent the history and practice governing airport activity by pointing our attention to the variety of speech activity that it claims historically occurred at various "transportation nodes" such as rail stations, bus stations, wharves, and Ellis Island. Even if we were inclined to accept petitioner's historical account describing speech activity at these locations, an account respondent contests, we think that such evidence is of little import for two reasons. First, much of the evidence is irrelevant to *public* fora analysis, because sites such as bus and rail terminals traditionally have had *private* ownership. The development of privately owned parks that ban speech activity would not change the public fora status of publicly held parks. But the reverse is also true. The practices of privately held transportation centers do not bear on the government's regulatory authority over a publicly owned airport.

Second, the relevant unit for our inquiry is an airport, not "transportation nodes" generally. When new methods of transportation develop, new methods for accommodating that transportation are also likely to be needed. And with each new step, it therefore will be a new inquiry whether the transportation necessities are compatible with various kinds of expressive activity. To make a category of "transportation nodes," therefore, would unjustifiably elide what may prove to be critical differences of which we should rightfully take account.

---

3. We deal here only with ISKCON's petition raising the permissibility of solicitation. Respondent's cross-petition concerning the leafletting ban is disposed of in the companion case, *Lee v. International Society for Krishna Consciousness, Inc.*, 91–339.

The "security magnet," for example, is an airport commonplace that lacks a counterpart in bus terminals and train stations. And public access to air terminals is also not infrequently restricted—just last year the Federal Aviation Administration required airports for a 4-month period to limit access to areas normally publicly accessible. To blithely equate airports with other transportation centers, therefore, would be a mistake. * * *

As commercial enterprises, airports must provide services attractive to the marketplace. In light of this, it cannot fairly be said that an airport terminal has as a principal purpose "promoting the free exchange of ideas." To the contrary, the record demonstrates that Port Authority management considers the purpose of the terminals to be the facilitation of passenger air travel, not the promotion of expression. Even if we look beyond the intent of the Port Authority to the manner in which the terminals have been operated, the terminals have never been dedicated (except under the threat of court order) to expression in the form sought to be exercised here: *i.e.*, the solicitation of contributions and the distribution of literature. * * * Thus, we think that neither by tradition nor purpose can the terminals be described as satisfying the standards we have previously set out for identifying a public forum.

The restrictions here challenged, therefore, need only satisfy a requirement of reasonableness. * * *

We have on many prior occasions noted the disruptive effect that solicitation may have on business. "Solicitation requires action by those who would respond: The individual solicited must decide whether or not to contribute (which itself might involve reading the solicitor's literature or hearing his pitch), and then, having decided to do so, reach for a wallet, search it for money, write a check, or produce a credit card." *Kokinda.* Passengers who wish to avoid the solicitor may have to alter their path, slowing both themselves and those around them. The result is that the normal flow of traffic is impeded. This is especially so in an airport, where "air travelers, who are often weighted down by cumbersome baggage * * * may be hurrying to catch a plane or to arrange ground transportation." Delays may be particularly costly in this setting, as a flight missed by only a few minutes can result in hours worth of subsequent inconvenience.

In addition, face-to-face solicitation presents risks of duress that are an appropriate target of regulation. The skillful, and unprincipled, solicitor can target the most vulnerable, including those accompanying children or those suffering physical impairment and who cannot easily avoid the solicitation. The unsavory solicitor can also commit fraud through concealment of his affiliation or through deliberate efforts to shortchange those who agree to purchase. Compounding this problem is the fact that, in an airport, the targets of such activity frequently are on tight schedules. This in turn makes such visitors unlikely to stop and formally complain to airport authorities. As a result, the airport faces considerable difficulty in achieving its legitimate interest in monitoring solicitation activity to assure that travelers are not interfered with unduly.

The Port Authority has concluded that its interest in monitoring the activities can best be accomplished by limiting solicitation and distribution to the sidewalk areas outside the terminals. This sidewalk area is frequented by an overwhelming percentage of airport users. Thus the resulting access of those who would solicit the general public is quite complete. In turn we think it would be odd to conclude that the Port Authority's terminal regulation is unreasonable despite the Port Authority having otherwise assured access to an area universally traveled. * * *

Moreover, "the justification for the Rule should not be measured by the disorder that would result from granting an exemption solely to ISKCON." For if petitioner is given access, so too must other groups. "Obviously, there would be a much larger threat to the State's interest in crowd control if all other religious, nonreligious, and noncommercial organizations could likewise move freely." As a result, we conclude that the solicitation ban is reasonable. * * *

JUSTICE O'CONNOR, concurring in 91-155 [on the solicitation issue] and concurring in the judgment in 91-339 [on the distribution of literature issue]. * * *

In the decision below, the Court of Appeals upheld a ban on solicitation of funds within the airport terminals operated by the Port Authority of New York and New Jersey, but struck down a ban on the repetitive distribution of printed or written material within the terminals. I would affirm both parts of that judgment.

I concur in the Court's opinion in No. 91-155 and agree that publicly owned airports are not public fora. * * *

That airports are not public fora, however, does not mean that the government can restrict speech in whatever way it likes. * * *

"The reasonableness of the Government's restriction [on speech in a nonpublic forum] must be assessed in light of the purpose of the forum and all the surrounding circumstances." *Cornelius.* " '[C]onsideration of a forum's special attributes is relevant to the constitutionality of a regulation since the significance of the governmental interest must be assessed in light of the characteristic nature and function of the particular forum involved.' " *Kokinda.* In this case, the "special attributes" and "surrounding circumstances" of the airports operated by the Port Authority are determinative. Not only has the Port Authority chosen *not* to limit access to the airports under its control, it has created a huge complex open to travelers and nontravelers alike. The airports house restaurants, cafeterias, snack bars, coffee shops, cocktail lounges, post offices, banks, telegraph offices, clothing shops, drug stores, food stores, nurseries, barber shops, currency exchanges, art exhibits, commercial advertising displays, bookstores, newsstands, dental offices and private clubs. The International Arrivals Building at JFK Airport even has two branches of Bloomingdale's.

We have said that a restriction on speech in a nonpublic forum is "reasonable" when it is "consistent with the [government's] legitimate interest in 'preserv[ing] the property * * * for the use to which it is lawfully dedicated.' " *Perry.* * * * In my view, the Port Authority is operating a shopping mall as well as an airport. The reasonableness inquiry, therefore, is not whether the restrictions on speech are "consistent with * * * preserving the property" for air travel, but whether they are reasonably related to maintaining the multipurpose environment that the Port Authority has deliberately created.

Applying that standard, I agree with the Court in No. 91-155 that the ban on solicitation is reasonable. * * *

In my view, however, the regulation banning leafletting—or, in the Port Authority's words, the "continuous or repetitive * * * distribution of * * * printed or written material"—cannot be upheld as reasonable on this record. I therefore concur in the judgment in No. 91-339 striking down that prohibition. While the difficulties posed by solicitation in a nonpublic forum are sufficiently obvious that its regulation may "rin[g] of common-sense," the same is not necessarily true of leafletting. To the contrary, we have expressly noted that leafletting does not entail the same kinds of problems presented by face-to-face solicitation. Specifically, "[o]ne need not ponder the contents of a leaflet or pamphlet in order mechanically to take it out of someone's hand * * *. 'The distribution of literature does not require that the recipient stop in order to receive the message the speaker wishes to convey; instead the recipient is free to read the message at a later time.'" With the possible exception of avoiding litter, it is difficult to point to any problems intrinsic to the act of leafletting that would make it naturally incompatible with a large, multipurpose forum such as those at issue here. * * *

Moreover, the Port Authority has not offered any justifications or record evidence to support its ban on the distribution of pamphlets alone. Its argument is focused instead on the problems created when literature is distributed in conjunction with a solicitation plea. Although we do not "requir[e] that * * * proof be present to justify the denial of access to a nonpublic forum on grounds that the proposed use may disrupt the property's intended function," *Perry*, we have required some explanation as to why certain speech is inconsistent with the intended use of the forum. [Here,] the Port Authority has provided no independent reason for prohibiting leafletting, and the record contains no information from which we can draw an inference that would support its ban. Because I cannot see how peaceful pamphleteering is incompatible with the multipurpose environment of the Port Authority airports, I cannot accept that a total ban on that activity is reasonable without an explanation as to why such a restriction "preserv[es] the property" for the several uses to which it has been put.

Of course, it is still open for the Port Authority to promulgate regulations of the time, place, and manner of leafletting which are "content-neutral, narrowly tailored to serve a significant government interest, and leave open ample alternative channels of communication." For example, during the many years that this litigation has been in progress, the Port Authority has not banned *sankirtan* completely from JFK International Airport, but has restricted it to a relatively uncongested part of the airport terminals, the same part that houses the airport chapel. In my view, that regulation meets the standards we have applied to time, place, and manner restrictions of protected expression.

I would affirm the judgment of the Court of Appeals in both No. 91–155 and No. 91–339.

JUSTICE KENNEDY, with whom JUSTICE BLACKMUN, JUSTICE STEVENS, and JUSTICE SOUTER join as to Part I, concurring in the judgment.

While I concur in the judgment affirming in this case, my analysis differs in substantial respects from that of the Court. In my view the airport corridors and shopping areas outside of the passenger security zones, areas operated by the Port Authority, are public forums, and speech in those places is entitled to protection against all government regulation inconsistent with public forum principles. The Port Authority's blanket prohibition on the distribution or sale of literature cannot meet those stringent standards, and I agree it is invalid under the First and Fourteenth Amendments. The Port Authority's rule disallowing in-person solicitation of money for immediate payment, however, is in my view a narrow and valid regulation of the time, place, and manner of protected speech in this forum, or else is a valid regulation of the nonspeech element of expressive conduct. I would sustain the Port Authority's ban on solicitation and receipt of funds.

I

[The Court's] analysis is flawed at its very beginning. It leaves the government with almost unlimited authority to restrict speech on its property by doing nothing more than articulating a non-speech-related purpose for the area, and it leaves almost no scope for the development of new public forums absent the rare approval of the government. The Court's error lies in its conclusion that the public-forum status of public property depends on the government's defined purpose for the property, or on an explicit decision by the government to dedicate the property to expressive activity. In my view, the inquiry must be an objective one, based on the actual, physical characteristics and uses of the property. * * *

The First Amendment is a limitation on government, not a grant of power. Its design is to prevent the government from controlling speech. Yet under the Court's view the authority of the government to control speech on its property is paramount, for in almost all cases the critical step in the Court's analysis is a classification of the property that turns on the government's own definition or decision, unconstrained by an independent duty to respect the speech its citizens can voice there. The Court acknowledges as much, by reintroducing today into our First Amendment law a strict doctrinal line between the proprietary and regulatory functions of government which I thought had been abandoned long ago.

The Court's approach is contrary to the underlying purposes of the public forum doctrine. The liberties protected by our doctrine derive from the Assembly, as well as the Speech and Press Clauses of the First Amendment, and are essential to a functioning democracy. See Kalven, *The Concept of the Public Forum: Cox v. Louisiana,* 1965 S.Ct.Rev. 1, 14, 19. Public places are of necessity the locus for discussion of public issues, as well as protest against arbitrary government action. At the heart of our jurisprudence lies the principle that in a free nation citizens must have the right to gather and speak with other persons in public places. The recognition that certain government-owned property is a public forum provides open notice to citizens that their freedoms may be exercised there without fear of a censorial government, adding tangible reinforcement to the idea that we are a free people. * * *

The Court's analysis rests on an inaccurate view of history. The notion that traditional public forums are property which have public discourse as their principal purpose is a most doubtful fiction. The types of property that we have recognized as the quintessential public forums are streets, parks, and sidewalks. It would seem apparent that the principal purpose of streets and sidewalks, like airports, is to facilitate transportation, not public discourse. [Similarly,] the purpose for the creation of public parks may be as much for beauty and open space as for discourse. Thus under the Court's analysis, even the quintessential public forums would appear to lack the necessary elements of what the Court defines as a public forum.

The effect of the Court's narrow view of the first category of public forums is compounded by its description of the second purported category, the so-called "designated" forum. The requirements for such a designation are so stringent that I cannot be certain whether the category has any content left at all. In any event, it seems evident that under the Court's analysis today few if any types of property other than those already recognized as public forums will be accorded that status. * * *

One of the places left in our mobile society that is suitable for discourse is a metropolitan airport. It is of particular importance to recognize that such spaces are public forums because in these days an airport is one of the few government-owned spaces where many persons have extensive contact with other members of the public. Given that private spaces of similar character are not subject to the dictates of the First Amendment, it is critical that we preserve these areas for protected speech. In my view, our public forum doctrine must recognize this reality, and allow the creation of public forums which do not fit within the narrow tradition of streets, sidewalks, and parks.

Under the proper circumstances I would accord public forum status to other forms of property, regardless of its ancient or contemporary origins and whether or not it fits within a narrow historic tradition. If the objective, physical characteristics of the property at issue and the actual public access and uses which have been permitted by the government indicate that expressive activity would be appropriate and compatible with those uses, the property is a public forum. * * * The possibility of some theoretical inconsistency between expressive activities and the property's uses should not bar a finding of a public forum, if those inconsistencies can be avoided through simple and permitted regulations.

The second category of the Court's jurisprudence, the so-called designated forum, provides little, if any, additional protection for speech. Where government property does not satisfy the criteria of a public forum, the government retains the power to dedicate the property for speech, whether for all expressive activity or for limited purposes only. I do not quarrel with the fact that speech must often be restricted on property of this kind to retain the purpose for which it has been designated. And I recognize that when property has been designated for a particular expressive use, the government may choose to eliminate that designation. But this increases the need to protect speech in other places, where discourse may occur free of such restrictions. In some sense the government always retains authority to close a public forum, by selling the property, changing its physical character, or changing its principal use. Otherwise the State would be prohibited from closing a park, or eliminating a street or sidewalk, which no one has understood the public forum doctrine to require. The difference is that when property is a protected public forum the State may not by fiat assert broad control over speech or expressive activities; it must alter the objective physical character or uses of the property, and bear the attendant costs, to change the property's forum status.

Under this analysis, it is evident that the public spaces of the Port Authority's airports are public forums. First, the District Court made detailed findings regarding the physical similarities between the Port Authority's airports and public streets. These findings show that the public spaces in the airports are broad, public thoroughfares full of people and lined with stores and other commercial activities. An airport corridor is of course not a street, but that is not the proper inquiry. The question is one of physical similarities, sufficient to suggest that the airport corridor should be a public forum for the same reasons that streets and sidewalks have been treated as public forums by the people who use them.

Second, the airport areas involved here are open to the public without restriction. Plaintiffs do not seek access to the secured areas of the airports, nor do I suggest that these areas would be public forums. And while most people who come to the Port Authority's airports do so for a reason related to air travel, either because they are passengers or because they are picking up or dropping off passengers, this does not distinguish an airport from streets or sidewalks, which most people use for travel. * * *

Third, and perhaps most important, it is apparent from the record, and from the recent history of airports, that when adequate time, place, and manner regulations are in place, expressive activity is quite compatible with the uses of major airports. The Port Authority's primary argument to the contrary is that the problem of congestion in its airports' corridors makes expressive activity inconsistent with the airports' primary purpose, which is to facilitate air travel. The First Amendment is often inconvenient. But that is besides the point. Inconvenience does not absolve the government of its obligation to tolerate speech. * * *

The danger of allowing the government to suppress speech is shown in the case now before us. A grant of plenary power allows the government to tilt the dialogue heard by the public, to exclude many, more marginal voices. The first challenged Port Authority regulation establishes a flat prohibition on "[t]he sale or distribution of flyers, brochures, pamphlets, books or any other printed or written material," if conducted within the airport terminal, "in a continuous or repetitive manner." We have long recognized that the right to distribute flyers and literature lies at the heart of the liberties guaranteed by the Speech and Press Clauses of the First Amendment. The Port Authority's rule, which prohibits almost all such activity, is among the most restrictive possible of those liberties. The regulation is in fact so broad and restrictive of speech, Justice O'Connor finds it void even under the standards applicable to government regulations in nonpublic forums. I have no difficulty deciding the regulation cannot survive the far more stringent rules applicable to regulations in public forums. The regulation is not drawn in narrow terms and it does not leave open ample alternative channels for communication. * * *

II

It is my view, however, that the Port Authority's ban on the "solicitation and receipt of funds" within its airport terminals should be upheld under the standards applicable to speech regulations in public forums. The regulation may be upheld as either a reasonable time, place, and manner restriction, or as a regulation directed at the nonspeech element of expressive conduct. The two standards have considerable overlap in a case like this one. * * *

I am in full agreement with the statement of the Court that solicitation is a form of protected speech. If the Port Authority's solicitation regulation prohibited all speech which requested the contribution of funds, I would conclude that it was a direct, content-based restriction of speech in clear violation of the First Amendment. The Authority's regulation does not prohibit all solicitation, however; it prohibits the "solicitation and receipt of funds." I do not understand this regulation to prohibit all speech that solicits funds. It reaches only personal solicitations for immediate payment of money. Otherwise, the "receipt of funds" phrase would be written out of the provision. The regulation does not cover, for example, the distribution of preaddressed envelopes along with a plea to contribute money to the distributor or his organization. As I understand the restriction it is directed only at the physical exchange of money, which is an element of conduct interwoven with otherwise expressive solicitation. In other words, the regulation permits expression that solicits funds, but limits the manner of that expression to forms other than the immediate receipt of money.

So viewed, I believe the Port Authority's rule survives our test for speech restrictions in the public forum. * * *

[T]he government interest in regulating the sales of literature[, however,] is not as powerful as in the case of solicitation. The danger of a fraud arising from such sales is much more limited than from pure solicitation, because in the case of a sale the nature of the exchange tends to be clearer to both parties. Also, the Port Authority's sale regulation is not as narrowly drawn as the solicitation rule, since it does not specify the receipt of money as a critical element of a violation. And perhaps most important, the flat ban on sales of literature leaves open fewer alternative channels of communication than the Port Authority's more limited prohibition on the solicitation and receipt of funds. Given the practicalities and ad hoc nature of much expressive activity in the public forum, sales of literature must be completed in one transaction to be workable. Attempting to collect money at another time or place is a far less plausible option in the context of a sale than when soliciting donations, because the literature sought to be sold will under normal circumstances be distributed within the forum.

* * *

Against all of this must be balanced the great need, recognized by our precedents, to give the sale of literature full First Amendment protection. We have long recognized that to prohibit distribution of literature for the mere reason that it is sold would leave organizations seeking to spread their message without funds to operate. "It should be remembered that the pamphlets of Thomas Paine were not distributed free of charge." *Murdock*. The effect of a rule of law distinguishing between sales and distribution would be to close the marketplace of ideas to less affluent organizations and speakers, leaving speech as the preserve of those who are able to fund themselves. One of the primary purposes of the public forum is to provide persons who lack access to more sophisticated media the opportunity to speak. A prohibition on sales forecloses that opportunity for the very persons who need it most. And while the same arguments might be made regarding solicitation of funds, the answer is that the Port Authority has not prohibited all solicitation, but only a narrow class of conduct associated with a particular manner of solicitation. * * *

JUSTICE SOUTER, with whom JUSTICE BLACKMUN and JUSTICE STEVENS join, concurring in the judgment in No. 91-339 [on the distribution of literature issue] and dissenting in No. 91-155 [on the solicitation issue].

I join in Part I of Justice Kennedy's opinion and the judgment of affirmance in No. 91-339. I agree with Justice Kennedy's view of the rule that should determine what is a public forum and with his conclusion that the public areas of the airports at issue here qualify as such. * * *

From the Court's conclusion in No. 91-155, however, sustaining the total ban on solicitation of money for immediate payment, I respectfully dissent.

[T]he respondent comes closest to justifying the restriction as one furthering the government's interest in preventing coercion and fraud.[1] The claim to be

---

1. Respondent also attempts to justify its regulation on the alternative basis of "interference with air travelers," referring in particular to problems of "annoyance," and "congestion." The First Amendment inevitably requires people to put up with annoyance and uninvited persuasion. Indeed, in such cases we need to scrutinize restrictions on speech with special care. In their degree of congestion, most of the public spaces of these airports are probably more comparable to public streets than to the fairground as we described it in *Heffron v. International Society for Krishna Consciousness, Inc.* Consequently, the congestion argument, which was held there to justify a regulation confining solicitation to a fixed location, should have less force here. Be that as it may, the conclusion of a majority of the Court today that the Constitution forbids the ban on the sale [Ed. Does the majority of the Court conclude that the Constitution forbids the ban on the *sale* of literature?] as well as the distribution, of leaflets puts to rest respondent's argument that con-

preventing coercion is weak to start with. While a solicitor can be insistent, a pedestrian on the street or airport concourse can simply walk away or walk on. * * * Since there is here no evidence of any type of coercive conduct, over and above the merely importunate character of the open and public solicitation, that might justify a ban, the regulation cannot be sustained to avoid coercion.

As for fraud, our cases do not provide government with plenary authority to ban solicitation just because it could be [fraudulent.] * * * The evidence of fraudulent conduct here is virtually nonexistent. It consists of one affidavit describing eight complaints, none of them substantiated, "involving some form of fraud, deception, or larceny" over an entire 11-year period between 1975 and 1986, during which the regulation at issue here was, by agreement, not enforced. Petitioners claim, and respondent does not dispute, that by the Port Authority's own calculation, there has not been a single claim of fraud or misrepresentation since 1981. * * *

Even assuming a governmental interest adequate to justify some regulation, the present ban would fall when subjected to the requirement of narrow tailoring. Thus, in *Schaumburg* we said: "The Village's legitimate interest in preventing fraud can be better served by measures less intrusive than a direct prohibition on solicitation. Fraudulent misrepresentations can be prohibited and the penal laws used to punish such conduct directly. * * *"

[Finally,] I do not think the Port Authority's solicitation ban leaves open the "ample" channels of communication required of a valid content-neutral time, place and manner restriction. A distribution of preaddressed envelopes is unlikely to be much of an alternative. The practical reality of the regulation, which this Court can never ignore, is that it shuts off a uniquely powerful avenue of communication for organizations like the International Society for Krishna Consciousness, and may, in effect, completely prohibit unpopular and poorly funded groups from receiving funds in response to protected solicitation. * * *

Accordingly, I would reverse the judgment of the Court of Appeals in No. 91-155, and strike down the ban on solicitation.

LEE v. INTERNATIONAL SOCIETY FOR KRISHNA CONSCIOUSNESS, INC.

___ U.S. ___, 112 S.Ct. 2709, ___ L.Ed.2d ___ (1992).

PER CURIAM.

For the reasons expressed in the opinions of Justice O'Connor, Justice Kennedy, and Justice Souter in *International Society for Krishna Consciousness, Inc. v. Lee,* the judgment of the Court of Appeals holding that the ban on distribution of literature in the Port Authority airport terminals is invalid under the First Amendment is

Affirmed.

CHIEF JUSTICE REHNQUIST, with whom JUSTICE WHITE, JUSTICE SCALIA and JUSTICE THOMAS join, dissenting.

Leafletting presents risks of congestion similar to those posed by solicitation. It presents, in addition, some risks unique to leafletting. And of course, as with

---

gestion justifies a total ban on solicitation. While there may, of course, be congested locations where solicitation could severely compromise the efficient flow of pedestrians, the proper response would be to tailor the restrictions to those choke points.

solicitation, these risks must be evaluated against a backdrop of the substantial congestion problem facing the Port Authority and with an eye to the cumulative impact that will result if all groups are permitted terminal access. Viewed in this light, I conclude that the distribution ban, no less than the solicitation ban, is reasonable. I therefore dissent from the Court's holding striking the distribution ban.

I will not trouble to repeat in detail all that has been stated in No. 91-155, *International Society for Krishna Consciousness, Inc. v. Lee,* describing the risks and burdens flowing to travelers and the Port Authority from permitting solicitation in airport terminals. Suffice it to say that the risks and burdens posed by leafletting are quite similar to those posed by solicitation. The weary, harried, or hurried traveler may have no less desire and need to avoid the delays generated by having literature foisted upon him than he does to avoid delays from a financial solicitation. And while a busy passenger perhaps may succeed in fending off a leafletter with minimal disruption to himself by agreeing simply to take the proffered material, this does not completely ameliorate the dangers of congestion flowing from such leafletting. Others may choose not simply to accept the material but also to stop and engage the leafletter in debate, obstructing those who follow. Moreover, those who accept material may often simply drop it on the floor once out of the leafletter's range, creating an eyesore, a safety hazard, and additional cleanup work for airport staff. See *City Council of Los Angeles v. Taxpayers for Vincent,* 466 U.S. 789, 816-817 (1984) (aesthetic interests may provide basis for restricting speech).

In addition, a differential ban that permits leafletting but prohibits solicitation, while giving the impression of permitting the Port Authority at least half of what it seeks, may in fact prove for the Port Authority to be a much more Pyrrhic victory. Under the regime that is today sustained, the Port Authority is obliged to permit leafletting. But monitoring leafletting activity in order to ensure that it is *only* leafletting that occurs, and not also soliciting, may prove little less burdensome than the monitoring that would be required if solicitation were permitted. At a minimum, therefore, I think it remains open whether at some future date the Port Authority may be able to reimpose a complete ban, having developed evidence that enforcement of a differential ban is overly burdensome. Until now it has had no reason or means to do this, since it is only today that such a requirement has been announced. * * *

Notes and Questions

In order to prevent voter intimidation and election fraud, Tennessee prohibits either the soliciting of votes or the display or distribution of campaign materials within 100 feet of the entrance to a polling place. Is the campaign-free zone, a public forum? Is the permitting of charitable or religious speech (including solicitation) or commercial speech while banning election speech (but not exit polling) impermissible content discrimination?

BURSON v. FREEMAN, ___ U.S. ___, 112 S.Ct. 1846, 119 L.Ed.2d 5 (1992) upheld the statute. BLACKMUN, J., joined by Rehnquist, C.J., and White and Kennedy, JJ., argued that the 100 foot zone was a public forum, that the regulation was based on the content of the speech, that the state was required to show that its statute was necessary to achieve a compelling state interest and narrowly drawn to achieve that end, and determined that this was the "rare case" in which strict scrutiny against content regulation could be satisfied: "There is [ample evidence] that political candidates have used campaign workers to commit voter intimidation or electoral fraud. In contrast, there is simply no evidence that political candidates have used other forms of solicitation or exit polling to commit such electoral abuses. States adopt laws to address the problems that confront them. The First Amendment does not require States to regulate for problems that do not exist. * * *

"Here, the State, as recognized administrator of elections, has asserted that the exercise of free speech rights conflicts with another fundamental right, the right to cast a ballot in an election free from the taint of intimidation and fraud. A long history, a substantial consensus, and simple common sense shows that some restricted zone around polling places is necessary to protect that fundamental right. Given the conflict between those two rights, we hold that requiring solicitors to stand 100 feet [a] from the entrances to polling places does not constitute an unconstitutional compromise." [b]

SCALIA, J., agreed with Blackmun, J., that the regulation was justified, but maintained that the area around a polling place is not a public forum: "If the category of 'traditional public forum' is to be a tool of analysis rather than a conclusory label, it must remain faithful to its name and derive its content from *tradition*. Because restrictions on speech around polling places are as venerable a part of the American tradition as the secret ballot, [Tennessee's statute] does not restrict speech in a traditional public forum, and the 'exacting scrutiny' that the Court purports to apply is inappropriate. Instead, I believe that the [statute] though content-based, is constitutional because it is a reasonable, viewpoint-neutral regulation of a non-public forum."

STEVENS, J., joined by O'Connor and Souter, J., did not address the question of whether the area around a polling place was a public forum, but agreed with Blackmun, J., that the regulation could not be upheld without showing that it was necessary to serve a compelling state interest by means narrowly tailored to that end. He contended that the existence of the secret ballot was a sufficient safeguard against intimidation [c] and that the fear of fraud from last minute campaigning could not be reconciled with *Mills v. Alabama* (prohibition on election day editorials unconstitutional). In addition, Stevens, J., argued that the prohibition disproportionately affects candidates with "fewer resources, candidates from lesser visibility offices, and 'grassroots' candidates" who specially profit from "last-minute campaigning near the polling place. * * * The hubbub of campaign workers outside a polling place may be a nuisance, but it is also the sound of a vibrant democracy."

a. Blackmun, J., argued that the question of whether the state should be required to set a smaller zone, perhaps 25 feet, would put the state to an unreasonable burden of proof, and that the difference between such zones was not of constitutional moment.

b. Kennedy, J., concurring, reaffirmed the views he had put forward in *Simon and Schuster*, but noted that the first amendment must appropriately give way in some cases where other constitutional rights are at stake. Thomas, J., took no part.

c. Stevens, J., argued that the record showed no evidence of intimidation or abuse, nor did it offer a basis for denying election advocacy, while permitting other forms of political advocacy, e.g., environmental advocacy. He maintained that the plurality had shifted the strict scrutiny standard from the state to the candidate who wished to speak.

SECTION: GOVERNMENT SUPPORT OF SPEECH

SUBSIDIES AND TAX EXPENDITURES

CON LAW: P. 944, after note 3

AMER CON: P. 709, after note 2

RTS & LIB: P. 673, after note 3

LEATHERS v. MEDLOCK, ___ U.S. ___, 111 S.Ct. 1438, 113 L.Ed.2d 494 (1991), per O'CONNOR, J., held that Arkansas' extension of its sales tax to cable television services, while exempting the print media, did not violate the first amendment: "Cable television provides to its subscribers news, information, and entertainment. It is engaged in 'speech' under the First Amendment, and is, in much of its operation, part of the 'press.' That it is taxed differently from other media does not by itself, however, raise First Amendment concerns. Our cases have held that a tax that discriminates among speakers is constitutionally suspect only in certain circumstances. * * *

"[*Grosjean, Minneapolis Star,* and *Arkansas Writers'*] demonstrate that differential taxation of First Amendment speakers is constitutionally suspect when it threatens to suppress the expression of particular ideas or viewpoints. Absent a compelling justification, the government may not exercise its taxing power to single out the press. See *Grosjean; Minneapolis Star.* The press plays a unique role as a check on government abuse, and a tax limited to the press raises concerns about censorship of critical information and opinion. A tax is also suspect if it targets a small group of speakers. See *Minneapolis Star; Arkansas Writers'.* Again, the fear is censorship of particular ideas or viewpoints. Finally, for reasons that are obvious, a tax will trigger heightened scrutiny under the First Amendment if it discriminates on the basis of the content of taxpayer speech.

"The Arkansas tax at issue here presents none of these types of discrimination. The Arkansas sales tax is a tax of general applicability. It applies to receipts from the sale of all tangible personal property and a broad range of services, unless within a group of specific exemptions. [Furthermore,] there is no indication in this case that Arkansas has targeted cable television in a purposeful attempt to interfere with its First Amendment activities. Nor is the tax one that is structured so as to raise suspicion that it was intended to do so. Unlike the taxes involved in *Grosjean* and *Minneapolis Star,* the Arkansas tax has not selected a narrow group to bear fully the burden of the tax.

"The tax is also structurally dissimilar to the tax involved in *Arkansas Writers'.* In that case, only 'a few' Arkansas magazines paid the State's sales tax. * * *

"The danger from a tax scheme that targets a small number of speakers is the danger of censorship; a tax on a small number of speakers runs the risk of affecting only a limited range of views. The risk is similar to that from content-based regulation: it will distort the market for ideas. [There] is no comparable danger from a tax on the services provided by [the] approximately 100 suppliers of cable television services. This is not a tax structure that resembles a penalty for particular speakers or particular ideas.

"Finally, Arkansas' sales tax is not content based. There is nothing in the language of the statute that refers to the content of mass media communications. Moreover, the record establishes that cable television offers subscribers a variety of programming that presents a mixture of news, information, and entertainment. It contains no evidence, nor is it contended, that this material differs systematically in its message from that communicated by satellite broadcast programming, newspapers, or magazines.

"Because the Arkansas sales tax presents none of the First Amendment difficulties that have led us to strike down differential taxation in the past, cable petitioners can prevail only if the Arkansas tax scheme presents 'an additional basis' for concluding that the State has violated petitioners' First Amendment rights. Petitioners argue that such a basis exists here: Arkansas' tax discriminates among media [and] within a medium [if it is assumed that cable and satellite television are the same medium]. Petitioners argue that such intermedia and intramedia discrimination, even in the absence of any evidence of intent to suppress speech or of any effect on the expression of particular ideas, violates the First Amendment. Our cases do not support such a rule.

"*Regan v. Taxation with Representation of Washington* stands for the proposition that a tax scheme that discriminates among speakers does not implicate the First Amendment unless it discriminates on the basis of ideas. [On] the record in *Regan*, there appeared [no] 'hostile and oppressive discrimination.' We explained that '[t]he case would be different if Congress were to discriminate invidiously in its subsidies in such a way as to aim at the suppression of dangerous ideas.'

"That a differential burden on speakers is insufficient by itself to raise First Amendment concerns is evident as well from *Mabee v. White Plains Publishing Co.*, 327 U.S. 178, 66 S.Ct. 511, 90 L.Ed. 607 (1946), and *Oklahoma Press Publishing Co. v. Walling*, 327 U.S. 186, 66 S.Ct. 494, 90 L.Ed. 614 (1946). Those cases do not involve taxation, but they do involve government action that places differential burdens on members of the press. The Fair Labor Standards Act of 1938, 52 Stat. 1060, as amended, 29 U.S.C. § 201 *et seq.*, applies generally to newspapers as to other businesses, but it exempts from its requirements certain small papers. § 213(a)(8). Publishers of larger daily newspapers argued that the differential burden thereby placed on them violates the First Amendment. The Court upheld the exemption because there was no indication that the government had singled out the press for special treatment or that the exemption was a ' "deliberate and calculated device" ' to penalize a certain group of newspapers, *Mabee*, quoting *Grosjean*.

"Taken together, *Regan*, *Mabee*, and *Oklahoma Press* establish that differential taxation of speakers, even members of the press, does not implicate the First Amendment unless the tax is directed at, or presents the danger of suppressing, particular ideas. That was the case in *Grosjean, Minneapolis Star,* and *Arkansas Writers',* but it is not the case here."[a]

MARSHALL, J., joined by Blackmun, J., dissented: "Because cable competes with members of the print and electronic media in the larger information market, the power to discriminate between these media triggers the central concern underlying the nondiscrimination principle: the risk of covert censorship. The nondiscrimination principle protects the press from censorship prophylactically, condemning any selective-taxation scheme that presents the '*potential* for abuse' by the State, *Minneapolis Star,* independent of any actual 'evidence of an improper censorial motive,' *Arkansas Writers' Project*; see

---

a. The Court remanded for a determination whether the distinction between cable and satellite services violated equal protection. The issue had not been reached by the lower court.

Minneapolis Star, ('Illicit legislative intent is not the *sine qua non* of a violation of the First Amendment'). * * *

"The majority dismisses the risk of governmental abuse under the Arkansas tax scheme on the ground that the number of media actors exposed to the tax is 'large.' [To] start, the majority's approach provides no meaningful guidance on the intermedia scope of the nondiscrimination principle. From the majority's discussion, we can infer that three is a sufficiently 'small' number of affected actors to trigger First Amendment problems and that one hundred is too 'large' to do so. But the majority fails to pinpoint the magic number *between* three and one hundred actors above which discriminatory taxation can be accomplished with impunity. The suggestion that the First Amendment prohibits selective taxation that 'resembles a penalty' is no more helpful. A test that turns on whether a selective tax 'penalizes' a particular medium presupposes some baseline establishing that medium's entitlement to equality of treatment with other media. The majority never develops any theory of the State's obligation to treat like-situated media equally, except to say that the State must avoid discriminating against too 'small' a number of media actors.

"In addition, the majority's focus on absolute numbers fails to reflect the concerns that inform the nondiscrimination principle. The theory underlying the majority's 'small versus large' test is that 'a tax on the services provided by a large number of cable operators offering a wide variety of programming throughout the State,' poses no 'risk of affecting only a limited range of views'. This assumption is unfounded. The record in this case furnishes ample support for the conclusion that the State's cable operators make unique contributions to the information market. See, e.g., App. 82 (testimony of cable operator that he offers 'certain religious programming' that 'people demand . . . because they otherwise could not have access to it'); id. at 138 (cable offers Spanish-language information network); id. at 150 (cable broadcast of local city council meetings). The majority offers no reason to believe that programs like these are duplicated by other media. Thus, to the extent that selective taxation makes it harder for Arkansas' 100 cable operators to compete with Arkansas' 500 newspapers, magazines, and broadcast television and radio stations, Arkansas' discriminatory tax *does* 'risk . . . affecting only a limited range of views,' and may well 'distort the market for ideas' in a manner akin to direct 'content-based regulation.'

"The majority also mistakenly assesses the impact of Arkansas' discriminatory tax as if the State's 100 cable operators comprised 100 additional actors in a *statewide* information market. In fact, most communities are serviced by only a single cable operator. Thus, in any given locale, Arkansas' discriminatory tax may disadvantage a *single* actor, a 'small' number even under the majority's calculus.

"Even more important, the majority's focus on absolute numbers ignores the potential for abuse inherent in the State's power to discriminate based on *medium identity*. So long as the disproportionately taxed medium is sufficiently 'large,' nothing in the majority's test prevents the State from singling out a particular medium for higher taxes, either because the State does not like the character of the services that the medium provides or because the State simply wishes to confer an advantage upon the medium's competitors. [F]or all we know, the legislature's initial decision selectively to tax cable may have been prompted by a [plea] from traditional broadcast media to curtail competition from the emerging cable industry. If the legislature did indeed respond to such importunings, the tax would implicate government censorship as surely as if the government itself disapproved of the new competitors.

"The majority, however, does not flinch at the prospect of intermedia discrimination. * * *

"At a minimum, the majority incorrectly conflates our cases on selective taxation of the press and our cases on the selective taxation (or subsidization) of speech generally. *Regan* holds that the government does not invariably violate the Free Speech Clause when it selectively subsidizes one group of speakers according to content-neutral criteria. This power, when exercised with appropriate restraint, inheres in government's legitimate authority to tap the energy of expressive activity to promote the public welfare.

"But our cases on the selective taxation of the *press* strike a different posture. Although the Free Press Clause does not guarantee the press a preferred position over other speakers, the Free Press Clause does 'protec[t] [members of press] from invidious discrimination.' L. Tribe, *American Constitutional Law* § 12–20, at 963 (2d ed. 1988). Selective taxation is precisely that. In light of the Framers' specific intent 'to preserve an untrammeled press as a vital source of public information,' *Grosjean,* our precedents recognize that the Free Press Clause imposes a special obligation on government to avoid disrupting the integrity of the information market.[4]"

SIMON & SCHUSTER, INC. v. NEW YORK STATE CRIME VICTIMS BOARD
___ U.S. ___, 112 S.Ct. 501, 116 L.Ed.2d 476 (1991).

JUSTICE O'CONNOR delivered the opinion of the Court.

In the summer of 1977, New York was terrorized by a serial killer popularly known as the Son of Sam. The hunt for the Son of Sam received considerable publicity, and by the time David Berkowitz was identified as the killer and apprehended, the rights to his story were worth a substantial amount. Berkowitz's chance to profit from his notoriety while his victims and their families remained uncompensated did not escape the notice of New York's Legislature. The State quickly enacted the statute at issue, N.Y.Exec.Law § 632–a (McKinney 1982 and Supp.1991).

The statute was intended to "ensure that monies received by the criminal under such circumstances shall first be made available to recompense the victims of that crime for their loss and suffering." As the author of the statute explained, "[i]t is abhorrent to one's sense of justice and decency that an individual * * * can expect to receive large sums of money for his story once

---

4. The majority's reliance on *Mabee v. White Plains Publishing Co.,* and *Oklahoma Press Publishing Co. v. Walling,* is also misplaced. At issue in those cases was a provision that exempted small newspapers with primarily local distribution from the Fair Labor Standards Act of 1938 (FLSA). In upholding the provision, the Court noted that the exemption promoted a legitimate interest in placing the exempted papers "on a parity with other small town enterprises" that also were not subject to regulation under the FLSA. In *Minneapolis Star,* we distinguished these cases on the ground that, unlike the FLSA exemption, Minnesota's discrimination between large and small newspapers did not derive from, or correspond to, any *general* state policy to benefit small businesses. Similarly, Arkansas' discrimination against cable operators derives not from any general, legitimate state policy unrelated to speech but rather from the simple decision of state officials to treat one information medium differently from all others. Thus, like the schemes in *Arkansas Writers' Project* and *Minneapolis Star,* but unlike the scheme at issue in *Mabee* and *Oklahoma Press,* the Arkansas tax scheme must be supported by a compelling interest to survive First Amendment scrutiny. Cf. *United States v. O'Brien.*

he is captured—while five people are dead, [and] other people were injured as a result of his conduct."

The Son of Sam law, as later amended, requires any entity contracting with an accused or convicted person for a depiction of the crime to submit a copy of the contract to respondent Crime Victims Board, and to turn over any income under that contract to the Board. * * *

Subsection (10) broadly defines "person convicted of a crime" to include "any person convicted of a crime in this state either by entry of a plea of guilty or by conviction after trial *and any person who has voluntarily and intelligently admitted the commission of a crime for which such person is not prosecuted.*" § 632–a(10)(b) (emphasis added). Thus a person who has never been accused or convicted of a crime in the ordinary sense, but who admits in a book or other work to having committed a crime, is within the statute's coverage.

As recently construed by the New York Court of Appeals, however, the statute does not apply to victimless crimes. * * *

A statute is presumptively inconsistent with the First Amendment if it imposes a financial burden on speakers because of the content of their speech. *Leathers v. Medlock.* As we emphasized in invalidating a content-based magazine tax, "official scrutiny of the content of publications as the basis for imposing a tax is entirely incompatible with the First Amendment's guarantee of freedom of the press." *Arkansas Writers' Project, Inc. v. Ragland.* * * *

The Son of Sam law is such a content-based statute. It singles out income derived from expressive activity for a burden the State places on no other income, and it is directed only at works with a specified content. [The] Board tries unsuccessfully to distinguish the Son of Sam law from the discriminatory tax at issue in *Arkansas Writers' Project.* While the Son of Sam law escrows all of the speaker's speech-derived income for at least five years, rather than taxing a percentage of it outright, this difference can hardly serve as the basis for disparate treatment under the First Amendment. Both forms of financial burden operate as disincentives to speak; indeed, in many cases it will be impossible to discern in advance which type of regulation will be more costly to the speaker. * * *

Finally, the Board claims that even if the First Amendment prohibits content-based financial regulation specifically of the *media,* the Son of Sam law is different, because it imposes a general burden on any "entity" contracting with a convicted person to transmit that person's speech. This argument falters on both semantic and constitutional grounds. Any "entity" that enters into such a contract becomes by definition a medium of communication, if it wasn't one already. In any event, the characterization of an entity as a member of the "media" is irrelevant for these purposes. The Government's power to impose content-based financial disincentives on speech surely does not vary with the identity of the speaker.

The Son of Sam law establishes a financial disincentive to create or publish works with a particular content. In order to justify such differential treatment, "the State must show that its regulation is necessary to serve a compelling state interest and is narrowly drawn to achieve that end." *Arkansas Writers' Project.* * * *

There can be little doubt [that] the State has a compelling interest in ensuring that victims of crime are compensated by those who harm them. Every State has a body of tort law serving exactly this interest. The State's interest in preventing wrongdoers from dissipating their assets before victims can recover explains the existence of the State's statutory provisions for prejudgment remedies and orders of restitution. * * *

The State likewise has an undisputed compelling interest in ensuring that criminals do not profit from their crimes. Like most if not all States, New York has long recognized the "fundamental equitable principle," *Children of Bedford v. Petromelis,* 77 N.Y.2d, at 727, 570 N.Y.S.2d, at 460, 573 N.E.2d, at 548, that "[n]o one shall be permitted to profit by his own fraud, or to take advantage of his own wrong, or to found any claim upon his own iniquity, or to acquire property by his own crime." *Riggs v. Palmer,* 115 N.Y. 506, 511–512, 22 N.E. 188, 190 (1889). The force of this interest is evidenced by the State's statutory provisions for the forfeiture of the proceeds and instrumentalities of crime.

The parties debate whether book royalties can properly be termed the profits of crime, but that is a question we need not address here. For the purposes of this case, we can assume without deciding that the income escrowed by the Son of Sam law represents the fruits of crime. We need only conclude that the State has a compelling interest in depriving criminals of the profits of their crimes, and in using these funds to compensate victims.

The Board attempts to define the State's interest more narrowly, as "ensuring that criminals do not profit from storytelling about their crimes before their victims have a meaningful opportunity to be compensated for their injuries." Here the Board is on far shakier ground. The Board cannot explain why the State should have any greater interest in compensating victims from the proceeds of such "storytelling" than from any of the criminal's other assets. Nor can the Board offer any justification for a distinction between this expressive activity and any other activity in connection with its interest in transferring the fruits of crime from criminals to their victims. Thus even if the State can be said to have an interest in classifying a criminal's assets in this manner, that interest is hardly compelling. * * *

In short, the State has a compelling interest in compensating victims from the fruits of the crime, but little if any interest in limiting such compensation to the proceeds of the wrongdoer's speech about the crime. We must therefore determine whether the Son of Sam law is narrowly tailored to advance the former, not the latter, objective. * * *

As a means of ensuring that victims are compensated from the proceeds of crime, the Son of Sam law is significantly overinclusive. [Had] the Son of Sam law been in effect at the time and place of publication, it would have escrowed payment for such works as The Autobiography of Malcolm X, which describes crimes committed by the civil rights leader before he became a public figure; Civil Disobedience, in which Thoreau acknowledges his refusal to pay taxes and recalls his experience in jail; and even the Confessions of Saint Augustine, in which the author laments "my past foulness and the carnal corruptions of my soul," one instance of which involved the theft of pears from a neighboring vineyard. *Amicus* Association of American Publishers, Inc., has submitted a sobering bibliography listing hundreds of works by American prisoners and ex-prisoners, many of which contain descriptions of the crimes for which the authors were incarcerated, including works by such authors as Emma Goldman and Martin Luther King, Jr. * * * The argument that a statute like the Son of Sam law would prevent publication of *all* of these works is hyperbole—some would have been written without compensation—but the Son of Sam law clearly reaches a wide range of literature that does not enable a criminal to profit from his crime while a victim remains uncompensated.**

[The judgment] of the Court of Appeals is accordingly

Reversed.[a]

JUSTICE KENNEDY, concurring in the judgment.

The New York statute we now consider imposes severe restrictions on authors and publishers, using as its sole criterion the content of what is written. The regulated content has the full protection of the First Amendment and this, I submit, is itself a full and sufficient reason for holding the statute unconstitutional. In my view it is both unnecessary and incorrect to ask whether the State can show that the statute " 'is necessary to serve a compelling state interest and is narrowly drawn to achieve that end.' " That test or formulation derives from our equal protection jurisprudence and has no real or legitimate place when the Court considers the straightforward question whether the State may enact a burdensome restriction of speech based on content only, apart from any considerations of time, place, and manner or the use of public forums.

Here a law is directed to speech alone where the speech in question is not obscene, not defamatory, not words tantamount to an act otherwise criminal, not an impairment of some other constitutional right, not an incitement to lawless action, and not calculated or likely to bring about imminent harm the State has the substantive power to prevent. No further inquiry is necessary to reject the State's argument that the statute should be upheld.

Borrowing the compelling interest and narrow tailoring analysis is ill-advised when all that is at issue is a content-based restriction, for resort to the test might be read as a concession that States may censor speech whenever they believe there is a compelling justification for doing so. Our precedents and traditions allow no such inference. * * *

There are a few legal categories in which content-based regulation has been permitted or at least contemplated. These include obscenity, see, *e.g., Miller;* defamation, see, *e.g., Dun & Bradstreet, Inc. v. Greenmoss Builders, Inc.;* incitement, see, *e.g., Brandenburg v. Ohio,* 395 U.S. 444, 89 S.Ct. 1827, 23 L.Ed.2d 430 (1969); or situations presenting some grave and imminent danger the government has the power to prevent, see, *e.g., Near v. Minnesota.* These are, however, historic and traditional categories long familiar to the bar, although with respect to the last category it is most difficult for the government to prevail. See *New York Times Co. v. United States.* While it cannot be said with certainty that the foregoing types of expression are or will remain the only ones that are without

** Because the Son of Sam law is so overinclusive, we need not address the Board's contention that the statute is content neutral under our decisions in *Ward v. Rock Against Racism* and *Renton v. Playtime Theatres, Inc.* In these cases, we determined that statutes were content neutral where they were intended to serve purposes unrelated to the content of the regulated speech, despite their incidental effects on some speakers but not others. Even under *Ward* and *Renton,* however, regulations must be "narrowly tailored" to advance the interest asserted by the State. A regulation is not "narrowly tailored"—even under the more lenient tailoring standards applied in *Ward* and *Renton*—where, as here, "a substantial portion of the burden on speech does not serve to advance [the State's content-neutral] goals." Thus whether the Son of Sam law is analyzed as content neutral under *Ward* or content based under *Leathers,* it is too overinclusive to satisfy the requirements of the First Amendment. And, in light of our conclusion in this case, we need not decide whether, as Justice Blackmun suggests, the Son of Sam law is underinclusive as well as overinclusive. Nor does this case present a need to address Justice Kennedy's discussion of what is a longstanding debate on an issue which the parties before us have neither briefed nor argued.

a. Blackmun, J., concurred. Thomas, J., did not participate.

First Amendment protection, as evidenced by the proscription of some visual depictions of sexual conduct by children, see *New York v. Ferber,* the use of these traditional legal categories is preferable to the sort of ad hoc balancing that the Court henceforth must perform in every case if the analysis here used becomes our standard test.

As a practical matter, perhaps we will interpret the compelling interest test in cases involving content regulation so that the results become parallel to the historic categories I have discussed, although an enterprise such as today's tends not to remain *pro forma* but to take on a life of its own. When we leave open the possibility that various sorts of content regulations are appropriate, we discount the value of our precedents and invite experiments that in fact present clear violations of the First Amendment, as is true in the case before us.

To forgo the compelling interest test in cases involving direct content-based burdens on speech would not, of course, eliminate the need for difficult judgments respecting First Amendment issues. Among the questions we cannot avoid the necessity of deciding are: whether the restricted expression falls within one of the unprotected categories discussed above; whether some other constitutional right is impaired, see *Nebraska Press Assn. v. Stuart;* whether, in the case of a regulation of activity which combines expressive with nonexpressive elements, the regulation aims at the activity or the expression, compare *United States v. O'Brien* with *Texas v. Johnson;* whether the regulation restricts speech itself or only the time, place, or manner of speech, see *Ward v. Rock Against Racism;* and whether the regulation is in fact content-based or content-neutral. See *Boos v. Barry.* However difficult the lines may be to draw in some cases, here the answer to each of these questions is clear.

The case before us presents the opportunity to adhere to a surer test for content-based cases and to avoid using an unnecessary formulation, one with the capacity to weaken central protections of the First Amendment. * * *

RUST v. SULLIVAN
___ U.S. ___, 111 S.Ct. 1759, 114 L.Ed.2d 233 (1991).

CHIEF JUSTICE REHNQUIST delivered the opinion of the Court.

These cases concern a facial challenge to Department of Health and Human Services (HHS) regulations which limit the ability of Title X fund recipients to engage in abortion-related activities. * * *

In 1970, Congress enacted Title X of the Public Health Service Act (Act), 84 Stat. 1506, as amended, 42 U.S.C. §§ 300–300a–41, which provides federal funding for family-planning services. The Act authorizes the Secretary to "make grants to and enter into contracts with public or non-profit private entities to assist in the establishment and operation of voluntary family planning projects which shall offer a broad range of acceptable and effective family planning methods and services." 42 U.S.C. § 300(a). Grants and contracts under Title X must "be made in accordance with such regulations as the Secretary may promulgate." 42 U.S.C. § 300a–4. Section 1008 of the Act, however, provides that "[n]one of the funds appropriated under this subchapter shall be used in programs where abortion is a method of family planning." 42 U.S.C. § 300a–6. * * *

In 1988, the Secretary promulgated new regulations designed to provide "'clear and operational guidance' to grantees about how to preserve the distinction between Title X programs and abortion as a method of family planning." 53 Fed.Reg. 2923–2924 (1988). * * *

The regulations attach three principal conditions on the grant of federal funds for Title X projects. First, the regulations specify that a "Title X project may not provide counseling concerning the use of abortion as a method of family planning or provide referral for abortion as a method of family planning." 42 CFR § 59.8(a)(1) (1989). Because Title X is limited to preconceptional services, the program does not furnish services related to childbirth. Only in the context of a referral out of the Title X program is a pregnant woman given transitional information. § 59.8(a)(2). Title X projects must refer every pregnant client "for appropriate prenatal and/or social services by furnishing a list of available providers that promote the welfare of the mother and the unborn child." Id. The list may not be used indirectly to encourage or promote abortion, "such as by weighing the list of referrals in favor of health care providers which perform abortions, by including on the list of referral providers health care providers whose principal business is the provision of abortions, by excluding available providers who do not provide abortions, or by 'steering' clients to providers who offer abortion as a method of family planning." § 59.8(a)(3). The Title X project is expressly prohibited from referring a pregnant woman to an abortion provider, even upon specific request. One permissible response to such an inquiry is that "the project does not consider abortion an appropriate method of family planning and therefore does not counsel or refer for abortion." § 59.8(b)(5).

Second, the regulations broadly prohibit a Title X project from engaging in activities that "encourage, promote or advocate abortion as a method of family planning." § 59.10(a). Forbidden activities include lobbying for legislation that would increase the availability of abortion as a method of family planning, developing or disseminating materials advocating abortion as a method of family planning, providing speakers to promote abortion as a method of family planning, using legal action to make abortion available in any way as a method of family planning, and paying dues to any group that advocates abortion as a method of family planning as a substantial part of its activities.

Third, the regulations require that Title X projects be organized so that they are "physically and financially separate" from prohibited abortion activities. § 59.9. To be deemed physically and financially separate, "a Title X project must have an objective integrity and independence from prohibited activities. Mere bookkeeping separation of Title X funds from other monies is not sufficient." Id. The regulations provide a list of nonexclusive factors for the Secretary to consider in conducting a case-by-case determination of objective integrity and independence, such as the existence of separate accounting records and separate personnel, and the degree of physical separation of the project from facilities for prohibited activities.

[Petitioners] are Title X grantees and doctors who supervise Title X funds suing on behalf of themselves and their patients. Respondent is the Secretary of the Department of Health and Human Services. [Petitioners] contend that the regulations violate the First Amendment by impermissibly discriminating based on viewpoint because they prohibit "all discussion about abortion as a lawful option—including counseling, referral, and the provision of neutral and accurate information about ending a pregnancy—while compelling the clinic or counselor to provide information that promotes continuing a pregnancy to term." They assert that the regulations violate the "free speech rights of private health care organizations that receive Title X funds, of their staff, and of their patients" by impermissibly imposing "viewpoint-discriminatory conditions on government subsidies" and thus "penaliz[e] speech funded with non-Title X monies." Because "Title X continues to fund speech ancillary to pregnancy testing in a manner that is not even-handed with respect to views and information about abortion, it invidiously discriminates on the basis of viewpoint." Relying on *Regan v. Taxation With Representation of Wash.,* and *Arkansas Writers' Project, Inc. v. Ragland,* petitioners also assert that while the Government may place certain conditions on the receipt of federal subsidies, it may not "discriminate invidiously in its subsidies in such a way as to 'ai[m] at the suppression of dangerous ideas.'" *Regan.*

There is no question but that the statutory prohibition contained in § 1008 is constitutional. [The] Government can, without violating the Constitution, selectively fund a program to encourage certain activities it believes to be in the public interest, without at the same time funding an alternate program which seeks to deal with the problem in another way.[a] In so doing, the Government has not discriminated on the basis of viewpoint; it has merely chosen to fund one activity to the exclusion of the other. "[A] legislature's decision not to subsidize the exercise of a fundamental right does not infringe the right." *Regan.* * * *

The challenged regulations implement the statutory prohibition by prohibiting counseling, referral, and the provision of information regarding abortion as a method of family planning. They are designed to ensure that the limits of the federal program are observed. The Title X program is designed not for prenatal care, but to encourage family planning. A doctor who wished to offer prenatal care to a project patient who became pregnant could properly be prohibited from doing so because such service is outside the scope of the federally funded program. The regulations prohibiting abortion counseling and referral are of the same ilk; "no funds appropriated for the project may be used in programs where abortion is a method of family planning," and a doctor employed by the project may be prohibited in the course of his project duties from counseling abortion or referring for abortion. This is not a case of the Government "suppressing a dangerous idea," but of a prohibition on a project grantee or its employees from engaging in activities outside of its scope.

To hold that the Government unconstitutionally discriminates on the basis of viewpoint when it chooses to fund a program dedicated to advance certain permissible goals, because the program in advancing those goals necessarily discourages alternate goals, would render numerous government programs constitutionally suspect. When Congress established a National Endowment for Democracy to encourage other countries to adopt democratic principles, 22 U.S.C. § 4411(b), it was not constitutionally required to fund a program to encourage competing lines of political philosophy such as Communism and Fascism. Petitioners' assertions ultimately boil down to the position that if the government chooses to subsidize one protected right, it must subsidize analogous counterpart rights. But the Court has soundly rejected that proposition. Within far broader limits than petitioners are willing to concede, when the government appropriates public funds to establish a program it is entitled to define the limits of that program.

We believe that petitioners' reliance upon our decision in *Arkansas Writers' Project* is misplaced. That case involved a state sales tax which discriminated

---

a. The Court cited *Maher v. Roe* [Con Law, p. 463, Amer Con, p. 304, Rts & Lib. p. 192 (constitutional for government to subsidize childbirth without subsidizing abortions)] and *Harris v. McRae* [Con Law, p. 465, Amer Con, p. 305, Rts & Lib. p. 194 (accord)].

between magazines on the basis of their content. Relying on this fact, and on the fact that the tax "targets a small group within the press," contrary to our decision in *Minneapolis Star,* the Court held the tax invalid. But we have here not the case of a general law singling out a disfavored group on the basis of speech content, but a case of the Government refusing to fund activities, including speech, which are specifically excluded from the scope of the project funded.

Petitioners rely heavily on their claim that the regulations would not, in the circumstance of a medical emergency, permit a Title X project to refer a woman whose pregnancy places her life in imminent peril to a provider of abortions or abortion-related services. This case, of course, involves only a facial challenge to the regulations, and we do not have before us any application by the Secretary to a specific fact situation. On their face, we do not read the regulations to bar abortion referral or counseling in such circumstances. * * *

Petitioners also contend that the restrictions on the subsidization of abortion-related speech contained in the regulations are impermissible because they condition the receipt of a benefit, in this case Title X funding, on the relinquishment of a constitutional right, the right to engage in abortion advocacy and counseling. * * *

[H]ere the government is not denying a benefit to anyone, but is instead simply insisting that public funds be spent for the purposes for which they were authorized. The Secretary's regulations do not force the Title X grantee to give up abortion-related speech; they merely require that the grantee keep such activities separate and distinct from Title X activities. Title X expressly distinguishes between a Title X *grantee* and a Title X *project.* The grantee, which normally is a health care organization, may receive funds from a variety of sources for a variety of purposes. The grantee receives Title X funds, however, for the specific and limited purpose of establishing and operating a Title X project. 42 U.S.C. § 300(a). The regulations govern the scope of the Title X *project's* activities, and leave the grantee unfettered in its other activities. The Title X *grantee* can continue to perform abortions, provide abortion-related services, and engage in abortion advocacy; it simply is required to conduct those activities through programs that are separate and independent from the project that receives Title X funds. 42 CFR 59.9 (1989).

In contrast, our "unconstitutional conditions" cases involve situations in which the government has placed a condition on the *recipient* of the subsidy rather that on a particular program or service, thus effectively prohibiting the recipient from engaging in the protected conduct outside the scope of the federally funded program. [By] requiring that the Title X grantee engage in abortion-related activity separately from activity receiving federal funding, Congress has, consistent with our teachings in *League of Women Voters* and *Regan,* not denied it the right to engage in abortion-related activities. Congress has merely refused to fund such activities out of the public fisc, and the Secretary has simply required a certain degree of separation from the Title X project in order to ensure the integrity of the federally funded program.

The same principles apply to petitioners' claim that the regulations abridge the free speech rights of the grantee's staff. Individuals who are voluntarily employed for a Title X project must perform their duties in accordance with the regulation's restrictions on abortion counseling and referral. The employees remain free, however, to pursue abortion-related activities when they are not acting under the auspices of the Title X project. The regulations, which govern solely the scope of the Title X project's activities, do not in any way restrict the activities of those persons acting as private individuals. The employees' freedom of expression is limited during the time that they actually work for the project; but this limitation is a consequence of their decision to accept employment in a project, the scope of which is permissibly restricted by the funding authority.

This is not to suggest that funding by the Government, even when coupled with the freedom of the fund recipients to speak outside the scope of the Government-funded project, is invariably sufficient to justify government control over the content of expression. For example, this Court has recognized that the existence of a Government "subsidy," in the form of Government-owned property, does not justify the restriction of speech in areas that have "been traditionally open to the public for expressive activity," or have been "expressly dedicated to speech activity." Similarly, we have recognized that the university is a traditional sphere of free expression so fundamental to the functioning of our society that the Government's ability to control speech within that sphere by means of conditions attached to the expenditure of Government funds is restricted by the vagueness and overbreadth doctrines of the First Amendment, *Keyishian v. Board of Regents*. It could be argued by analogy that traditional relationships such as that between doctor and patient should enjoy protection under the First Amendment from government regulation, even when subsidized by the Government. We need not resolve that question here, however, because the Title X program regulations do not significantly impinge upon the doctor-patient relationship. Nothing in them requires a doctor to represent as his own any opinion that he does not in fact hold. Nor is the doctor-patient relationship established by the Title X program sufficiently all-encompassing so as to justify an expectation on the part of the patient of comprehensive medical advice. The program does not provide post-conception medical care, and therefore a doctor's silence with regard to abortion cannot reasonably be thought to mislead a client into thinking that the doctor does not consider abortion an appropriate option for her. The doctor is always free to make clear that advice regarding abortion is simply beyond the scope of the program. In these circumstances, the general rule that the Government may choose not to subsidize speech applies with full force. * * *

JUSTICE BLACKMUN, with whom JUSTICE MARSHALL joins, with whom JUSTICE STEVENS joins as to Parts II [b] and III,[c] and with whom JUSTICE O'CONNOR joins as to Part I,[d] dissenting. * * *

II

A

Until today, the Court never has upheld viewpoint-based suppression of speech simply because that suppression was a condition upon the acceptance of public funds. Whatever may be the Government's power to condition the receipt of its largess upon the relinquishment of constitutional rights, it surely does not extend to a condition that suppresses the recipient's cherished freedom of speech based solely upon the content or viewpoint of that speech. * * *

It cannot seriously be disputed that the counseling and referral provisions at issue in the present cases constitute content-based regulation of speech. Title X

---

b. Part II discussed freedom of speech and portions of it are set out below.

c. Part III argued that the regulations violated the fifth amendment due process clause.

d. Part I contended that the regulations were not authorized by the statute. O'Connor, J., and Stevens, J., each filed separate dissents advancing the same contention.

grantees may provide counseling and referral regarding any of a wide range of family planning and other topics, save abortion.

The Regulations are also clearly viewpoint-based. While suppressing speech favorable to abortion with one hand, the Secretary compels anti-abortion speech with the other. For example, the Department of Health and Human Services' own description of the Regulations makes plain that "Title X projects are *required* to facilitate access to prenatal care and social services, including adoption services, that might be needed by the pregnant client to promote her well-being and that of her child, while making it abundantly clear that the project is not permitted to promote abortion by facilitating access to abortion through the referral process." 53 Fed.Reg. 2927 (1988) (emphasis added).

Moreover, the Regulations command that a project refer for prenatal care each woman diagnosed as pregnant, irrespective of the woman's expressed desire to continue or terminate her pregnancy. 42 CFR § 59.8(a)(2) (1990). If a client asks directly about abortion, a Title X physician or counselor is required to say, in essence, that the project does not consider abortion to be an appropriate method of family planning. § 59.8(b)(4). Both requirements are antithetical to the First Amendment. See *Wooley v. Maynard*.

The Regulations pertaining to "advocacy" are even more explicitly viewpoint-based. These provide: "A Title X project may not *encourage, promote or advocate* abortion as a method of family planning." § 59.10 (emphasis added). They explain: "This requirement prohibits actions to *assist* women to obtain abortions or *increase* the availability or accessibility of abortion for family planning purposes." § 59.10(a) (emphasis added). The Regulations do not, however, proscribe or even regulate anti-abortion advocacy. These are clearly restrictions aimed at the suppression of "dangerous ideas."

Remarkably, the majority concludes that "the Government has not discriminated on the basis of viewpoint; it has merely chosen to fund one activity to the exclusion of another." But the majority's claim that the Regulations merely limit a Title X project's speech to preventive or preconceptional services rings hollow in light of the broad range of non-preventive services that the Regulations authorize Title X projects to provide.[2] By refusing to fund those family-planning projects that advocate abortion *because* they advocate abortion, the Government plainly has targeted a particular viewpoint. The majority's reliance on the fact that the Regulations pertain solely to funding decisions simply begs the question. Clearly, there are some bases upon which government may not rest its decision to fund or not to fund. For example, the Members of the majority surely would agree that government may not base its decision to support an activity upon considerations of race. As demonstrated above, our cases make clear that ideological viewpoint is a similarly repugnant ground upon which to base funding decisions.

The majority's reliance upon *Regan* in this connection is [misplaced]. That case stands for the proposition that government has no obligation to subsidize a private party's efforts to petition the legislature regarding its views. Thus, if the challenged Regulations were confined to non-ideological limitations upon the use of Title X funds for lobbying activities, there would exist no violation of the First Amendment. The advocacy Regulations at issue here, however, are not limited

---

2. In addition to requiring referral for prenatal care and adoption services, the Regulations permit general health services such as physical examinations, screening for breast cancer, treatment of gynecological problems, and treatment for sexually transmitted diseases. 53 Fed.Reg. 2927 (1988). None of the latter are strictly preventive, preconceptional services.

to lobbying but extend to all speech having the effect of encouraging, promoting, or advocating abortion as a method of family planning. § 59.10(a). Thus, in addition to their impermissible focus upon the viewpoint of regulated speech, the provisions intrude upon a wide range of communicative conduct, including the very words spoken to a woman by her physician. By manipulating the content of the doctor/patient dialogue, the Regulations upheld today force each of the petitioners "to be an instrument for fostering public adherence to an ideological point of view [he or she] finds unacceptable." *Wooley v. Maynard.* This type of intrusive, ideologically based regulation of speech goes far beyond the narrow lobbying limitations approved in *Regan,* and cannot be justified simply because it is a condition upon the receipt of a governmental benefit.[3]

B

The Court concludes that the challenged Regulations do not violate the First Amendment rights of Title X staff members because any limitation of the employees' freedom of expression is simply a consequence of their decision to accept employment at a federally funded project. But it has never been sufficient to justify an otherwise unconstitutional condition upon public employment that the employee may escape the condition by relinquishing his or her job.

* * *

The majority attempts to circumvent this principle by emphasizing that Title X physicians and counselors "remain free . . . to pursue abortion-related activities when they are not acting under the auspices of the Title X project." "The regulations," the majority explains, "do not in any way restrict the activities of those persons acting as private individuals." Under the majority's reasoning, the First Amendment could be read to tolerate *any* governmental restriction upon an employee's speech so long as that restriction is limited to the funded workplace. This is a dangerous proposition, and one the Court has rightly rejected in the past.

In *Abood,* it was no answer to the petitioners' claim of compelled speech as a condition upon public employment that their speech outside the workplace remained unregulated by the State.[e] Nor was the public employee's First Amendment claim in *Rankin v. McPherson* derogated because the communication that her employer sought to punish occurred during business hours.[f] At the least, such conditions require courts to balance the speaker's interest in the message against those of government in preventing its dissemination.

3. The majority attempts to obscure the breadth of its decision through its curious contention that "the Title X program regulations do not significantly impinge upon the doctor-patient relationship." That the doctor-patient relationship is substantially burdened by a rule prohibiting the dissemination by the physician of pertinent medical information is beyond serious dispute. This burden is undiminished by the fact that the relationship at issue here is not an "all-encompassing" one. A woman seeking the services of a Title X clinic has every reason to expect, as do we all, that her physician will not withhold relevant information regarding the very purpose of her visit. To suggest otherwise is to engage in uninformed fantasy. Further, to hold that the doctor-patient relationship is somehow incomplete where a patient lacks the resources to seek comprehensive healthcare from a single provider is to ignore the situation of a vast number of Americans. As Justice Marshall has noted in a different context: "It is perfectly proper for judges to disagree about what the Constitution requires. But it is disgraceful for an interpretation of the Constitution to be premised upon unfounded assumptions about how people live." *United States v. Kras* (dissenting opinion).

e. *Abood v. Detroit Board of Education* [Con Law, p. 1018, Amer Con p. 776, Rts & Lib p. 747 (compelled funding of ideological activities of union violates freedom of speech)].

f. *Rankin* [Con Law, p. 1017, Amer Con p. 775, Rts & Lib p. 746 (expressed hope that assassination attempt of president be successful is protected speech when uttered in private to fellow employee during working hours)].

In the cases at bar, the speaker's interest in the communication is both clear and vital. In addressing the family-planning needs of their clients, the physicians and counselors who staff Title X projects seek to provide them with the full range of information and options regarding their health and reproductive freedom. Indeed, the legitimate expectations of the patient and the ethical responsibilities of the medical profession demand no less. "The patient's right of self-decision can be effectively exercised only if the patient possesses enough information to enable an intelligent choice. . . . The physician has an ethical obligation to help the patient make choices from among the therapeutic alternatives consistent with good medical practice." Current Opinions, the Council on Ethical and Judicial Affairs of the American Medical Association ¶ 8.08 (1989).

* * *

The Government's articulated interest in distorting the doctor/patient dialogue—ensuring that federal funds are not spent for a purpose outside the scope of the program—falls far short of that necessary to justify the suppression of truthful information and professional medical opinion regarding constitutionally protected conduct.[4] Moreover, the offending Regulation is not narrowly tailored to serve this interest. For example, the governmental interest at stake could be served by imposing rigorous bookkeeping standards to ensure financial separation or adopting content-neutral rules for the balanced dissemination of family-planning and health information. By failing to balance or even to consider the free speech interests claimed by Title X physicians against the Government's asserted interest in suppressing the speech, the Court falters in its duty to implement the protection that the First Amendment clearly provides for this important message.

C

Finally, it is of no small significance that the speech the Secretary would suppress is truthful information regarding constitutionally protected conduct of vital importance to the listener. One can imagine no legitimate governmental interest that might be served by suppressing such information. * * *

SECTION: THE RIGHT NOT TO SPEAK, THE RIGHT TO ASSOCIATE, AND THE RIGHT NOT TO ASSOCIATE

THE RIGHT NOT TO BE ASSOCIATED WITH PARTICULAR IDEAS

CON LAW: P. 1004, after second paragraph of fn. e

AMER CON: P. 762, after second paragraph of fn. e

RTS & LIB: P. 733, after second paragraph of fn. e

Do doctors have a first amendment right to resist state mandated disclosures to patients considering abortions? Consider joint opinion of O'Connor, Kennedy, and Souter, JJ., in *Planned Parenthood v. Casey,* in this Supplement supra: "[A] requirement that a doctor give a woman certain information as part of obtaining her consent to an abortion is, for constitutional purposes, no different from a requirement that a doctor give certain specific information about any medical procedure. All that is left of petitioners' argument is an asserted First Amendment right of a physician not to provide information about the risks of abortion, and childbirth, in a manner mandated by the State. To be sure, the physician's First Amendment rights not to speak are implicated, see *Wooley v. Maynard,* but

4. It is to be noted that the Secretary has made no claim that the Regulations at issue reflect any concern for the health or welfare of Title X clients.

only as part of the practice of medicine, subject to reasonable licensing and regulation by the State. We see no constitutional infirmity in the requirement that the physician provide the information mandated by the State here."

FREEDOM OF ASSOCIATION AND EMPLOYMENT

CON LAW: P. 1021, after note 1

AMER CON: P. 779, after note 1

RTS & LIB: P. 750, after note 1

LEHNERT v. FERRIS FACULTY ASS'N, ___ U.S. ___, 111 S.Ct. 1950, 114 L.Ed.2d 572 (1991), per BLACKMUN, J., again addressed the question of which union expenditures (such as lobbying, union conventions, newsletters, the costs of affiliating with state and national unions or of preparing for an illegal strike) could appropriately be charged to non-union members of a bargaining unit: "[C]hargeable activities must (1) be 'germane' to collective bargaining activity; (2) be justified by the government's vital policy interest in labor peace and avoiding 'free riders'; and (3) not significantly add to the burdening of free speech that is inherent in the allowance of an agency or union shop."

SCALIA, J., joined by O'Connor, Kennedy, and Souter, JJ., concurring in part and dissenting in part, argued for a different test, namely that contributions could constitutionally be compelled only for the costs of performing the union's statutory duties.

CON LAW: P. 1021, addition to fn. b

AMER CON: P. 779, addition to fn. b

RTS & LIB: P. 750, addition to fn. b

Renne v. Geary, ___ U.S. ___, 111 S.Ct. 2331, 115 L.Ed.2d 288 (1991) vacated the 9th circuit's decision on the ground the case was not justiciable. Marshall, J., joined by Blackmun, J., dissenting, argued that a ban on party endorsements in nonpartisan elections was overbroad. White, J., dissenting, argued that the first amendment does not require the state to include references to party endorsements in its official voter pamphlets and, like the majority, did not reach the question of whether a state could ban party endorsements in nonpartisan elections.

GOVERNMENT MANDATED DISCLOSURES AND FREEDOM OF ASSOCIATION

REPORTER'S PRIVILEGE

CON LAW: P. 1045, after note 5

AMER CON: P. 803, after note 5

RTS & LIB: P. 774, after note 5

Dan Cohen, an active Republican associated with Wheelock Whitney's Independent–Republican gubernatorial campaign provided the St. Paul Pioneer Press Dispatch and the Minneapolis Star and Tribune with information about the Democratic–Farmer–Labor candidate for Lieutenant Governor after reporters had promised him anonymity. Cohen gave public court records to the papers involving charges of unlawful assembly and petit theft. The unlawful assembly charges turned out to arise out of the candidate's participation in a civil rights protest, and were eventually dismissed. The petit theft conviction was for leaving a store without paying for $6.00 worth of sewing equipment. The judgment had since been vacated.

After some discussion concerning the misleading way in which the materials had been presented and debate about whether publication of the source's identity was appropriate under the circumstances, the papers published a story in which they named Cohen and mentioned his connection to the Whitney campaign. In response to Cohen's law suit against the publishers, the Minnesota Supreme Court found no claim for fraudulent misrepresentation or breach of contract. It further ruled that a cause of action based on promissory estoppel would be barred by the first amendment.

COHEN v. COWLES MEDIA CO., ___ U.S. ___, 111 S.Ct. 2513, 115 L.Ed.2d 586 (1991), per WHITE, J., reversed: "Respondents [newspaper publishers] rely on the proposition that 'if a newspaper lawfully obtains truthful information about a matter of public significance then state officials may not constitutionally punish publication of the information, absent a need to further a state interest of the highest order.' *Smith v. Daily Mail.* That proposition is unexceptionable, and it has been applied in various cases that have found insufficient the asserted state interests in preventing publication of truthful, lawfully obtained information. See, *e.g., The Florida Star v. B.J.F.; Smith v. Daily Mail.*

"This case however, is not controlled by this line of cases but rather by the equally well-established line of decisions holding that generally applicable laws do not offend the First Amendment simply because their enforcement against the press has incidental effects on its ability to gather and report the news. As the cases relied on by respondents recognize, the truthful information sought to be published must have been lawfully acquired. The press may not with impunity break and enter an office or dwelling to gather news. Neither does the First Amendment relieve a newspaper reporter of the obligation shared by all citizens to respond to a grand jury subpoena and answer questions relevant to a criminal investigation, even though the reporter might be required to reveal a confidential source. *Branzburg v. Hayes.* The press, like others interested in publishing, may not publish copyrighted material without obeying the copyright laws. See *Zacchini v. Scripps–Howard Broadcasting Co.* Similarly, the media must obey the National Labor Relations Act, *Associated Press v. NLRB,* and the Fair Labor Standards Act, *Oklahoma Press Publishing Co. v. Walling;* may not restrain trade in violation of the antitrust laws, *Associated Press v. United States;* and must pay non-discriminatory taxes. *Minneapolis Star and Tribune Co. v. Minnesota Commissioner of Revenue.* It is therefore beyond dispute that '[t]he publisher of a newspaper has no special immunity from the application of general laws. He has no special privilege to invade the rights and liberties of others.' *Associated Press v. NLRB.* Accordingly, enforcement of such general laws against the press is not subject to stricter scrutiny than would be applied to enforcement against other persons or organizations.

"There can be little doubt that the Minnesota doctrine of promissory estoppel is a law of general applicability. It does not target or single out the press. Rather, in so far as we are advised, the doctrine is generally applicable to the daily transactions of all the citizens of Minnesota. The First Amendment does not forbid its application to the press.

"Justice Blackmun suggests that applying Minnesota promissory estoppel doctrine in this case will 'punish' Respondents for publishing truthful information that was lawfully obtained. This is not strictly accurate because compensatory damages are not a form of punishment, as were the criminal sanctions at issue in *Smith*. If the contract between the parties in this case had contained a liquidated damages provision, it would be perfectly clear that the payment to petitioner would represent a cost of acquiring newsworthy material to be published at a profit, rather than a punishment imposed by the State. The payment of compensatory damages in this case is constitutionally indistinguishable from a generous bonus paid to a confidential news source. In any event, as indicated above, the characterization of the payment makes no difference for First Amendment purposes when the law being applied is a general law and does not single out the press. Moreover, Justice Blackmun's reliance on cases like *The Florida Star* and *Smith v. Daily Mail* is misplaced. In those cases, the State itself defined the content of publications that would trigger liability. Here, by contrast, Minnesota law simply requires those making promises to keep them. The parties themselves, as in this case, determine the scope of their legal obligations and any restrictions which may be placed on the publication of truthful information are self-imposed.

"Also, it is not at all clear that Respondents obtained Cohen's name 'lawfully' in this case, at least for purposes of publishing it. Unlike the situation in *The Florida Star*, where the rape victim's name was obtained through lawful access to a police report, respondents obtained Cohen's name only by making a promise which they did not honor. The dissenting opinions suggest that the press should not be subject to any law, including copyright law for example, which in any fashion or to any degree limits or restricts the press' right to report truthful information. The First Amendment does not grant the press such limitless protection.

"Nor is Cohen attempting to use a promissory estoppel cause of action to avoid the strict requirements for establishing a libel or defamation claim. As the Minnesota Supreme Court observed here, 'Cohen could not sue for defamation because the information disclosed [his name] was true.' Cohen is not seeking damages for injury to his reputation or his state of mind. He sought damages in excess of $50,000 for a breach of a promise that caused him to lose his job and lowered his earning capacity. Thus this is not a case like *Hustler Magazine, Inc. v. Falwell*, where we held that the constitutional libel standards apply to a claim alleging that the publication of a parody was a state-law tort of intentional infliction of emotional distress.

"Respondents and *amici* argue that permitting Cohen to maintain a cause of action for promissory estoppel will inhibit truthful reporting because news organizations will have legal incentives not to disclose a confidential source's identity even when that person's identity is itself newsworthy. Justice Souter makes a similar argument. But if this is the case, it is no more than the incidental, and constitutionally insignificant, consequence of applying to the press a generally applicable law that requires those who make certain kinds of promises to keep them. Although we conclude that the First Amendment does not confer on the press a constitutional right to disregard promises that would otherwise be enforced under state law, we reject Cohen's request that in reversing the Minnesota Supreme Court's judgment we reinstate the jury verdict awarding him $200,000 in compensatory damages. The Minnesota Supreme Court's incorrect conclusion that the First Amendment barred Cohen's claim may well have truncated its consideration of whether a promissory estoppel claim had otherwise been established under Minnesota law and whether Cohen's jury verdict could be upheld on a promissory estoppel basis. Or perhaps the State Constitution may be construed to shield the press from a promissory estoppel cause of action such as this one. These are matters for the Minnesota Supreme Court to address and resolve in the first instance on remand."

BLACKMUN, J., joined by Marshall and Souter, JJ., dissented: "The majority concludes that this case is not controlled by the decision in *Smith v. Daily Mail* to the effect that a State may not punish the publication of lawfully obtained, truthful information 'absent a need to further a state interest of the highest order.' Instead, we are told, the controlling precedent is 'the equally well-established line of decisions holding that generally applicable laws do not offend the First Amendment simply because their enforcement against the press has incidental effects on its ability to gather and report the news.' I disagree.

"I do not read the decision of the Supreme Court of Minnesota to create any exception to or immunity from the laws of that State for members of the press. In my view, the court's decision is premised, not on the identity of the speaker, but on the speech itself. Thus, the court found it to be of 'critical significance,' that 'the promise of anonymity arises in the classic First Amendment context of the quintessential public debate in our democratic society, namely, a political source involved in a political campaign.' Necessarily, the First Amendment protection afforded respondents would be equally available to non-media defendants. See, *e.g., Lovell v. Griffin* ('The liberty of the press is not confined to newspapers and periodicals. . . . The press in its historic connotation comprehends every sort of publication which affords a vehicle of information and opinion'). The majority's admonition that ' "[t]he publisher of a newspaper has no special immunity from the application of general laws," ' and its reliance on the cases that support that principle, are therefore misplaced.

"In *Branzburg*, for example, this Court found it significant that 'these cases involve no intrusions upon speech or assembly, no * * * restriction on what the press may publish, and no express or implied command that the press publish what it prefers to withhold. * * * [N]o penalty, civil or criminal, related to the content of published material is at issue here.' Indeed, '[t]he sole issue before us' in *Branzburg* was 'the obligation of reporters to respond to grand jury subpoenas as other citizens do and to answer questions relevant to an investigation into the commission of crime.' See also *Associated Press v. NLRB; Associated Press v. United States; Citizen Publishing Co. v. United States.* In short, these cases did *not* involve the imposition of liability based upon the content of speech.[1]

"Contrary to the majority, I regard our decision in *Hustler Magazine, Inc. v. Falwell*, to be precisely on point. There, we found that the use of a claim of intentional infliction of emotional distress to impose liability for the publication of a satirical critique violated the First Amendment. There was no doubt that Virginia's tort of intentional infliction of emotional distress was 'a law of general applicability' unrelated to the suppression of speech. Nonetheless, a unanimous

---

1. The only arguable exception is *Zacchini v. Scripps–Howard Broadcasting Co.* In *Zacchini*, a performer sued a news organization for appropriation of his "right to publicity value of his performance," after it broadcast the entirety of his act on local television. This Court held that the First Amendment did not bar the suit. We made clear, however, that our holding did not extend to the reporting of *information* about an event of public interest. We explained that "if * * * respondent had merely reported that petitioner was performing at the fair and described or commented on his act, with or without showing his picture on television, we would have a very different case." Thus, *Zacchini* cannot support the majority's conclusion that "a law of general applicability," may not violate the First Amendment when employed to penalize the dissemination of truthful information or the expression of opinion.

Court found that, when used to penalize the expression of opinion, the law was subject to the strictures of the First Amendment.

"As in *Hustler,* the operation of Minnesota's doctrine of promissory estoppel in this case cannot be said to have a merely 'incidental' burden on speech; the publication of important political speech *is* the claimed violation. Thus, as in *Hustler,* the law may not be enforced to punish the expression of truthful information or opinion.[4] In the instant case, it is undisputed that the publication at issue was true.

"To the extent that truthful speech may ever be sanctioned consistent with the First Amendment, it must be in furtherance of a state interest 'of the highest order.' *Smith.* Because the Minnesota Supreme Court's opinion makes clear that the State's interest in enforcing its promissory estoppel doctrine in this case was far from compelling, I would affirm that court's decision."

SOUTER, J., joined by Marshall, Blackmun, and O'Connor, JJ., dissented: "I agree with Justice Blackmun that this case does not fall within the line of authority holding the press to laws of general applicability where commercial activities and relationships, not the content of publication, are at issue. Even such general laws as do entail effects on the content of speech, like the one in question, may of course be found constitutional, but only, as Justice Harlan observed, 'when [such effects] have been justified by subordinating valid governmental interests, a prerequisite to constitutionality which has necessarily involved a weighing of the governmental interest involved. . . . Whenever, in such a context, these constitutional protections are asserted against the exercise of valid governmental powers a reconciliation must be effected, and that perforce requires an appropriate weighing of the respective interests involved.' *Konigsberg v. State Bar of California.*

"Thus, '[t]here is nothing talismanic about neutral laws of general applicability,' *Employment Division v. Smith* (O'Connor, J., concurring in judgment), for such laws may restrict First Amendment rights just as effectively as those directed specifically at speech itself. Because I do not believe the fact of general applicability to be dispositive, I find it necessary to articulate, measure, and compare the competing interests involved in any given case to determine the legitimacy of burdening constitutional interests, and such has been the Court's recent practice in publication cases. See *Hustler; Zacchini.*

"Nor can I accept the majority's position that we may dispense with balancing because the burden on publication is in a sense 'self-imposed' by the newspaper's voluntary promise of confidentiality. This suggests both the possibility of waiver, the requirements for which have not been met here, as well as a conception of First Amendment rights as those of the speaker alone, with a value that may be measured without reference to the importance of the information to public discourse. * * *

"The importance of this public interest is integral to the balance that should be struck in this case. There can be no doubt that the fact of Cohen's identity

---

4. The majority argues that, unlike the criminal sanctions we considered in *Smith v. Daily Mail*, the liability at issue here will not "punish" respondents in the strict sense of that word. While this may be true, we have long held that the imposition of civil liability based on protected expression constitutes "punishment" of speech for First Amendment purposes. * * *

Though they be civil, the sanctions we review in this case are no more justifiable as "a cost of acquiring newsworthy material," than were the libel damages at issue in *New York Times,* a permissible cost of disseminating newsworthy material.

expanded the universe of information relevant to the choice faced by Minnesota voters in that State's 1982 gubernatorial election, the publication of which was thus of the sort quintessentially subject to strict First Amendment protection. The propriety of his leak to respondents could be taken to reflect on his character, which in turn could be taken to reflect on the character of the candidate who had retained him as an adviser. An election could turn on just such a factor; if it should, I am ready to assume that it would be to the greater public good, at least over the long run.

"This is not to say that the breach of such a promise of confidentiality could never give rise to liability. One can conceive of situations in which the injured party is a private individual, whose identity is of less public concern than that of the petitioner; liability there might not be constitutionally prohibited. Nor do I mean to imply that the circumstances of acquisition are irrelevant to the balance, although they may go only to what balances against, and not to diminish, the First Amendment value of any particular piece of information.

"Because I believe the State's interest in enforcing a newspaper's promise of confidentiality insufficient to outweigh the interest in unfettered publication of the information revealed in this case, I respectfully dissent."

Chapter

FREEDOM OF RELIGION

SECTION: ESTABLISHMENT CLAUSE

OFFICIAL ACKNOWLEDGEMENT OF RELIGION

CON LAW: P. 1160, at end of Sec.
AMER CON: P. 893, at end of Sec.
RTS & LIB: P. 889, at end of Sec.

LEE v. WEISMAN, ___ U.S. ___, 112 S.Ct. 2649, ___ L.Ed.2d ___ (1992), per KENNEDY, J., held violative of the establishment clause the practice of public school officials inviting members of the clergy to offer invocation and benediction prayers at graduation ceremonies: "We can decide the case without reconsidering the general constitutional framework [in *Lemon*] by which public schools' efforts to accommodate religion are measured. [The] government involvement with religious activity in this case is pervasive, to the point of creating a state-sponsored and state-directed religious exercise in the public school [where] subtle coercive pressures exist and where the student had no real alternative which would have allowed her to avoid the fact or appearance of participation.

"[The] undeniable fact is that the school district's supervision and control of a high school graduation ceremony places public pressure, as well as peer pressure, on attending students to stand as a group or, at least, maintain respectful silence during the Invocation and Benediction. This pressure, though subtle and indirect, can be as real as any overt compulsion. [N]o doubt some persons who have no desire to join a prayer have little objection to standing as a sign of respect for those who do. But for the dissenter of high school age who has a reasonable perception that she is being forced by the State to pray in a manner her conscience will not allow, the injury is no less real. * * *

"Finding no violation under these circumstances would place objectors in the dilemma of participating, with all that implies, or protesting. * * * Research in psychology supports the common assumption that adolescents are often susceptible to pressure from their peers towards conformity, and that the influence is strongest in matters of social convention. To recognize that the choice imposed by the State constitutes an unacceptable constraint only acknowledges that the government may no more use social pressure to enforce orthodoxy than it may use more direct means. [That] the intrusion was in the course of promulgating religion that sought to be civic or non sectarian rather than pertaining to one sect does not lessen the offense or isolation to the objectors. At best it narrows their number, at worst increases their sense of isolation and affront.

"[I]n our society and in our culture high school graduation is one of life's most significant occasions. A school rule which excuses attendance is beside the point. Attendance may not be required by official decree, yet it is apparent that a student is not free to absent herself from the graduation exercise in any real sense of the term 'voluntary,' for absence would require forfeiture of these intangible benefits which have motivated the student through youth and all her high school years. [To] say that a student must remain apart from the ceremony at the opening invocation and closing benediction is to risk compelling conformity in an environment analogous to the classroom setting, where we have said the risk of compulsion is especially high. See *Engel* and *Schempp*. * * *

"Inherent differences between the public school system and a session of a State Legislature distinguish this case from *Marsh*. [The] atmosphere at the opening of a session of a state legislature where adults are free to enter and leave with little comment and for any number of reasons cannot compare with the constraining potential of the one school event most important for the student to attend. * * *

"We do not hold that every state action implicating religion is invalid if one or a few citizens find it offensive. People may take offense at all manner of religious as well as nonreligious messages, but offense alone does not in every case show a violation. We know too that sometimes to endure social isolation or even anger may be the price of conscience or nonconformity. But, by any reading of our cases, the conformity required of the student in this case was too high an exaction to withstand the test of the Establishment Clause."

BLACKMUN, J., joined by Stevens and O'Connor, JJ., concurred: "There can be 'no doubt' that the 'invocation of God's blessings' delivered at Nathan Bishop Middle School 'is a religious activity,' *Engel,* [and] that the government is advancing and promoting religion. As our prior decisions teach us, it is this that the Constitution prohibits. * * *

"But it is not enough that the government restrain from compelling religious practices: it must not engage in them either. [To] that end, our cases have prohibited government endorsement of religion, its sponsorship, and active involvement in religion, whether or not citizens were coerced to conform.

"I remain convinced that our jurisprudence is not misguided, and that it requires the decision reached by the Court today."

SOUTER, J., joined by Stevens and O'Connor, JJ., concurred to emphasize two points: First, "history neither contradicts nor warrants reconsideration of the settled principle that the Establishment Clause forbids support for religion in general no less than support for one religion or some."

Second, "state coercion of religious conformity, over and above state endorsement of religious exercise or belief, is [*not*] a necessary element of an Establishment Clause violation. [L]aws that coerce nonadherents to 'support or participate in any religion or its exercise,' would virtually by definition violate their right to religious free exercise. [Thus,] a literal application of the coercion test would render the Establishment Clause a virtual nullity * * *.

"The Framers adopted the Religion Clauses in response to a long tradition of coercive state support for religion, particularly in the form of tax assessments, but their special antipathy to religious coercion did not exhaust their hostility to the features and incidents of establishment. Indeed, Jefferson and Madison opposed any political appropriation of regligion, [and] saw that even without the tax collector's participation, an official endorsement of religion can impair religious liberty. [O]ne can call any act of endorsement a form of coercion, but only if one is willing to dilute the meaning of 'coercion' until there is no meaning left. [This] principle against favoritism and endorsement has become the foundation of Establishment Clause jurisprudence, ensuring that religious belief is irrelevant to every citizen's standing in the political community * * *.

"Religious students cannot complain that omitting prayers from their graduation ceremony would, in any realistic sense, 'burden' their spiritual callings. To be sure, many of them invest this rite of passage with spiritual significance, but they may express their religious feelings about it before and after the ceremony. They may even organize a privately sponsored baccalaureate if they desire the company of likeminded students. Because they accordingly have no need for the machinery of the State to affirm their beliefs, the government's sponsorship of prayer at the graduation ceremony is most reasonably understood as an official endorsement of religion and, in this instance, of theistic religion."

SCALIA, J., joined by Rehnquist, C.J., and White and Thomas, JJ., dissented: "Three terms ago, I joined an opinion recognizing that 'the meaning of the [Establishment] Clause is to be determined by reference to historical practices and understandings.' It said that '[a] test for implementing the protections of the Establishment Clause that, if applied with consistency, would invalidate longstanding traditions cannot be a proper reading of the Clause.' *Allegheny County* (Kennedy, J., concurring in judgment in part and dissenting in part).

"These views of course prevent me from joining today's opinion, which is conspicuously bereft of any reference to history [and] lays waste a tradition that is as old as public-school graduation ceremonies themselves, and that is a component of an even more longstanding American tradition of nonsectarian prayer to God at public celebrations generally.

"[Since] the Court does not dispute that students exposed to prayer at graduation ceremonies retain (despite 'subtle coercive pressures,') the free will to sit, there is absolutely no basis for the Court's decision. It is fanciful enough to say that 'a reasonable dissenter,' standing head erect in a class of bowed heads, 'could believe that the group exercise signified her own participation or approval of it.' It is beyond the absurd to say that she could entertain such a belief while pointedly declining to rise.

"But let us assume the very worst, that the nonparticipating graduate is 'subtly coerced' * * * to stand! Even that half of the disjunctive does not remotely establish a 'participation' (or an 'appearance of participation') in a religious exercise. * * *

"The deeper flaw in the Court's opinion does not lie in its wrong answer to the question whether there was state-induced 'peer-pressure' coercion; it lies, rather, in the Court's making violation of the Establishment Clause hinge on such a precious question. The coercion that was a hallmark of historical establishments of religion was coercion of religious orthodoxy and of financial support by force of *law and threat of penalty.* [I] concede that our constitutional tradition [has,] ruled out of order government-sponsored endorsement of religion—even when no legal coercion is present, and indeed even when no ersatz, 'peer-pressure' psycho-coercion is present—where the endorsement is sectarian, in the sense of specifying details upon which men and women who believe in a benevolent, omnipotent Creator and Ruler of the world, are known to differ (for example, the divinity of Christ). But there is simply no support for the proposition that the officially sponsored nondenominational invocation and benediction read by Rabbi Gutterman—with no one legally coerced to recite them—violated the Constitution of the United States. To the contrary, they are so characteristically American they could have come from the pen of George Washington or Abraham Lincoln himself.

"The Court relies on our 'school prayer' cases, *Engel* and *Schempp*. But whatever the merit of those cases, they do not support, much less compel, the Court's psycho-journey. In the first place, *Engel* and *Schempp* do not constitute an exception to the rule, distilled from historical practice, that public ceremonies may include prayer; rather, they simply do not fall within the scope of the rule (for the obvious reason that school instruction is not a public ceremony). Second, we have made clear our understanding that school prayer occurs within a framework in which legal coercion to attend school (i.e., coercion under threat of penalty) provides the ultimate backdrop. * * * Voluntary prayer at graduation—a one-time ceremony at which parents, friends and relatives are present—can hardly be thought to raise the same concerns.

"[Given] the odd basis for the Court's decision, invocations and benedictions will be able to be given at public-school graduations next June, as they have for the past century and a half, so long as school authorities make clear that anyone who abstains from screaming in protest does not necessarily participate in the prayers. All that is seemingly needed is an announcement, or perhaps a written insertion at the beginning of the graduation Program, to the effect that, while all are asked to rise for the invocation and benediction, none is compelled to join in them, nor will be assumed, by rising, to have done so."

Query: How would the *Lee* Court have decided the crèche issue in *Allegheny?* Has Kennedy, J.'s "coercion" approach prevailed over O'Connor, J.'s "endorsement" approach? See Choper, *Separation of Church and State: "New" Directions by the "New" Supreme Court,* 34 J. Church & State 363 (1992).

Chapter

EQUAL PROTECTION

SECTION: TRADITIONAL APPROACH

CON LAW: P. 1220, at end of note (b)

AMER CON: P. 936, at end of note (b)

RTS & LIB: P. 949, at end of note (b)

NORDLINGER v. HAHN, ___ U.S. ___, 112 S.Ct. 2326, ___ L.Ed.2d ___ (1992), per BLACKMUN, J., held that California's "acquisition value" system for initially assessing property (Proposition 13) "rationally furthers the State's ["legitimate"] interests in neighborhood stability and the protection of property owners' reliance interests." As in *Allegheny,* Proposition 13 "resulted in dramatic disparities in taxation of properties of comparable value." But "the Equal Protection Clause is satisfied so long as there is a plausible policy reason for the classification, *Fritz,* [and] *Allegheny* was the rare case where the facts precluded any plausible inference that the reason for the unequal assessment practice was to achieve the benefits of an acquisition-value tax scheme. By contrast, Proposition 13 was enacted precisely to achieve the benefits."

THOMAS, J., concurred in upholding Proposition 13 but would have "confronted [*Allegheny*] directly": "Even if the assessor did violate West Virginia law, she would not have violated the Equal Protection Clause. A violation of state law does not by itself constitute a violation of the Federal Constitution."

STEVENS, J., dissented: "[T]he selective provision of benefits based on the timing of one's membership in a class (whether that class be the class of residents or the class of property owners) is rarely a 'legitimate state interest.' Similarly situated neighbors have an equal right to share in the benefits of local government. It would obviously be unconstitutional to provide one with more or better fire or police protection than the other; it is just as plainly unconstitutional to require one to pay five times as much in property taxes as the other for the same government services. In my opinion, the severe inequalities created by Proposition 13 are arbitrary and unreasonable and do not rationally further a legitimate state interest."

SECTION: RACE AND ETHNIC ANCESTRY

DE JURE vs. DE FACTO DISCRIMINATION

CON LAW: P. 1243, at end of note 3

RTS & LIB: P. 972, at end of note 3

GEORGIA v. McCOLLUM, ___ U.S. ___, 112 S.Ct. 2348, ___ L.Ed.2d ___ (1992), per BLACKMUN, J., extended *Batson* and *Edmonson v. Leesville Concrete Co.*, p. 183 of this Supplement, to peremptory challenges by a criminal defendant: "Just as public confidence in criminal justice is undermined by a conviction in a trial where racial discrimination has occurred in jury selection, so is public confidence undermined where a defendant, assisted by racially discriminatory peremptory strikes, obtains an acquittal."

O'Connor and Scalia, JJ., dissented on the ground that there was no "state action" (as discussed in her dissent in *Edmonson*). Rehnquist, C.J. and Thomas, J., agreed, but concurred in the judgment because "*Edmonson* governs this case." On the merits, THOMAS, J., added: "In *Strauder,* we put the rights of defendants foremost. Today's decision, while protecting jurors, leaves defendants with less means of protecting themselves. [B]lack criminal defendants will rue the day that this court ventured down this road that inexorably will lead to the elimination of peremptory strikes."

CON LAW: P. 1241, at end of note 1(a)

AMER CON: P. 952, before note (b)

RTS & LIB: P. 970, at end of note 1(a)

Deference to factfinder: The trial court's decision on the ultimate question of discriminatory intent represents a finding of fact of the sort accorded great deference on appeal, particularly on issues of credibility. *Hernandez v. New York*, ___ U.S. ___, 111 S.Ct. 1859, 114 L.Ed.2d 395 (1991).

REMEDYING SEGREGATION

CON LAW: P. 1265, after note (c)

AMER CON: P. 971, before *Keyes*

RTS & LIB: P. 994, after note (c)

(d) In FREEMAN v. PITTS, ___ U.S. ___, 112 S.Ct. 1430, 118 L.Ed.2d 108 (1992), the district court had found that the De Kalb County (GA) School System had "achieved unitary status [with] regard to student assignments, transportation, physical facilities, and extracurricular activities," but not in respect to "teacher and principal assignments, resource allocation, and quality of education." The Court, per KENNEDY, J.,—emphasizing that "returning schools to the control of local authorities at the earliest practicable date is essential to restore their true accountability in our government system"—held that "while retaining jurisdiction over the case, the court [may] withdraw judicial supervision with respect to discrete categories in which the school district has achieved compliance with a court-ordered desegregation plan [and] need not retain active control over every aspect of school administration until a school district has demonstrated unitary status in all facets of its system.

"[Among] the factors which must inform the sound discretion of the court in ordering partial withdrawal are the following: whether there has been full and satisfactory compliance with the decree in those aspects of the system where supervision is to be withdrawn; whether retention of judicial control is necessary or practicable to achieve compliance with the decree in other facets of the school system; and whether the school district has demonstrated, [its] good faith commitment to the whole of the court's decree * * *.

"As the de jure violation becomes more remote in time and these demographic changes intervene, it becomes less likely that a current racial imbalance in a school district is a vestige of the prior de jure system. The causal link between current conditions and the prior violation is even more attenuated if the school district has demonstrated its good faith. [It] was appropriate for the District Court to examine the reasons for the racial imbalance before ordering an impractical, and no doubt massive, expenditure of funds to achieve racial balance after 17 years of efforts to implement the comprehensive plan in a district where there were fundamental changes in demographics, changes not attributable to the former de jure regime or any later actions by school officials. The District Court's determination to order instead the expenditure of scarce resources in areas such as the quality of education, where full compliance had not yet been achieved, underscores the uses of discretion in framing equitable remedies. * * *

"There was no showing that racial balance [in student assignments] was an appropriate mechanism to cure other deficiencies in this case. It is true that the school district was not in compliance with respect to faculty assignments, but the record does not show that student reassignments would be a feasible or practicable way to remedy this defect."

SCALIA, J., concurred: "Racially imbalanced schools are [the] product of a blend of public and private actions, and any assessment that they would not be segregated, or would not be *as* segregated, in the absence of a particular one of those factors is guesswork. [Only] in rare cases such as this one and *Spangler,* where the racial imbalance had been temporarily corrected after the abandonment of de jure segregation, can it be asserted with any degree of confidence that the past discrimination is no longer playing a proximate role. Thus, allocation of the burden of proof foreordains the result in almost all of the 'vestige of past discrimination' cases. [Our] post-*Green* cases provide that, once state-enforced school segregation is shown to have existed in a jurisdiction in 1954, there arises a presumption, effectively irrebuttable (because the school district cannot prove the negative), that any current racial imbalance is the product of that violation, at least if the imbalance has continuously existed.

"In the context of elementary and secondary education, [the] extent and recency of the prior discrimination, and the improbability that young children (or their parents) would use 'freedom of choice' plans to disrupt existing patterns 'warrant[ed] a presumption [that] schools that are substantially disproportionate in their racial composition' were remnants of the de jure system. *Swann.*

"But granting the merits of this approach at the time of *Green,* it is now 25 years later. [Since] a multitude of private factors has shaped school systems in the years after abandonment of de jure segregation—normal migration, population growth (as in this case), 'white flight' from the inner cities, increases in the costs of new facilities—the percentage of the current makeup of school systems attributable to the prior, government-enforced discrimination has diminished with each passing year, to the point where it cannot realistically be assumed to be a significant factor.

"[While] we must continue to prohibit, without qualification, all racial discrimination in the operation of public schools, and to afford remedies that eliminate not only the discrimination but its identified consequences, we should consider laying aside the extraordinary, and increasingly counterfactual, presumption of *Green*. We must soon revert to the ordinary principles [that] plaintiffs alleging Equal Protection violations must prove intent and causation and not merely the existence of racial disparity, see *Washington v. Davis*."

SOUTER, J., concurred, emphasizing that "racial imbalance in student assignments caused by demographic change is not insulated from federal judicial oversight where the demographic change is itself caused ["by past school segregation and the patterns of thinking that segregation creates"], and before deciding to relinquish supervision and control over student assignments, a district court should make findings on the presence or absence of this relationship."

BLACKMUN, J., joined by Stevens and O'Connor, JJ., concurred only in the judgment, stressing that "the District Court's jurisdiction should continue until the school board demonstrates full compliance with the Constitution." Although disagreeing with the conclusion of the court of appeals that retaining jurisdiction means that the district court should "continually order reassignment of students," nonetheless the district court must assure that the school district "has met its burden of proving [that] the current racial imbalance in the schools is [not] attributable in part to the former de jure segregated regime or any later action by school officials." Thomas, J., did not participate.

CON LAW: P. 1279, at end of Sec.

AMER CON: P. 981, at end of Sec.

RTS & LIB: P. 1008, at end of Sec.

UNITED STATES v. FORDICE, ___ U.S. ___, 112 S.Ct. 2727, ___ L.Ed.2d ___ (1992), per WHITE, J., involved Mississippi's public university system which maintained five almost completely white and three almost exclusively black schools: "That college attendance is by choice and not by assignment does not mean that a race-neutral admissions policy cures the constitutional violation of a dual system. [If] the State perpetuates policies and practices traceable to its prior system that continue to have segregative effects—whether by influencing student enrollment decisions or by fostering segregation in other facets of the university system—and such policies are without sound educational justification and can be practicably eliminated, the State has not satisfied its burden of proving that it has dismantled its prior system."

The Court remanded the case for review "in light of the proper standard," but did "address four policies of the present system: * * *

"The present admission standards are not only traceable to the de jure system and were originally adopted for a discriminatory purpose, but they also have present discriminatory effects. Every Mississippi resident under 21 seeking admission to the university system must take the ACT. Any applicant who scores at least 15 qualifies for automatic admission to [the] historically white institutions. [I]n 1985, 72 percent of Mississippi's white high school seniors achieved an ACT composite score of 15 or better, while less than 30 percent of black high school seniors earned that score. It is not surprising then that Mississippi's universities remain predominantly identifiable by race.

"[The] courts below made little if any effort to justify in educational terms those particular disparities in entrance requirements or to inquire whether it was practicable to eliminate them.

"[The] record also indicated that the disparity between black and white students' high school grade averages was much narrower than the gap between their average ACT scores, thereby suggesting that an admissions formula which included grades would increase the number of black students eligible for automatic admission to all of Mississippi's public universities. * * *

"A second aspect of the present system that necessitates further inquiry is the widespread duplication of programs. [It] can hardly be denied that such duplication was part and parcel of the prior dual system of higher education—the whole notion of 'separate but equal' required duplicative programs in two sets of schools—and that the present unnecessary duplication is a continuation of that practice. *Brown* and its progeny, however, established that the burden of proof falls on the State, and not the aggrieved plaintiffs, to establish that it has dismantled its prior de jure segregated system. The court's holding that petitioners could not establish the constitutional defect of unnecessary duplication, therefore, improperly shifted the burden away from the State. * * *

"We next address [the fact that in] 1981, the State assigned certain missions to Mississippi's public universities as they then existed. [We] do not suggest that absent discriminatory purpose the assignment of different missions to various institutions in a State's higher education system would raise an equal protection issue where one or more of the institutions become or remain predominantly black or white. But here the issue is whether the State has sufficiently dismantled its prior dual system; and when combined with the differential admission practices and unnecessary program duplication, it is likely that the mission designations interfere with student choice and tend to perpetuate the segregated system. On remand, the court should inquire whether it would be practicable and consistent with sound educational practices to eliminate any such discriminatory effects of the State's present policy of mission assignments.

"Fourth, the State attempted to bring itself into compliance with the Constitution by continuing to maintain and operate all eight higher educational institutions. [O]n remand this issue should be carefully explored by inquiring and determining whether retention of all eight institutions itself affects student choice and perpetuates the segregated higher education system, whether maintenance of each of the universities is educationally justifiable, and whether one or more of them can be practicably closed or merged with other existing institutions."

THOMAS, J., concurred, emphasizing that "we do not foreclose the possibility that there exists 'sound educational justification' for maintaining historically black colleges as such. * * * Obviously, a State cannot maintain such traditions by closing particular institutions, historically white or historically black, to particular racial groups. Nonetheless, it hardly follows that a State cannot operate a diverse assortment of institutions—including historically black institutions—open to all on a race-neutral basis, but with established traditions and programs that might disproportionately appeal to one race or another. No one, I imagine, would argue that such institutional diversity is without 'sound educational justification,' or that it is even remotely akin to program duplication, which is designed to separate the races for the sake of separating the races." [a]

SCALIA, J., concurred on the ground that "the District Court should have required Mississippi to prove that its continued use of ACT requirements does not have a racially exclusionary purpose and effect," but dissented from "the

a. O'Connor, J., also filed a brief concurrence.

Court's [applying] to universities the amorphous standard adopted for primary and secondary schools in *Green.* * * *

Bazemore's standard for dismantling a dual system ought to control here: discontinuation of discriminatory practices and adoption of a neutral admissions policy. To use *Green* nomenclature, modern racial imbalance remains a 'vestige' of past segregative practices in Mississippi's universities, in that the previously mandated racial identification continues to affect where students choose to enroll—just as it surely affected which clubs students chose to join in *Bazemore.* We tolerated this vestigial effect in *Bazemore,* squarely rejecting the view that the State was obliged to correct 'the racial segregation resulting from [its prior] practice[s].' (Brennan, J., dissenting in part). And we declined to require the State, as the Court has today, to prove that no holdover practices of the de jure system, e.g., program offerings in the different clubs, played a role in the students' decisions of which clubs to join. [Like] the club attendance in *Bazemore* (and unlike the school attendance in *Green*), attending college is voluntary, not a legal obligation, and which institution particular students attend is determined by their own choice."

SECTION: SPECIAL SCRUTINY FOR OTHER CLASSIFICATIONS

MENTAL RETARDATION

CON LAW: P. 1376, addition to note 2

GREGORY v. ASHCROFT, ___ U.S. ___, 111 S.Ct. 2395, 115 L.Ed.2d 410 (1991), per O'CONNOR, J., upheld Missouri's mandatory requirement for judges at age 70: "Petitioners are correct to assert their claim at the level of rational basis. This Court has said repeatedly that age is not a suspect classification under the Equal Protection Clause. *Murgia; Cleburne.* Nor do petitioners claim that they have a fundamental interest in serving as judges. * * * It is an unfortunate fact of life that physical and mental capacity sometimes diminish with age. * * * The Missouri mandatory retirement provision, like all legal classifications, is founded on a generalization. It is far from true that all judges suffer significant deterioration in performance at age 70. It is probably not true that most do. It may not be true at all. But a state ' "does not violate the Equal Protection Clause merely because the classifications made by its laws are imperfect." ' *Murgia.*" [a]

SECTION: "FUNDAMENTAL RIGHTS"

RESTRICTIONS ON PARTIES AND CANDIDATES

CON LAW: P. 1418, addition to fn. c

RTS & LIB: P. 1147, addition to fn. c

After *Socialist Workers Party,* Illinois law was amended to require the collection of 25,000 signatures (or 5% of the electorate, whichever is less) to run candidates from a new party in any electoral district or for any statewide office. Cook County, Illinois is divided into two districts: an area corresponding to the city of Chicago and another covering the suburbs. Petitioners gathered 44,000 signatures in the city part of the district and 7,800 signatures in the suburban part of the district. The election board held that peti-

a. Blackmun, J., joined by Stevens, J., dissenting on federal statutory grounds, did not reach the equal protection issue.

tioners could run candidates in the Chicago district and for county wide offices, but not for positions in the suburban district. Constitutional? See Norman v. Reed, ___ U.S. ___, 112 S.Ct. 698, 116 L.Ed.2d 711 (1992). Can petitioners be disabled from running for any positions in Cook County because of their failure to gather 25,000 signatures in the suburban district? See id. Because of their failure to provide a full slate of candidates? For discussion, see id. (not reaching the question).

CON LAW: P. 1419, after Lubin

RTS & LIB: P. 1148, after Lubin

BURDICK v. TAKUSHI, ___ U.S. ___, 112 S.Ct. 2059, ___ L.Ed.2d ___ (1992), per WHITE, J., upheld a Hawaii ban on write in voting in circumstances where the system provided for "easy [candidate access to the ballot] until the cutoff date for the filing of nominating petitions, two months before the primary." Petitioner's desire to cast a protest vote for Donald Duck was rejected: "[T]he function of the election process is 'to winnow out and finally reject all but the chosen candidates,' not to provide a means of giving vent to 'short-range political goals, pique, or personal quarrels.'" White, J., found the prohibition to be a "legitimate means of averting sore-loser candidacies" in general elections and a reasonable means of avoiding party raiding in the primaries.

KENNEDY, J., joined by Blackmun and Stevens, JJ., dissenting, denied that access for third party and independent candidacies was easy under the Hawaii system, argued that the interest in avoiding "sore-loser" candidacies did not justify an approach that threatened legitimate candidacies, contended that the party raiding concern could be averted by other means, and observed that Hawaii is de facto a one party state (controlled by the Democratic party) in which many elections are uncontested and suggested that the right to cast a meaningful vote was important (even though he considered the right to cast a protest vote to be insubstantial): "The majority's approval of Hawaii's ban is ironic at a time when the new democracies in foreign countries strive to emerge from an era of sham elections in which the name of the ruling party candidate was the only one on the ballot. Hawaii does not impose as severe a restriction on the right to vote, but it imposes a restriction that has a haunting similarity in its tendency to exact severe penalties for one who does anything but vote the dominant party ballot."

CONFINEMENT OF "FUNDAMENTAL RIGHTS"

CON LAW: P. 1463, after Mathews

AMER CON: P. 1144, after Mathews

RTS & LIB: P. 1193 after Mathews

Louisiana law provided that a criminal defendant found not guilty by reason of insanity was to be committed to a mental hospital until he could prove that he was not dangerous—even if the defendant was no longer insane. FOUCHA v. LOUISIANA, p. 97 of this Supplement, supra, found the law violated due process. After arguing the Louisiana's law violated due process, WHITE, J., joined by Blackmun, Stevens, and Souter, JJ., also argued that Louisiana's scheme violated equal protection: "Louisiana law [does] not provide for similar confinement for other classes of persons who have committed criminal acts and who cannot later prove they would not be dangerous. Criminals who have completed their terms, or about to do so, are an obvious and larger category of such persons. [Freedom from physical restraint being a fundamental right, the

State must have a particularly convincing reason, which it has not put forward, for such discrimination against insanity acquittees who are no longer mentally ill."

O'CONNOR, J., concurring, who had also joined White, J., in finding the statute to violate due process, stated: "Equal protection principles may set additional limits on the confinement of sane but dangerous acquittees. Although I think it unnecessary to reach equal protection issues on the facts before us, the permissibility of holding an acquittee who is not mentally ill longer than a person convicted of the same crimes could be imprisoned is open to serious question."

THOMAS, J., joined by Rehnquist, C.J., and Scalia, J., dissented: "I fully agree with Justice O'Connor that there would be a serious question of rationality had Louisiana sought to institutionalize a sane acquittee for a period longer than he might have been imprisoned if convicted. But that is simply not the case here." [a]

a. Kennedy, J., also dissented.

Chapter

THE CONCEPT OF STATE ACTION

SECTION: RECENT DEVELOPMENTS

CON LAW: P. 1527, add to fn. a

AMER CON: P. 1179, add to fn. a

RTS & LIB: P. 1256, add to fn. a

See also *Connecticut v. Doehr*, ___ U.S. ___, 111 S.Ct. 2105, 115 L.Ed.2d 1 (1991), holding that a state statute authorizing prejudgment attachment of real estate upon plaintiff's *ex parte* showing that there is probable cause to sustain the validity of his or her claim—without a showing of extraordinary circumstances, and without a requirement that the person seeking the attachment post a bond—violated due process. Petitioner sought an attachment on respondent's home in conjunction with a civil action for assault and battery that he was seeking to institute against respondent in the same court. On the strength of statements in petitioner's affidavit, the court found probable cause and ordered the attachment. Only after the sheriff attached his property did respondent receive notice of the attachment, which informed him of his right to a postattachment hearing. Rather than pursue this action, respondent filed a federal action, successfully arguing that the state statute violated due process.

CON LAW: P. 1535, at end

AMER CON: P. 1186, at end

RTS & LIB: P. 1264, at end

EDMONSON v. LEESVILLE CONCRETE CO., ___ U.S. ___, 111 S.Ct. 2077, 114 L.Ed.2d 660 (1991), per KENNEDY, J., held that use by a private litigant in a civil trial of a peremptory challenge to exclude jurors on the basis of race violated "the excluded jurors' equal protection rights": "We [ask] first whether the claimed constitutional deprivation resulted from the exercise of a right or privilege having its source in state authority; and second, whether the private party charged with the deprivation could be described in all fairness as a state actor.

"There can be no question that the [first] inquiry is satisfied here. By their very nature, peremptory challenges have no significance outside a court of law. [They] are permitted only when the government, by statute or decisional law, deems it appropriate to allow parties to exclude a given number of persons who otherwise would satisfy the requirements for service on the petit jury.

"[Second], in determining whether a particular action or course of conduct is governmental in character, it is relevant to examine the following: the extent to which the actor relies on governmental assistance and benefits, see *Burton;* whether the actor is performing a traditional governmental function, see *Terry; Marsh*; and whether the injury caused is aggravated in a unique way by the incidents of governmental authority, see *Shelley* * * *.

"Although private use of state-sanctioned private remedies or procedures does not rise, by itself, to the level of state action, our cases have found state action when private parties make extensive use of state procedures with 'the overt, significant assistance of state officials.' See *Lugar.* It cannot be disputed that, without the overt, significant participation of the government, the peremptory challenge system, as well as the jury trial system of which it is a part, simply could not exist. [The] government summons jurors, constrains their freedom of movement, and subjects them to public scrutiny and examination. The party who exercises a challenge invokes the formal authority of the court, which must discharge the prospective juror, thus effecting the 'final and practical denial' of the excluded individual's opportunity to serve on the petit jury. [By] enforcing a discriminatory peremptory challenge, the court 'has not only made itself a party to the [biased act], but has elected to place its power, property and prestige behind the [alleged] discrimination.' *Burton.* In so doing, the government has 'create[d] the legal framework governing the [challenged] conduct,' [*Tarkanian*], and in a significant way has involved itself with invidious discrimination.

"[Further, a] traditional function of government is evident here. The peremptory challenge is used in selecting an entity that is a quintessential governmental body, having no attributes of a private actor. The jury exercises the power of the court and of the government that confers the court's jurisdiction. [If] a government confers on a private body the power to choose the government's employees or officials, the private body will be bound by the constitutional mandate of race neutrality [*Terry*].

"[I]n most civil cases, the initial decision whether to sue at all, the selection of counsel, and any number of ensuing tactical choices in the course of discovery and trial may be without the requisite governmental character to be deemed state action. That cannot be said of the exercise of peremptory challenges, however; when private litigants participate in the selection of jurors, they serve an important function within the government and act with its substantial assistance. If peremptory challenges based on race were permitted, persons could be required by summons to be put at risk of open and public discrimination as a condition of their participation in the justice system. The injury to excluded jurors would be the direct result of governmental delegation and participation.

"Finally, we note that the injury caused by the discrimination is made more severe because the government permits it to occur within the courthouse itself. Few places are a more real expression of the constitutional authority of the government than a courtroom, where the law itself unfolds."

O'CONNOR, J., joined by Rehnquist, C.J., and Scalia, J., dissented: "The peremptory challenge 'allows parties,' in this case *private* parties, to exclude potential jurors. It is the nature of a peremptory that its exercise is left wholly within the discretion of the litigant. [The] peremptory is, by design, an enclave of private action in a government-managed proceeding.

"The Court amasses much ostensible evidence of the Federal Government's 'overt, significant participation' in the peremptory process. [The] bulk of the practices the Court describes—the establishment of qualifications for jury service, the location and summoning of prospective jurors, the jury wheel, the voter lists, the jury qualification forms, the per diem for jury service—are independent of the statutory entitlement to peremptory strikes, or of their use. All of this government action is in furtherance of the Government's distinct obligation to provide a qualified jury; the Government would do these things even if there were no peremptory challenges. All of this activity, as well as the trial judge's control over voir dire, are merely prerequisites to the use of a peremptory challenge; they do not constitute participation *in* the challenge. That these actions may be necessary to a peremptory challenge—in the sense that there could be no such challenge without a venire from which to select—no more makes the challenge state action than the building of roads and provision of public transportation makes state action of riding on a bus.

"[The] government 'normally can be held responsible for a private decision only when it has exercised coercive power or has provided such significant encouragement, either overt or covert, that the choice must in law be deemed to be that of the State.' *Blum*. [Thus, in *Shelley,* the coercive power of the State was necessary in order to enforce the private choice of those who had created the covenants. [A] judge does not 'significantly encourage' discrimination by the mere act of excusing a juror in response to an unexplained request.

"There is another important distinction between *Shelley* and this case. The state courts in *Shelley* used coercive force to impose conformance on parties who did not wish to discriminate. 'Enforcement' of peremptory challenges, on the other hand, does not compel anyone to discriminate; the discrimination is wholly a matter of private choice. * * *

"A peremptory challenge by a private litigant [is] not a traditional government function. [In] order to constitute state action under this doctrine, private conduct must not only comprise something that the government traditionally does, but something that *only* the government traditionally does. Even if one could fairly characterize the use of a peremptory strike as the performance of the traditional government function of jury selection, it has never been exclusively the function of the government to select juries; peremptory strikes are older than the Republic. * * *

"Constitutional 'liability attaches only to those wrongdoers who carry a badge of authority of [the government] and represent it in some capacity.' *Tarkanian*. A government attorney who uses a peremptory challenge on behalf of the client is, by definition, representing the government. The challenge thereby becomes state action. It is antithetical to the nature of our adversarial process, however, to say that a private attorney acting on behalf of a private client represents the government for constitutional purposes."

Chapter

LIMITATIONS ON JUDICIAL POWER AND REVIEW

SECTION: CASE OR CONTROVERSY

STANDING AND RIPENESS

INJURY REQUIRED FOR STANDING; SUITS BY TAXPAYERS AND CITIZENS

CON LAW: P. 1611, after note (c)

AMER CON: P. 1243, after note (c)

RTS & LIB: P. 1321, after note (c)

(d) As indicated in fn. c after *SCRAP*, the Endangered Species Act authorizes "any person" to enjoin violations. The Act requires that federal agencies consult with executive branch officials to ensure that any action funded by the agency is not likely to jeopardize endangered species. *LUJAN v. DEFENDERS OF WILDLIFE*, ___ U.S. ___, 112 S.Ct. 2130, ___ L.Ed.2d ___ (1992), per SCALIA, J., held that the case-or-controversy requirement prevented a challenge by environmental groups to a federal administrative regulation exempting projects funded in foreign nations: "The question presented here is whether the public interest in proper administration of the laws (specifically, in agencies' observance of a particular, statutorily prescribed procedure) can be converted into an individual right by a statute that denominates it as such, and that permits all citizens (or, for that matter, a subclass of citizens who suffer no distinctive concrete harm) to sue. If the concrete injury requirement has the separation-of-powers significance we have always said, the answer must be obvious: To permit Congress to convert the undifferentiated public interest in executive officers' compliance with the law into an 'individual right' vindicable in the courts is to permit Congress to transfer from the President to the courts the Chief Executive's most important constitutional duty, to 'take Care that the Laws be faithfully executed,' Art. II, § 3. * * *

"Nothing in this contradicts the principle that '[the] injury required by Art. III may exist solely by virtue of statutes creating legal rights, the invasion of which creates standing.' *Warth*. Both of the cases used by *Linda R.S.* as an illustration of that principle involved Congress's elevating to the status of legally cognizable injuries concrete, de facto injuries that were previously inadequate in law (namely, injury to an individual's personal interest in living in a racially integrated community, see *Trafficante,* and injury to a company's interest in marketing its product free from competition. As we said in *Sierra Club,* '[Statutory] broadening [of] the categories of injury that may be alleged in support of standing is a different matter from abandoning the requirement that the party seeking review must himself have suffered an injury.' Whether or not the principle set forth in *Warth* can be extended beyond that distinction, it is clear that in suits against the government, at least, the concrete injury requirement must remain."

KENNEDY, J., joined by Souter, J., joined the opinion, adding: "Congress has the power to define injuries and articulate chains of causation that will give rise to a case or controversy where none existed before, and I do not read the Court's opinion to suggest a contrary view. See *Warth.* In exercising this power, however, Congress must at the very least identify the injury it seeks to vindicate and relate the injury to the class of persons entitled to bring suit. The citizen-suit provision of the Endangered Species Act does not meet these minimal requirements, because while the statute purports to confer a right on 'any person [to] enjoin [the] United States and any other governmental instrumentality or agency [who] is alleged to be in violation of any provision of this chapter,' it does not of its own force establish that there is an injury in 'any person' by virtue of any 'violation.'"

BLACKMUN, J., joined by O'Connor, J., dissented: "There may be factual circumstances in which a congressionally imposed procedural requirement is so insubstantially connected to the prevention of a substantive harm that it cannot be said to work any conceivable injury to an individual litigant. But, as a general matter, the courts owe substantial deference to Congress' substantive purpose in imposing a certain procedural requirement."

Stevens, J., dissented from the Court's reasoning on separate grounds.

Appendix A

THE JUSTICES OF THE SUPREME COURT

CON LAW: P. [10], after Taney, Roger B.

RTS & LIB: P. [10], after Taney, Roger B.

    THOMAS, CLARENCE (1948–___); Bush (1991–___); Ga.Rep.; Mo., Assistant Attorney General (3); U.S., Chair, E.E.O.C. (8), *Judge, Court of Appeals* (1½).

Appendix B

THE CONSTITUTION OF THE UNITED STATES

CON LAW: P. [26], after Amendment XXVI
AMER CON: P. [26], after Amendment XXVI
RTS & LIB: P. [26], after Amendment XXVI

Amendment XXVII [?] *

No law, varying compensation for the services of Senators and Representatives, shall take effect, until an election of Representatives shall have intervened.

---

* On May 7, 1992, more than 200 years after it was first proposed by James Madison, the Twenty-Seventh Amendment was ratified by a 38th State (Michigan). Although Congress set no time limit for ratification of this amendment, ten of the *other* amendments proposed at the same time (1789)—now known as the Bill of Rights—were ratified in a little more than two years. After all this time, is the ratification of the Twenty-Seventh Amendment valid? Does it matter that many of the states that ratified the Amendment did not exist at the time it was first proposed?

Appendix C

NEW YORK v. UNITED STATES

May Congress compel states to regulate a matter within both state and federal regulatory powers? NEW YORK v. UNITED STATES, ___ U.S. ___, 112 S.Ct. 2408, ___ L.Ed.2d ___ (1992), per O'CONNOR, J., ruled "No" 6 to 3. Congress had sought through the Low Level Radioactive Waste Amendment Act of 1985 to solve the shortage of sites for disposal of the millions of cubic feet of such waste created every year by various industries, hospitals, research institutions, and government activities. In 1985 only three such disposal sites were in operation—in Nevada, Washington and South Carolina. Sixteen other states had entered into interstate compacts with one of those three for use of their sites, but there were no assured outlets for disposal of low-level radioactive waste generated in the other 31 states.

The 1985 Act required the three existing sites "to make disposal capacity available for low level radioactive waste generated by any source" through the end of 1992. To induce, and if necessary to coerce, all states to create their own sites or make arrangements by interstate compact to use those of other states Congress used three types of incentive: (1) Financial incentives authorized states to collect a surcharge on all such waste received from other states; a portion of the surcharge was paid into a federal escrow fund for payments to those states that achieved a series of deadlines in development of sites for the disposal of such waste within their own state. These financial incentives were upheld unanimously as within the federal commerce, taxing and spending powers and consistent with the tenth amendment.

(2) The "access" incentives authorized states with sites to repeatedly double the surcharge for such waste from states that failed to meet a series of dated deadlines to either develop their own sites or join an interstate compact for use of another state's site. States that failed to meet the 1990 deadline could be denied access altogether. These access incentives were upheld unanimously: "As a simple regulation, this provision would be within the power of Congress to authorize the States to discriminate against interstate commerce. Where federal regulation of private activity is within the scope of the Commerce Clause, we have recognized the ability of Congress to offer states the choice of regulating that activity according to federal standards or having state law pre-empted by federal regulation. See *Hodel; FERC v. Mississippi.* This is the choice presented to nonsited States by the Act's second set of incentives: States may either regulate the disposal of radioactive waste according to federal standards by attaining local or regional self-sufficiency, or their residents who produce radio-

active waste will be subject to federal regulation authorizing sited States and regions to deny access to their disposal sites."

(3) The third so-called "incentive" provided that after January 1, 1996, if a state or compact region is unable to provide for the disposal of all low level radioactive waste generated there, "each state in which such waste is generated, upon the request of the generator or owner of the waste, shall take title to the waste, be obligated to take possession of the waste, and shall be liable in damages" incurred by the generator or owner for the states failure to take possession of the waste.

New York challenged the Act after Congress had approved 9 regional compacts encompassing 42 states; all six compacts with unfinished sites and four of the unaffiliated states were on schedule, having satisfied the statutory deadlines. The principal focus of the opinion ruled the "lake title" provision unconstitutional:

"Congress exercises its conferred powers subject to the limitations contained in the Constitution. Thus, for example, under the Commerce Clause Congress may regulate publishers engaged in interstate commerce, but Congress is constrained in the exercise of that power by the First Amendment. The Tenth Amendment likewise restrains the power of Congress, but this limit is not derived from the text of the Tenth Amendment itself, which, as we have discussed, is essentially a tautology. Instead, the Tenth Amendment confirms that the power of the Federal Government is subject to limits that may, in a given instance, reserve power to the States. The Tenth Amendment thus directs us to determine, as in this case, whether an incident of state sovereignty is protected by a limitation on an Article I [power].

"This framework has been sufficiently flexible over the past two centuries to allow for enormous changes in the nature of government. The Federal Government undertakes activities today that would have been unimaginable to the Framers in two senses; first, because the Framers would not have conceived that any government would conduct such activities; and second, because the Framers would not have believed that the Federal Government, rather than the States, would assume such responsibilities. Yet the powers conferred upon the Federal Government by the Constitution were phrased in language broad enough to allow for the expansion of the Federal Government's [role].

"The actual scope of the Federal Government's authority with respect to the States has changed over the years, [but] the constitutional structure underlying and limiting that authority has not. In the end, just as a cup may be half empty or half full, it makes no difference whether one views the question at issue in this case as one of ascertaining the limits of the power delegated to the Federal Government under the affirmative provisions of the Constitution or one of discerning the core of sovereignty retained by the States under the Tenth Amendment. Either way, we must determine whether [any] provisions of the Low-Level Radioactive Waste Policy Amendments Act of 1985 oversteps the boundary between federal and state [authority].

"Most of our recent cases interpreting the Tenth Amendment have concerned the authority of Congress to subject state governments to generally applicable laws. The Court's jurisprudence in this area has traveled an unsteady path. See *Maryland v. Wirtz; National League of Cities; Garcia.* This case presents no occasion to apply or revisit the holdings of any of these cases, as this is not a case in which Congress has subjected a State to the same legislation applicable to private parties.

"This case instead concerns the circumstances under which Congress may use the States as implements of regulation; that is, whether Congress may direct or otherwise motivate the States to regulate in a particular field or a particular way. Our cases have established a few principles that guide our resolution of the issue.

"As an initial matter, Congress may not simply 'commandee[r] the legislative processes of the States by directly compelling them to enact and enforce a federal regulatory program.' *Hodel.* [While] Congress has substantial powers to govern the Nation directly, including in areas of intimate concern to the States, the Constitution has never been understood to confer upon Congress the ability to require the States to govern according to Congress' instructions. See *Coyle v. Oklahoma,* 221 U.S. 559, 565, 91 S.Ct. 688, 689, 55 L.Ed. 853 (1911).

"[This] is not to say that Congress lacks the ability to encourage a State to regulate in a particular way, or that Congress may not hold out incentives to the States as a method of influencing a State's policy choices. Our cases have identified a variety of methods, short of outright coercion, by which Congress may urge a State to adopt a legislative program consistent with federal interests. Two of these methods are of particular relevance here.

"First, under Congress' spending power, 'Congress may attach conditions on the receipt of federal funds.' *South Dakota v. Dole.* [Second], where Congress has the authority to regulate private activity under the Commerce Clause, we have recognized Congress' power to offer States the choice of regulating that activity according to federal standards or having state law pre-empted by federal regulation. *Hodel.* [By] either of these two methods, as by any other permissible method of encouraging a State to conform to federal policy choices, the residents of the State retain the ultimate decision as to whether or not the State will [comply].

"By contrast, where the Federal Government compels States to regulate, the accountability of both state and federal officials is diminished. If the citizens of New York, for example, do not consider that making provision for the disposal of radioactive waste is in their best interest, they may elect state officials who share their view. That view can always be preempted under the Supremacy Clause if is contrary to the national view, but in such a case it is the Federal Government that makes the decision in full view of the public, and it will be federal officials that suffer the consequences if the decision turns out to be detrimental or unpopular. But where the Federal Government directs the States to regulate, it may be state officials who will bear the brunt of public disapproval, while the federal officials who devised the regulatory program may remain insulated from the electoral ramifications of their decision. Accountability is thus diminished when, due to federal coercion, elected state officials cannot regulate in accordance with the views of the local electorate in matters not preempted by federal regulation. See La Pierre, *Political Accountability in the National Political Process—The Alternative to Judicial Review of Federalism Issues,* 80 Nw.U.L.Rev. 577, 639–665 (1985). * * *

"The take title provision offers state governments a 'choice' of either accepting ownership of waste or regulating according to the instructions of Congress. Respondents do not claim that the Constitution would authorize Congress to impose either option as a freestanding requirement. On one hand, the Constitution would not permit Congress simply to transfer radioactive waste from generators to state governments. Such a forced transfer, standing alone, would in principle be no different than a congressionally compelled subsidy from state governments to radioactive waste producers. The same is true of the provision requiring the States to become liable for the generators' damages. Standing alone, this provision would be indistinguishable from an Act of Congress directing the States to assume the liabilities of certain state residents. Either type of federal action would 'commandeer' state governments into the service of federal regulatory purposes, and would for this reason be inconsistent with the Constitution's division of authority between federal and state governments. On the other hand, the second alternative held out to state governments—regulating pursuant to Congress' direction—would, standing alone, present a simple command to state governments to implement legislation enacted by Congress. As we have seen, the Constitution does not empower Congress to subject state governments to this type of instruction.

"Because an instruction to state governments to take title to waste, standing alone, would be beyond the authority of Congress, and because a direct order to regulate, standing alone, would also be beyond the authority of Congress, it follows that Congress lacks the power to offer the States a choice between the two. Unlike the first two sets of incentives, the take title incentive does not represent the conditional exercise of any congressional power enumerated in the Constitution. In this provision, Congress has not held out the threat of exercising its spending power or its commerce power; it has instead held out the threat, should the States not regulate according to one federal instruction, of simply forcing the States to submit to another federal instruction. A choice between two unconstitutionally coercive regulatory techniques is no choice at all. Either way, 'the Act commandeers the legislative processes of the States by directly compelling them to enact and enforce a federal regulatory program,' *Hodel,* an outcome that has never been understood to lie within the authority conferred upon Congress by the Constitution.

"Respondents emphasize the latitude given to the States to implement Congress' plan. The Act enables the States to regulate pursuant to Congress' instructions in any number of different ways. States may avoid taking title by contracting with sited regional compacts, by building a disposal site alone or as part of a compact, or by permitting private parties to build a disposal site. States that host sites may employ a wide range of designs and disposal methods, subject only to broad federal regulatory limits. This line of reasoning, however, only underscores the critical alternative a State lacks. A State may not decline to administer the federal program. No matter which path the State chooses, it must follow the direction of Congress.

"The take title provision appears to be unique. No other federal statute has been cited which offers a state government no option other than that of implementing legislation enacted by Congress. Whether one views the take title provision as lying outside Congress' enumerated powers, or as infringing upon the core of state sovereignty reserved by the Tenth Amendment, the provision is inconsistent with the federal structure of our Government established by the Constitution.

"[The] United States argues that the Constitution's prohibition of congressional directives to state governments can be overcome where the federal interest is sufficiently important to justify state submission. This argument contains a kernel of truth: In determining whether the Tenth Amendment limits the ability of Congress to subject state governments to generally applicable laws, the Court has in some cases stated that it will evaluate the strength of federal interests in light of the degree to which such laws would prevent the State from functioning as a sovereign; that is, the extent to which such generally applicable laws would impede a state government's responsibility to represent and be accountable to the citizens of the State.

"[But] whether or not a particularly strong federal interest enables Congress to bring state governments within the orbit of generally applicable federal regulation, no Member of the Court has ever suggested that such a federal interest would enable Congress to command a state government to enact state regulation. No matter how powerful the federal interest involved, the Constitution simply does not give Congress the authority to require the States to regulate. The Constitution instead gives Congress the authority to regulate matters directly and to pre-empt contrary state regulation. Where a federal interest is sufficiently strong to cause Congress to legislate, it must do so directly; it may not conscript state governments as its [agents].

"Respondents note that the Act embodies a bargain among the sited and unsited States, a compromise to which New York was a willing participant and from which New York has reaped much benefit. Respondents then pose what appears at first to be a troubling question: How can a federal statute be found an unconstitutional infringement of State sovereignty when state officials consented to the statute's enactment?

"The answer follows from an understanding of the fundamental purpose served by our Government's federal structure. The Constitution does not protect the sovereignty of States for the benefit of the States or state governments as abstract political entities, or even for the benefit of the public officials governing the States. To the contrary, the Constitution divides authority between federal and state governments for the protection of individuals. State sovereignty is not just an end in itself: 'Rather, federalism secures to citizens the liberties that derive from the diffusion of sovereign power.' *Coleman v. Thompson,* 501 U.S. ___, 111 S.Ct. 2546, 2570, 115 L.Ed.2d 640 (1991) (Blackmun, J., dissenting) at 2781. [The] constitutional authority of Congress cannot be expanded by the 'consent' of the governmental unit whose domain is thereby narrowed, whether that unit is the Executive Branch or the States.

"State officials thus cannot consent to the enlargement of the powers of Congress beyond those enumerated in the Constitution. Indeed, the facts of this case raise the possibility that powerful incentives might lead both federal and state officials to view departures from the federal structure to be in their personal interests. Most citizens recognize the need for radioactive waste disposal sites, but few want sites near their homes. As a result, while it would be well within the authority of either federal or state officials to choose where the disposal sites will be, it is likely to be in the political interest of each individual official to avoid being held accountable to the voters for the choice of location. If a federal official is faced with the alternatives of choosing a location or directing the States to do it, the official may well prefer the latter, as a means of shifting responsibility for the eventual decision. If a state official is faced with the same set of alternatives—choosing a location or having Congress direct the choice of a location—the state official may also prefer the latter, as it may permit the avoidance of personal responsibility. The interests of public officials thus may not coincide with the Constitution's intergovernmental allocation of authority. Where state officials purport to submit to the direction of Congress in this manner, federalism is hardly being advanced. * * *"

WHITE, J., joined by BLACKMUN and STEVENS, J., dissented from the "take title" ruling and the reasoning supporting it. The dissenters described at length the extended negotiations between the states that led to the 1985 Act and disagreed with the majority's refusal to estop New York from challenging the Act. They viewed New York's participation in the negotiations and its actions under the Act as "approval of the interstate agreement process embodied in the 1980 and 1985 Acts" within the meaning of the interstate compact clause:

"[Even] were New York not to be estopped from challenging the take title provision's constitutionality, I am convinced that, seen as a term of an agreement entered into between the several States, this measure proves to be less constitutionally odious than the Court opines. First, the practical effect of New York's position is that because it is unwilling to honor its obligations to provide in-state storage facilities for its low-level radioactive waste, other States with such plants must accept New York's waste, whether they wish to or not. Otherwise, the many economically and socially beneficial producers of such waste in the State would have to cease their operations. The Court's refusal to force New York to accept responsibility for its own problem inevitably means that some other State's sovereignty will be impinged by it being forced, for public health reasons, to accept New York's low-level radioactive waste. I do not understand the principle of federalism to impede the National Government from acting as referee among the States to prohibit one from bullying another.

"Moreover, it is utterly reasonable that, in crafting a delicate compromise between the three overburdened States that provided low-level radioactive waste disposal facilities and the rest of the States, Congress would have to ratify some punitive measure as the ultimate sanction for noncompliance. The take title provision, though surely onerous, does not take effect if the generator of the waste does not request such action, or if the State lives up to its bargain of providing a waste disposal facility either within the State or in another State pursuant to a regional compact arrangement or a separate [contract].

"The Court announces that it has no occasion to revisit such decisions as *Gregory v. Ashcroft*, [infra], *South Carolina v. Baker; Garcia, EEOC v. Wyoming,* and *National League of Cities,* because 'this is not a case in which Congress has subjected a State to the same legislation applicable to private parties.' Although this statement sends the welcome signal that the Court does not intend to cut a wide swath through our recent Tenth Amendment precedents, it nevertheless is unpersuasive. I have several difficulties with the Court's analysis in this respect: [it] derives its rule from cases that do not support its analysis; it fails to apply the appropriate tests from the cases on which it purports to base its rule; and it omits any discussion of the most recent and pertinent test for determining the take title provision's constitutionality.

"The Court's distinction between a federal statute's regulation of States and private parties for general purposes, as opposed to a regulation solely on the activities of States, is unsupported by our recent Tenth Amendment cases. In no case has the Court rested its holding on such a distinction. Moreover, the Court makes no effort to explain why this purported distinction should affect the analysis of Congress' power under general principles of federalism and the Tenth Amendment. The distinction, facilely thrown out, is not based on any defensible theory. Certainly one would be hard-pressed to read the spirited exchanges between the Court and dissenting Justices in *National League of Cities,* and in *Garcia,* as having been based on the distinction now drawn by the Court. An incursion on state sovereignty hardly seems more constitutionally acceptable if the federal statute that 'commands' specific action also applies to private parties. The alleged diminution in state authority over its own affairs is not any less because the federal mandate restricts the activities of private parties.

"[The] Court purports to draw support for its rule against Congress 'commandeer[ing]' state legislative processes from a solitary statement in dictum in *Hodel.* 'As an initial matter, Congress may not simply "commandee[r] the legislative processes of the States by directly compelling them to enact and enforce a federal regulatory program."' (quoting *Hodel*). That statement was not necessary to the decision in *Hodel,* which involved the question whether the Tenth Amendment interfered with Congress' authority to pre-empt a field of activity that could also be subject to state regulation and not whether a federal statute could dictate certain actions by States; the language about 'commandeer[ing]' States was classic dicta. In holding that a federal statute regulating the activities of private coal mine operators was constitutional, the Court observed that '[i]t would . . . be a radical departure from long-established precedent for this Court to hold that the Tenth Amendment prohibits Congress from displacing state police power laws regulating private activity.'

"[The] Court also claims support for its rule from our decision in *FERC,* and quotes a passage from that case in which we stated that '"this Court never has sanctioned explicitly a federal command to the States to promulgate and enforce laws and regulations."' In so reciting, the Court extracts from the relevant passage in a manner that subtly alters the Court's meaning. In full, the passage reads: 'While this Court never has sanctioned explicitly a federal command to the States to promulgate and enforce laws and regulations, there are instances where the Court has upheld federal statutory structures that in effect directed state decisionmakers to take or to refrain from taking certain actions.' (citing *Fry v. United States,* 421 U.S. 542, 95 S.Ct. 1792, 44 L.Ed.2d 363 (1975)). The phrase highlighted by the Court merely means that we have not had the occasion to address whether Congress may 'command' the States to enact a certain law. Moreover, it should go without saying that the absence of any on-point precedent from this Court has no bearing on the question whether Congress has properly exercised its constitutional authority under Article I.

"Rather than seek guidance from *FERC* and *Hodel,* therefore, the more appropriate analysis should flow from *Garcia,* even if this case does not involve a congressional law generally applicable to both States and private parties. In *Garcia,* we stated the proper inquiry: '[W]e are convinced that the fundamental limitation that the constitutional scheme imposes on the Commerce Clause to protect the "States as States" is one of process rather than one of result. Any substantive restraint on the exercise of Commerce Clause powers must find its justification in the procedural nature of this basic limitation, and it must be tailored to compensate for possible failings in the national political process rather than to dictate a "sacred province of state autonomy."' [The] Court tacitly concedes that a failing of the political process cannot be shown in this case because it refuses to rebut the unassailable arguments that the States were well able to look after themselves in the legislative process that culminated in the 1985 Act's passage. The Court rejects this process-based argument by resorting to generalities and platitudes about the purpose of federalism being to protect individual rights.

"Ultimately, I suppose, the entire structure of our federal constitutional government can be traced to an interest in establishing checks and balances to prevent the exercise of tyranny against individuals. But these fears seem extremely far distant to me in a situation such as this. We face a crisis of national proportions in the disposal of low-level radioactive waste, and Congress has acceded to the wishes of the States by permitting local decisionmaking rather than imposing a solution from Washington. New York itself participated and supported passage of this legislation at both the gubernatorial and federal representative levels, and then enacted state laws specifically to comply with the deadlines and timetables agreed upon by the States in the 1985 Act. For me, the Court's civics lecture has a decidedly hollow ring at a time when action, rather than rhetoric, is needed to solve a national [problem].

"The ultimate irony of the decision today is that in its formalistically rigid obeisance to 'federalism,' the Court gives Congress fewer incentives to defer to the wishes of state officials in achieving local solutions to local problems. This legislation was a classic example of Congress acting as arbiter among the States in their attempts to accept responsibility for managing a problem of grave import. The States urged the National Legislature not to impose from Washington a solution to the country's low-level radioactive waste management problems. Instead, they sought a reasonable level of local and regional autonomy consistent with Art. I, s 10, cl. 3, of the Constitution. By invalidating the measure designed to ensure compliance for recalcitrant States, such as New York, the Court upsets the delicate compromise achieved among the States and forces Congress to erect several additional formalistic hurdles to clear before achieving exactly the same objective. Because the Court's justifications for undertaking this step are unpersuasive to me, I respectfully dissent."

JUSTICE STEVENS delivered a short additional dissent:

"[The] Federal Government directs state governments in many realms. The Government regulates state-operated railroads, state school systems, state prisons, state elections, and a host of other state functions. Similarly, there can be no doubt that, in time of war, Congress could either draft soldiers itself or command the States to supply their quotas of troops. I see no reason why Congress may not also command the States to enforce federal water and air quality standards or federal standards for the disposition of low-level radioactive wastes."

†